Book I

UFO-DYNAMICS

Psychiatric and Psychic Dimensions
of
The UFO Syndrome

by
Berthold Eric Schwarz, M.D.

1983

UFO-DYNAMICS
Book I

By Berthold E. Schwarz, M.D.

Copyright © 1983 by Berthold Eric Schwarz

Published by Rainbow Books / Betty Wright in association with Futura Printing, Inc.
2299 Riverside Dr. / POB 1069   517 E. Ocean Ave.
Moore Haven, FL 33471   P.O. Drawer 99
                                                               Boynton Beach, FL 33425-0099
Printed in the United States of America

Library of Congress:
Catalog Card No. 83-060103
ISBN: 0-935834-12-5

1st Printing 1983
2nd Printing 1983

Dedication

To our children, and their children's children and those who are yet unborn.

OTHER BOOKS BY BERTHOLD E. SCHWARZ, M.D.

Parent-Child Tensions, Berthold E. Schwarz & B.A. Ruggieri
   J.B. Lippincott Company
Psychic-Dynamics, Berthold E. Schwarz
   Pageant Press
The Jacques Romano Story, Berthold E. Schwarz
   University Books, Inc.
Parent-Child Telepathy, Berthold E. Schwarz
   Garrett Publications
You CAN Raise Decent Children, Berthold E. Schwarz
   & B.A. Ruggieri
   Arlington House
PSYCHIC-NEXUS, Psychic Phenomena in Psychiatry and
   and Everyday Life, Berthold E. Schwarz
   Van Nostrand Reinhold Co.
UFO-DYNAMICS, Psychiatric and Psychic Aspects of the
   UFO Syndrome, Berthold E. Schwarz, BOOK I & BOOK II,
   Rainbow Books/ Betty Wright in association with
   Futura, Inc.

Table of Contents

*Book II contains Chapters 16 through 25 plus Appendix and
Index for Books I and II.*

Preface

Increasingly through the years I have received numerous telephone calls and letters, sometimes desperate ones, asking my professional help about the medical-psychiatric aspects of close encounter or UFO contactee cases. Since many of these interesting people have been referred by various UFO groups, they had already been screened and many of them presented high-interest, intriguing phenomena. In all too many instances it has been frustrating because of distance and time, and the more desirable, detailed psychiatric work-ups and prolonged periods of observation could not be undertaken. However, these professional experiences have hammered home the message that close encounter UFO cases are not at all rare and there are no ready-made answers for them. The UFO syndrome poses complex, near-insoluble problems. But, these numerous examples have pointed out the urgent need for some organized collection of psychiatric studies which spell out various techniques and methods using actual, first-hand, concrete examples. Therefore, because of this vacuum, *UFO-DYNAMICS, the Psychiatric and Psychic Aspects of the UFO Syndrome,* is an attempt to fill that gap. No one person, let alone myself, with all my limitations, could ever dream of supplying the ultimate means of approaching the multi-dimensional UFO problem, however, possibly a book written for psychiatrists and other physicians and also including behavioral scientists and the intelligent layman, might serve as a beginning or introduction.

By presenting a collection of case-studies that I was intimately involved with and in some instances have followed over a period of years, I hope that the reader and skeptic who approaches this borderland subject of science, will be better able to pursue ufology from a broader perspective and by having an awareness of some of the psycho- and psychic-dynamic aspects he will be in a better position to refer cases to those who are competent and interested in this area.

Opinions do not develop overnight and as new data, material, and methods come about, ideas change also. Sometimes they flash back to earlier concepts which were tossed away and sometimes new combinations are arrived at. If anything can be said there appears to be great need for a multidisciplinarian approach in researching UFOs. It is counter-productive to become involved in Keystone-cops polemics when studying UFOs: i.e., did the Government know or did they harass witnesses? For, interesting as some of these aspects might be, they are basically side-issues. I personally doubt that the Government has the answers to UFOs locked up in dusty archival file cabinets or encoded in computer banks, any more than they have the "answers" to inflation, unemployment, poverty, etc. The individual UFO researcher might better reserve his energies and time for grappling with the world-wide, long-term questions about UFOs: who are they, where do they come from, and what is their purpose? Unconventional data can be subjected to scientific analysis but one need not be stuffy or any less scientific in his approach if he realizes that this particular kind of data calls for, at the least, an open-minded and often a uniquely adaptable approach; and that just because modern man cannot do or understand what UFOs are allegedly capable of doing, it does not mean that what is happening is not valid. In studying close encounter UFO cases one must cope with all these factors plus one's own reactions or tendencies to dissociate from this "unreal" reality — and much more. If the potential researcher really wants to get his feet wet, he might be surprised by his own involvement in the synchronicity and he might discover that some of the most absorbing material will be found almost in his own back yard. He will ask again and again what constitutes proof? How does one determine truth? Perhaps new generations of investigators, armed with innovative techniques and apparatus will be better able to explore these problems and bring us closer to answers and possibly, as an unanticipated bonus, practical benefits for mankind.

Berthold Eric Schwarz
Vero Beach, Florida 32964

Acknowledgements

Appreciation is given to the following organizations who permitted the re-printing of articles in toto or in part:

Aerial Phenomena Research Organization (APRO) for Psychiatric Aspects of Ufology, Proceedings of the Eastern UFO Symposium: 8-12, Jan. 23, 1971, Baltimore, Maryland; UFO Table Talk (Josh and the Psychiatrist), Proceedings of the 5th APRO UFO Symposium: 14-18, June 15, 1974, Pottstown, Pennsylvania.

Canadian UFO Report for UFO Forum, a Scientific Commentary Prepared by Brian C. Cannon, with P.M.H. Edwards, Ph.D., Rupert H. MacNeill, M.A., Peter M. Millman, Ph.D., and B.E. Schwarz, M.D., Vol. 1 (No. 8): 30-35, Fall 1970.

Flying Saucer Review for Gary Wilcox and the Ufonauts, Special Issue No. 3, Sept., 1969 "UFO Percipients," pp. 20-27; UFO Occupants: Fact or Fantasy?, Vol. 15 (No. 5): 14-18, Sept.-Oct., 1969; Possible UFO-induced Temporary Paralysis, Vol. 17 (No. 2); 4-9, March/April, 1971; "Beauty of the Night," Vol. 18 (No. 4): 5-9, 17, July/Aug., 1972; The Port Monmouth Landing, Vol. 17 (No. 3): 21-27, May/June 1971; Woodstock UFO Festival, 1966 (in two parts) Vol. 19 (No. 1): 3-6, Jan./Feb., 1973, and Vol. 19 (No. 2): 18-23, Mar./Apr., 1973; UFO Landing and Repair by Crew by Ted Bloecher (in two parts) Vol. 20 (No. 2): 21-26, Oct., 1974, and Vol. 20 (No. 3): 24-27, Dec., 1974; New Berlin UFO Landing and Repair by Crew, a Psychiatric-Paranormal Survey of the Principal Witness, Vol. 21 (Nos. 3, 4): 22-28, Nov. 1975; Berserk: A UFO-Creature Encounter, Vol. 20 (No. 1): 3-11, 1974; The Twilight side of a UFO Encounter, by Brent M. Raynes, Vol. 22 (No. 2): 11-14, July, 1976; The Maine UFO Encounter: Investigation Under Hypnosis by Shirley C. Fickett, Vol. 22 (No. 2): 14-17, July 1976; Comments on the Psychiatric-paranormal Aspects of the Maine Case, Vol. 22 (No. 2): 18-22, July 1976; The Man-In-Black Syndrome (in three parts), Vol. 23 (No. 4): 9-15, 1977, Vol. 23 (No. 5): 22-25, 1977, and Vol. 23 (No. 6): 26-29, 1977; Talks With Betty Hill: 1—Aftermath of Encounter, Vol. 23 (No. 2): 16-19, Aug., 1977; Talks With Betty Hill: 2—The things That Happen Around Her, Vol. 23 (No. 3): 11-14, Oct., 1977; Talks With Betty Hill: 3—Experiments and Conclusions, Vol. 23 (No. 4): 28-31, Jan., 1978; Stella Lansing's UFO Motion Pictures, Vol. 18 (No. 1): 3-12, 19, Jan./Feb., 1972; Stella Lansing's Movies: Four Entities and a Possible UFO, Special Issue No. 5: 2-10, 36, Nov., 1973; Stella Lansing's Clocklike UFO Patterns (in four parts), Vol. 20 (No. 4): 3-9, 1974, Vol. 20 (No. 5): 20-27 (1974 Series) Mar., 1975, Vol. 20 (No. 6): 18-22 (1974 series) April, 1975, Vol. 21 (No. 1): 14-17 June 1975; A Note on the Significance of Stella Lansing by I. Grattan-Guinness, Vol. 21 (No. 2): 18, 1975; "Mail Bag" (Dr. Schwarz and Mrs. Lansing attacked) David K. Bowman and Charles Bowen, Vol. 21 (No. 1): 29-30, 1975; Commentary on the August Roberts Mystery with further notes on Mrs. Lansing, Vol. 21 (No. 6): 18-19 (1975 series) April 1976.

Journal of the American Society of Psychosomatic Dentistry and Medicine for a UFO Motion Picture Experiment (at Betty Hill's "Landing Field") Vol. 26 (No. 2): 73-81, 1979; Clinical Observations on Telekinesis (in four parts), Vol. 27 (No. 1): 13-23, 1980, Vol. 27 (No. 2): 54-63, 1980, Vol. 27 (No. 3): 87-96, 1980, and Vol. 27 (No. 4): 110-123, 1980.

The Journal of the Medical Society of New Jersey for UFOs in New Jersey Vol. 66 (No. 8): 460-464, Aug., 1969.

MAGONIA for The Ethical Ufologist, No. 1: 13-14, 1979.

Medical Times for UFOs: Delusion or Dilemma? Vol. 96 (No. 10): 967-981, Oct., 1968, reprinted in FSR, Special Issue (Beyond Condon) No. 2: 46-52, June 1969.

Mutual UFO Network for saucers, Psi and psychiatry, Proceedings, UFO Symposium: 82-95, June 22, 1974, Akron, Ohio.

My thanks go to the many people who helped these researches in countless ways through the years. Sometimes it has been at formal meetings; through friendships; telephone calls; letter writing; field trips; and even on occasion people who had interviewed me happily consenting to my turning the tables on them and taping their opinions. Regretfully, no list could ever be complete, and in some instances my most noteworthy informants had to be anonymous. For these good people my gratitude or mere mention of their names could never be commensurate with their contributions. If there are any errors they are unintentional and I am alone responsible.

I am indebted to the following individuals who kindly permitted the inclusion of their original studies without which my own supplemental contributions would be woefully incomplete:

Ted Bloecher, Chapter 9, Report of a UFO Landing and Repair by Crews.

Shirley C. Fickett, Chapter 12, The Maine UFO Encounter.

Ivor Grattan-Guinness, Chapter 22, A Note on the Significance of Stella Lansing.

Brent Raynes, Chapter 11, The Twilight Side of a UFO Encounter.

Particular thanks go to Vilma E. Semsey, my secretary who has helped in many ways beyond the call of duty; my family, including my wife, son and daughter who are owed much for putting up with these time-consuming studies that entailed sacrifices on their parts and which sometimes made our family-home-office facility a hotel. Hopefully, some day, benefits will be forthcoming.

Introduction

UFODYNAMICS
By
Berthold E. Schwarz, M.D.

My purpose is to present a series of psychiatric studies on UFOs — first-hand field and office investigations of people who have claimed close sightings or encounters with UFOs. It is not my intention to rehash already published studies, many of which are based on arm-chair techniques. I will also introduce spontaneously occurring and, in selected instances, experimental UFO data using filmic and occasional audio tape techniques. Collaborative material where leading UFO investigators and recognized groups studied unusual cases with on-the-scene data collecting and interviewing will be collated with supplementary psychiatric studies, which hopefully will give some of the broader, if not at times hidden, dimensions to the problem. These studies will sometimes probe the role of the unconscious mind and related psychic aspects.

The modern era of flying saucers burst upon the scene in 1947, following Kenneth Arnold's sighting of flying discs near Mount Rainier in Washington. However, some UFO related side issues to his sightings were bizarre and dangerous, and they nearly cost him his life. Thirty years later at the FATE Magazine International Ufology Congress (1), in Chicago, Arnold reflected on these early events and stood firm by what he and Ray Palmer had reported in their paper, "The Coming of the Saucers (2)." Arnold was still unable to explain what had happened. When I met Arnold and Palmer at the Congress I was impressed by their openness, friendly manners, and courage in daring to tell the whole story at a time when their own reward would be ridicule, or skepticism. Few scientists would be, or apparently were, impressed. However, in my opinion Arnold and Palmer were light years ahead of their time.

These omissions or downplayings of UFO "side issues" by serious investigators were perhaps a sign of the times, which situation in recent years has been remedied. Unfortunately, however, many early ufological studies on the contactees, abductees, and alleged UFO landing/encounter cases frequently overlooked detailed information about the people who were involved, their reactions, previous relevant life experiences and health, their families, the effects of the UFO experience on subsequent behavior, and the frequent occurrence of puzzling, enigmatic, associated paranormal events. For the most part much potentially valuable material has been lost forever.

Although UFOs have received enormous world-wide attention, chiefly in such popular media as TV and movies, books and magazines, with some notable exceptions there have been surprisingly few serious studies by biologically and psychosocially oriented researchers or reports from physicians and behavioral scientists. Most of the earlier (and contemporary) researches have been undertaken by physical scientists who have prepared excellent papers on the techniques of measuring the physical attributes of UFOs and correlating them, when available, with visual, radar, infra red, electromagnetic and other data.

UFOs — flying saucers — constitute one of the most controversial subjects of our time. They can evoke ridicule and laughter, hilarious cartoons, fear, horror, awe, and flights of fantasy. Sometimes lurid accounts of UFO experiences can rival the most sensational chapters in science fiction. It is no wonder that the serious reader might ask whether UFOs are real, or if they exist only in imagination and are a delusion or hoax; or whether they come from other planets in distant solar systems and represent advanced technologies capable of defying gravity and performing aerodynamic feats such as great bursts of speed and an ability to make sudden stops or right angle turns — acts that are impossible to comprehend in light of present technology. If the reader is not stymied by these alleged facts, he might become further entangled in a mental boggle when he learns how UFOs are supposedly flown and manipulated by entities or humanoids of varying sizes, shapes, colors, and sometimes possessing apparent capabilities for superior intelligence and robot-like behavior. Many close encounters are also associated with telepathic communications, telekinesis, teleportation, precognition, materialization, dematerialization, and the causing or healing of diseases. It is no wonder that scientists, let alone intelligent laymen, have for the most part in the past discounted these sensational cases, for in the myriad reports there was always an alarming paucity of solid, objective, factual data. However, the contactee and abductee subjective data and landing accounts continue to provide sensational grist for the entertainment industry, for television, films, newspapers and magazines. It was no wonder then that there was a wide-spread failure to find early scientific recognition of UFOs as a legitimate subject for study. But, this is not quite the whole story, because despite this understandable attitude and the ostensibly negative findings of the Condon Report and the recommendations of the CIA chartered Robertson Committee,* people of all sorts, including reputable citizens and trained observers, still have continued to see UFOs and experience close encounters. UFOs did not end with the Condon Report and apparently will not go away.

---

*UFO Investigator, NICAP, Vol. 10 (No. 9): 2-3, December, 1979.

Although what is reported here comprises the bulk of the material that has been distilled from my files, I still have cabinets filled with typed protocols, films, and transcriptions of taped hypnotic interviews. For the present it is necessary that this be saved for the time capsule. However, all the data shows that the longer close-encounter cases are psychiatrically studied, the greater the yield of detailed, relevant, and sometimes hitherto ommitted (repressed) information. This seems related to the increasing complexity and yield of significant material from the prolonged treatment of patients in psychoanalytic psychotherapy and in contradistinction to the comparatively minimal information from one to two consultations.

It also soon became evident that in many instances UFO close encounters were often repeater experiences and that the initial sightings might really have been part of a UFO-human continuum: i.e., there were previous and subsequent UFO, psychic or Fortean experiences. Examples of this are found in the case of the most famous abductee of all, Mrs. Betty Hill's (Chapter 15) and Dr. Herbert Hopkin's (Chapter 14) chilling meetings with the Man-in-Black, which followed in the aftermath of the Maine Teleportation Case (Chapters 11 and 12). These near incredible events become even more exciting when one delves into the backgrounds and presumed past psychic experiences of these people. There must be some meaning to this singular relationship: the UFO-human equation. These and similar reports often rival the most intricate and tortured plots of detective stories, but they are quite suitable for psychiatric scrutiny. However, the reader will see that in all too many cases, although the UFO problem is expanded with tantalizing details, the mystery still remains unsolved. Nevertheless, the compilation of more data and extraction of additional clues from prolonged psychiatric study might pierce the impasse when this is coupled with understanding of possible psychic-dynamic mechanisms. This hope is not futile because many of the psychic findings associated with close encounter UFO cases have their striking parallels with otherwise non UFO related spontaneous psychic events. For example, numerous accounts of UFO-like data — without the term "UFO" — can be found in famed psychoanalyst and parapsychologist Nandor Fodor's *Encyclopedia of Psychic Science* (3), which was written more than fifty years ago. More up-to-date illustrations relevant to this situation can be found in PSYCHIC-NEXUS (4), a book about psychic phenomena in psychiatry and everyday life. PSYCHIC-NEXUS intentionally included a "sleeper" study about UFO contactee Mrs. Stella Lansing's motion pictures of UFOs. Therefore, for this work I have followed the same formula and included a chapter on Clinical Observations on Telekinesis. Much of that presumed psychical mind-over-matter data, which occurred spontaneously in clinical practice and in personal life, although admittedly simple compared to spectacular UFO associated material, was at core essentially the same. Both close encounter UFO and clinical telekinetic events seem to be charged with powerful emotional and interesting psycho and psychic dynamics.

Therefore, people who are interested in understanding close contact UFO cases should be thoroughly familiar with the psychopathology and psychic dynamics of psychical phenomena. Similarly, those who study psychic phenomena might find it valuable to know about the physical, behavioral and psychic aspects of UFOs. In reference to these matters, I have in my research files some poltergeist cases, where the involved people and their families have been psychiatrically studied, sometimes extending over three generations. Although these cases were referred solely for the purpose of investigating poltergeists, or for therapeutic intervention, the interesting UFO implications were: that in these "pure" uncontaminated poltergeist cases there were in fact instances of UFO-like, or Men-in-Black related phenomena. All that one had to do to elicit this information was to think of this possibility and then ask the pertinent questions — if that was necessary.

For instance, one poltergeist case involved alleged paranormal audiotapes with a passage containing a loud, clear, English accented voice, describing a local airplane's close call with a UFO. The group, which had been terrified by alleged clones of some of the protagonists (bilocation?), disappearing equipment and poltergeist activities, first learned about this near mishap from an alleged paranormal tape. The tape claimed information that was shortly confirmed by a local newpaper article — unless it was merely a coincidence of place, and circumstance. This episode was one of several in this case, which included repeated episodes of presumed telekinesis: e.g., a loaf of bread floating in a cabinet drawer, a key melting, shoe polish (?) writing on the picture window, a dime bending, etc. (Chapter 15, Part 3). To round out matters, there was also a UFO sighting by the involved mother and her daughter at the height of these observations. This event might have been related to other on-going psychopathological and biological factors that whetted my appetite to learn more about these matters, and I was not disappointed.

Many of the cases in this book will show how UFOs are frightfully complex and that whatever their physical parameters, which admittedly deserve intensive study, the *ufodynamics* — the psychiatric-psychic — aspects are no less attractive and in need of attention. Hopefully these combined approaches might awaken wider interests that will lead to practical discoveries toward the eventual understanding not only of UFOs and psychic phenomena, but also as to how these interrelated forces might be operative in the causation or healing of various diseases.

By the study of close encounter UFO cases physicians, behavioral scientists and intelligent laymen who are interested and conversant with psychiatric methodology might see some new and hitherto undisclosed patterns, and, beyond that, they might be sufficiently titillated to undertake their own investigations. UFO researchers comprise a diverse lot. They come from disparate disciplines and from all walks of life. Each in his own way has material to contribute. The interested reader is encouraged to study all viewpoints, for no one approach has a monopoly in tackling the problem and no one has yet found the answer.

Many of the UFO researchers are almost as individualistic as some of the people who claim close UFO experiences, and often the observers are as fascinating as the observed. Whatever the force behind UFOs, there is the frequent occurrence of synchronicity that seemingly binds, blinds, and baffles the observers and observed in the psychic nexus. They are the blind men and the elephant. Although they might not be aware of or admit it, they are seemingly interdependent in the psychic-dynamics of synchronicity, and this might be a major neglected clue to the UFO enigma.

Some of the more colorful popular UFO literature to the contrary, where sacred tenets and certitude is often proclaimed to the true believers, there is no need for fanaticism but much need for expanded effort and hard work. My hope is that what is presented in this book is not too dogmatic and that the reader can discern clear separation of factual from interpretive material, for this is just a beginning. Although a handful of cases does not carry the weight of a larger series, it is long overdue that first-hand psychiatric-parapsychiatric researches on the UFO-people interface be presented. Therefore, the reader will receive a smorgasbord that includes earlier, simpler studies which progress to more complicated ones with occasional extensive footnotes. Unfortunately, the implicit sensitivities and sometimes complexities of the material make this necessary. The reader who bravely wades through these minutiae should soon find out why this was done. Later, these simpler case reports are expanded to collaborative studies where outstanding investigators, such as Stan Gordon and his Westmoreland County UFO Study Group (Chapter 10), Ted Bloecher (Chapter 9), Shirley Fickett and Brent Raynes (Chapters 11 and 12) have thoroughly documented several unusual cases before psychiatric surveys were undertaken.

For those who might be curious about what a successful paragnost's reactions might be to UFO cases, I have included instances where Joseph Dunninger contributed his knowledge and skills as a telepathist and magician, and also as a crime sleuth, inventor of magical illusions and apparatus, and exposer of phony mediums. For the sake of readability exploratory interviews with negative results by Henry Gross (5), the successful Maine dowser, Gerard Croiset (6), Dorothy Allison,* and other "proven" paragnosts are not included.

Positive field and experimental studies are highlighted in the attention given to many of Mrs. Stella Lansing's motion picture films and UFO-like objects, and to alleged paranormal audio tapes (Chapters 10-23). I will also include personal experiences with Mrs. Lansing and other gifted motion picture photographers of UFOs or UFO-like percepts, and some clinically controlled experiments involving Mrs. Lansing, these "gifted" people, and trained observers. The reader might be tempted to try these experimental techniques on himself, and he might be surprised to discover his own latent abilities for filming UFO-like objects or possibly closely allied thoughtographic phenomena, and other paranormal effects, including audio tapes. For this can easily be done, and there is reason to believe that these potential abilities are probably widespread and not restricted to the "chosen few." Mrs. Lansing's filmed UFO-like objects and ufonauts (entities? humanoids?) beg for interpretation, and they could possibly be an important scientific sleeper in our midst. Those with backgrounds in the physical sciences will undoubtedly be able to devise experiments whereby the data can be better controlled and subjected to highly desirable, critical, qualitative, quantitative, and computer analysis which might help explain the phenomena. For example, if UFO-like filmic percepts are wholly or partially thoughtographic, psychic-dynamics might offer a useful working hypothesis for further experimentation; and these effects might be ultimately explained at the molecular level. It is stressed that nothing new has been *discovered* that violates natural laws; the problem is perhaps only our ignorance of what these natural laws might be. There is no need for UFOs and psychic-dynamics to be ensnarled in mind-body, "either or" dichotomies or in mumbo-jumbo; running away from the often interlocked relationships of UFOs and psychic-dynamics only betrays man's anxieties about himself and possibly his fear of having his identity compromised when he is reluctant to reach out and come to grips with the strange, Fortean, fascinating Unknown. Personally, nothing has been so intriguing, fatiguing, frustrating and infuriating as UFOs.

*Allison, D., and Jacobson, S.: **Dorothy Allison, A Psychic Story,** Jove Publications, Inc., New York, 1980, (paperback).

On the dark side of the UFO problem, some cases will illustrate potential dangers. However, it is not only the Men-in-Black and some of the bizarre things that happened or reputedly occurred in connection with the UFOs that comprised the prime peril, but the hazards of everyday living. Many times while on field trips I was more concerned about reckless automobile drivers, possibly under the influence of alcohol or drugs, careening around curves at late hours of the night. These risks in perspective, in my experience at least, are more real than presumed UFOs or UFO-like psychic aspects — such as pulsating spook lights on mountain ridges, orange globes seemingly coming out of nowhere and racing along the ground, a mongrel shepherd dog's sudden lunging at the door late at night and barking when no one is there, unaccountable UFO-related telephone calls, and unexpected meetings with strange people having information that one would not expect them to have and asking completely unanticipated questions with highly personal implications.

Although I will not burden the reader with all the frightening personal "coincidences," it is relevant to mention some events. For example, one Wednesday afternoon *on the day closest to my birthday*, and while getting out of my parked car to visit Dunninger in his home, situated on a dead-end street on the edge of the New Jersey Palisades, I was approached by a swarthy man in a black suit who asked me how he could get to Van Waggonen Avenue, Jersey City. This was surprising because I had never met a strange man in black before in this specific isolated location and nor was I ever asked about a place several miles away to which it was difficult to come up with directions. I was dealing with a thickly settled urban area. Although Dunninger and I had planned that day to discuss possible explanations of UFO-related events — the oddest part of this experience, *on the day of my visit which was closest to my birthday*, was that I was born on Van Waggonen Avenue, Jersey City! Coincidence? Probably, but then, there are so many like this when one really gets into first hand investigations of UFOs. Perhaps someone can devise suitable formulas to quantitate clinical controls.

All has not been so somber in studying UFOs, for some of the experiences had their lighter aspects, and to a psychiatrist they might even have been suggestive of deeper meanings. For example, one day when Mrs. Lansing was driving from Massachusetts to New Jersey for some filming experiments, she called me late in the afternoon to tell me that her car had broken down on the highway, that there was a gaping hole in the motor, and that despite the sudden danger in having her car stall in heavy traffic, she was all right. She told me where to meet her. My photographer friend, Augie Roberts, my fifteen-year-old son Eric, and I immediately drove to her rescue. When we arrived at the agreed-upon bowling alley, Mrs. Lansing was horribly upset. Naturally we thought it was connected to her close call with the automobile, but we soon learned otherwise. She had originally phoned from a road-side saloon, and she was all broken up because she did not know how to prevent fifteen-year-old Eric from coming with us and finding her at a place that featured topless dancers.

It has been gratifying to meet, over the years, many unusual people and hear about their UFO experiences, get to know their families, and learn how all these matters seemed to be in some way inter-related. Undoubtedly many of these people were disappointed because I could not give them ready explanations, if any understanding at all, about what happened to them. But, by using techniques that have proven useful in clinical psychiatry, I found that the people who had had close UFO experiences and who were exulted, exhausted, and depressed, frightened and perplexed, with no exceptions, were never harmed by the investigations, but in many cases they were helped by our mutual sharing and attempting to understand and explain various possibilities. If any people that I studied were ever harmed by their experiences, it was more likely that they suffered from the social complications of their UFO encounters. In some instances whole lives have been changed, not directly by the UFOs, as far as I could determine, but by the reactions to the extraordinary events themselves and often by what preceded or by what followed them. Although not scientifically validated, I can concur with the frequent observation that in some instances those who become intimately involved in UFO research seemed to be plagued with a series of continuing adversities. There is sufficient evidence here to justify its mention, and to point out the need for further research which will lead to either acceptance or rejection of this frightening clinical impression.

Most of the contactees I have studied were excellent hypnotic subjects and perhaps this is a clue to their experiences. For some, like Pulaski (Chapter 10) in the UFO creature encounter case, were spontaneously in and out of entrancement during their interviews. Could this proclivity for entrancement have opened them up for invasion by the UFO force? Or, possibly, could the contactees or combinations of people like them (their families and friends) who shared their interests in UFOs and who had similar dissociative traits been exploited by UFO forces in ways that split them further and opened them up for the development of psychic abilities such as telepathy, precognition, and telekinesis?

Although folie a deux, a condition where one person, usually a close relative, unconsciously imitates the emotional illness of the other, is not common in psychiatric practice, it is common to find patients with dissociative disorders who have other family members with similar features: e.g., sleepwalking, sleeptalking, amnesia and increased suggestibility. The needs of one family member seemingly oscillate and feed upon the psychodynamics of the other. They are mutually adaptive or symbiotic. For example, I once saw a wife for an hysterical crisis; years later her oldest daughter had similar problems; and still many years after that her husband was seen for amnesia. He sought hypnosis to "remember" where he had "lost" some important documents that belonged to his children and which he unconsciously did not want them to have. This symbiotic relationship might be similar to that of gifted paragnosts and their families. For example, the late Maine dowser Henry Gross (5) married a Yankee lady who also had high quality psychic events in her past history in addition to being raised in a haunted house. The Gross's daughter, Clara, also had alleged superior dowsing skills. Another example is Prof. Tenhaeff's superb paragnost Gerard Croiset (6), whose son, Gerard Jr., like his father, is endowed with specific psychic abilities for solving crimes, finding missing people, etc.

These interesting mechanisms bring to mind a UFO case which involved a young couple where the older, male contactee claimed he had been on board a space craft many times since he was a child. They came to me because of a four-hour period of amnesia during a most recent alleged close encounter of several hours duration. Study of their lives revealed that their UFO experience might have been chronologically and etiologically related to a series of recent "here-and-now" major traumas. However, the worst, most tragic feature of the case was that the young woman was symptom-free until she met her contactee boyfriend and came under his spell. Just previous to their professions of love he, while drunk, had killed her best friend in a bizarrely coincidental head-on auto collision. The male contactee confided to the young woman that he felt he was "chosen" by the UFOs to help humanity, and that by doing that, he would overcome all his handicaps. While allegedly entranced and transfixed by a glowing, hot UFO, which the couple claimed to see at the same time as the sun, they developed macular solar burns. The woman was seen by an opthalmologist who made the diagnosis and told her that she would be permanently, legally blind. On my testing of the couple, they could hardly read the largest, number 11-sized print on the eye card. Therefore, in this case, whatever the objective reality of their experience, it can be conjectured that the woman was mesmerized by her lover (folie a deux) and that she rejected common sense by joining him in gazing at the bright object. It should be stressed that those who are interested in UFOs should be well versed in the possible biological effects, and that people should not stare at bright objects or the sun and risk a catastrophe — macular solar burns — legal blindness.

To what extent these dissociative talents are inherited, or equally plausible, "learned" by identification and other complex psychopathological mechanisms — the perennial nature/nurture controversy — has yet to be resolved. However, these situations might be applicable to UFO contactee and their kin; and there are numerous examples in this book which support this curious relationship: i.e., premorbid, permissive environments favoring awareness and reception for UFO close encounters and Fortean-psychic phenomena. A more wide-spread instance of this might be the near-epidemic of UFO-creature cases in Pennsylvania, which might have its parallels in previous outbreaks in history — for example, the medieval St. Vitus' dance mania, or the odd goings-on described by Aldous Huxley in his Devils of Loudun (7). Do people with dissociative propensities have potential for a wide variety of experiences, depending on varying environmental factors (for example, pathological manifestations that occur in neuroses and psychoses, or appropriate states of consciousness for psychic phenomena)? Are the contactees, with their frequent histories for dissociative behavior, such as amnesia, blackouts, trips to other planets, states of sudden paralysis, communications with entities with strange sounding and sometimes mystical names, basically the same as persons with dissociative states manifested as fugues, multiple personalities and hypersuggestibility? Are contactees physical mediums for the creation of effects spreading from Big Foot with accompanying sulfur and brimstone (hallucinatory?) odors, and unexplainable three-toed tracks in the sand, to out-of-the-body-like experiences where they travel afar, or akin to Eisenbud's (8) into-our-experience body, like states of possession, visitations from materializing and dematerializing phantom beings, or apparently solid Men-in-Black? If the contactees are related to materialization mediums, how are they alike? If not, how do they differ? How do these phenomena tie in with such UFO physical effects as "fairy rings" (e.g., a circle of presumed dead vegetation, as in the Port Monmouth landing case), and presumed electromagnetic and radiation effects, etc., which must also be explained?

The reader, with sufficient data, might also wonder if contactees by virtue of having premorbid dissociative personalities are "chosen" by the force behind the phenomena. What is the relationship between the origin of UFOs and this hypothecated force? Are they the same? Could the UFO force be a projection from an independently functioning "freed" collective unconscious, in a way similar to the hypothetical generation of telekinetic episodes seen in a more limited or one-to-one physician-patient relationship (Chapter 24): How germane to the hypothesized creation of UFOs and their associated phenomena is the development of poltergeist effects by the deliberate conscious creation of a ghost, as in Prof. Owen's experiments (9)? If any entity or entities (telekinetic effects or poltergeists) could be split-off products of our unconscious, individually or collectively, which function independently as if in another dimension, why wouldn't they be capable, depending on myriad variables, of producing a variety of psychic and UFO-like phenomena? For example, one well-studied contactee, whom I had seen in psychiatric and hypnotic consultation, presented a complex history (sometimes involving other witnesses to multiple sightings) of alleged encounters with entities in her home, and because of the terror involved in one particular episode, involuntary micturition. An interesting clue for further study was provided by the contactee's teen-aged son, who had out-of-the-body experiences. During one of his unconscious peregrinations he "visited" his sweetheart. However, matters abruptly came to an end when the young woman called for help and her father came to her rescue with a shotgun.

If UFOs have been known throughout all of Man's recorded history and before (e.g., material based on archeological data, memory traces of lost civilizations as stressed by Velikovsky and others), why is it that for most of the modern era the popular opinion has held that they are extraterrestrial? Is it easier to see things outside ourselves, such extraterrestrial projections, rather than to recognize them as part of ourselves — measures that might compromise our identities, question our sense of individuality, and deny our humanity or our interdependency with our fellows (10)? How much easier when the entities often proclaim an abstruse origin for themselves rather than we force ourselves to examine their claims and look upon them as a personification of ourselves — or our unconscious repressed wishes, longings, fears. Is their message to be taken at face value? Or, as seems more likely in view of all the false leads and sometimes utter nonsense, is the medium really the message? Is the message the fact that strange things actually take place in our so-called sophisticated, modern, scientific age — events beyond man's capabilities and understanding? What is the significance of frequent contactee symbolisms and warnings to mankind, which tell him to mend his ways and that if he persists in his hostilities and in the destruction of the environment, he will be doomed to perish: "all hope abandon ye who enter here."

The handful of cases presented in this book can not answer these questions, but when considered with voluminous published material elsewhere, the techniques described here might help the reader to "sort" out the cases and see them from a different perspective. By studying a series of psychiatrically worked-up cases, the reader might better conclude how too little knowledge about UFOs could be dangerous, or, conversely, how widespread public knowledge about some of the cases could cause trouble: e.g., such acute effects as mass panic reactions, clogging sensitive lines of communication and blocking critically important messages of life and death, or of military importance; such chronic results as social decay, apathy, collapse of moral and religious values, unrealistic expectations of saviors from afar, or a sense of impending doom.

What is there in UFO landing cases that, when extrapolated to worldwide thousands of similar cases, might cause different countries, including the Communist states as well as our own free-world countries, to publicly avoid making definitive statements about their own vested interests and possible researches, and about any potential hazards and benefits? Why might it be dangerous to national security, if any government did have some answers and shared the data with other countries or private UFO institutes? The potentials of psychic warfare, mind control, or esoteric incitation of crowds to riot, antigravity effects, telekinetic fouling up of computers with accidental or intended release of missiles, nuclear detonations, etc., are, unfortunately, not phantasmagoria. For, what is known about UFOs strongly suggests that these are impossible possibilities.

If close involvement with UFOs or the societal pressures and confrontations can contribute, fortunately infrequently, to psychological disintegration, or to the precipitation of emotional disorders, or can even incite defensive acts with firearms, knives, or other weapons, intended or not, against "alien invaders" — how is this to be managed when one is confronted with situations where a man stands guard by his door with a rifle in his hands awaiting his illusory "alien" enemies? Or, to cite another example, how is one to deal with a middle-aged woman who, correctly or not, lives in terror of her UFO-contactee former husband's repeated attempts to murder her? No responsible, nor, certainly, any psychiatric, book on UFOs should avoid these questions, even if they only comprise a tiny minority overall of encounters. Nevertheless, these complications do occasionally occur and at the least they warrant footnotes to otherwise superficially considered straightforward and innocuous cases. How many cut-and-dried cases would really have similar potential dangers if they were psychiatrically probed? What constitutes a good clinical control for such data? How many "routine" encounter cases would have to be psychiatrically studied to get some idea of the frequency and magnitude of these risk factors? It should not be thought that this data is served, ready-made, on a silver platter. Unfortunately it is all too available to someone skilled in psychiatric interview techniques.

★ ★ ★

Years ago I had written the late rocket and space program expert, Dr. Wehrner von Braun, about setting up telepathic experiments from space between one of our astronauts and Dunninger. Although Dunninger was then in failing health, and beyond his peak, he was quite excited about this possible stunt, and in view of our ongoing investigations of his telepathic abilities he was itching to try this one, last feat as the super challenge of his career. Unfortunately, when I finally received an answer from one of Dr. von Braun's aides, I was informed, in so many words, that red tape and regulations would make this request impossible to fulfill.

Although some of our astronauts have reportedly seen strange objects or UFOs in space, to my knowledge none of the astronauts since retiring from the space program have given this matter any special consideration in detailed publications. It would seem that more interest in UFOs was stirred by the space program than the reverse, where interest in UFOs led to intensified space researches. However, it is of more than passing interest that Astronaut Edgar Mitchell conducted telepathic experiments in space with paragnosts on earth. After Mitchell retired from NASA, he founded his psychically oriented Institute of Noetic Sciences. He alone of the astronauts*+ seemed to have had this proclivity for psychic matters. However, the possibly UFO-related significance of this fact is vitiated by Mitchell's *prior* (before he made his flight) interest in psychic matters. When appropriate, further mention will be made of the astronauts in relation to psychiatry and UFOs.

---

*Unless one considers ex-astronaut Senator (New Mexico) Harrison Schmitt's interest in the cattle mutilation cases in this category. Schmitt, who holds a Ph.D. in geology from Harvard and who had walked on the moon, also said in an interview (**National Enquirer** 12/28/76): "We ought to be involved in a search to find out if there is any good evidence that UFOs really are space craft that are being piloted by extraterrestrial beings."

+The converse, where officialdom apparently leads the way, was brought to my attention by a recent Soviet emigre physician who informed me (BES) that a leading Eastern European parapsychologist has given lectures on psychical phenomena to the cosmonauts.

A few words about my background and interest in UFOs might be in order. As a psychiatrist this is important, for subjective reality should not be ignored in the guise of trying to be objective, strictly professional, and free of bias. Something should be said about the researcher's motives rather than whitewashing them with pious platitudes, glaring omissions, or pretention. Whether intended or not, it is all too easy to let one's opinions become prejudiced. The researcher is no less a human being and free of conscious if not unconscious prepossessions, despite his specialized occupation, than those he studies. When he fails to recognize these factors in himself as well as in others, he can easily become lost and blind to much that he searches for.

Because of the enormous paranormal element in close contact UFO cases and because of my background researching psychic phenomena in psychiatry and in every-day life for close to twenty years, I could no longer limit my curiosity to some occasional patient's or person's often dreary accounts of nocturnal lights, or to reading in the popular literature about alleged spectacular psi-related close UFO encounters. Alas, all this was secondhand experience at best. I had to know first-hand and get a piece of the action myself. Excluding Carl Jung, it seemed to me that astronomers, physicists, engineers, newspapermen, and just about everyone had an opinion on the mental status and supposed paranormal aspects of UFO cases — except psychiatrists.

At approximately this time Mrs. C.W., my wife's hairdresser, who knew of my interest in psychic matters and who had with her husband formerly invited me to investigate their haunted apartment, told me of the Presque Isle UFO-landing-monster case (Chapter 1), involving four adults and two infants. Mrs. C.W.'s in-laws knew some of the people in this happening and vouchsafed for their honesty and character. Later this celebrated case was mentioned in TIME and also in the Condon Report. However, what was said in those accounts was at odds from what I found to be the case.

Synchronicity,* in my opinion, is an unusual and mostly ignored aspect to UFO-related phenomena. It has "intervened," time and again, in ways that have been at times more interesting than the alleged close sightings or landing themselves. For example, one day, years ago, Floyd Farrant, my ophthalmologist friend, and I were stopped by a security

---

*Jung: "Synchronicity takes the coincidence of events in space and time as meaning more than mere chance, namely, a peculiar interdependence of objective events among themselves as well as with the subjective (psychic) states of the observer or observers."

guard while walking on a fork to a dirt road along an isolated reservoir wilderness in northern New Jersey. The officer asked us what direction we were walking; and then he said that if we continued on the path that we were on we would wind up in a nudist colony. He didn't want that to happen to somebody who had a Presbyterian [hospital] sticker on his windshield; the guard's late father was a Presbyterian minister. He suggested the alternate route as more suitable. In reposte I asked him if he had heard anything about UFO cases in the Pequannock Water Shed. At first he did not think I was serious, but when he could see my earnestness, he told me about the Jerry Simons case. Later, because of further possible synchronicity, I could fully document Simon's close UFO encounter and subsequent grave illness (Chapter 1). Fortunately, although Simons lived in the country, miles away from my home-office in Montclair, it developed that his personal physician was a friend of mine who lived in my home town as did the consulting neurologist. The pieces all fell into place, and with Simon's assent I could easily check his copious hospital records.

In a similar vein, when Ted Bloecher, the pioneer UFO investigator, asked me if I would look into his assiduously reported New Berlin UFO Landing and Repair by Crew case (Chapter 9), I finally selected — because it just worked out that way — my late mother's birthday. On the day before my planned trip, the patient I was seeing in consultation for the first time and who was unaware of my researches, informed me that she came from the exact isolated rural area of Pennsylvania. Her directions proved helpful. The clinical verification of the New Berlin case was supported by further unanticipated coincidences: it developed that my wife served on the same school board with a close relative of Mrs. Merriweather, the New Berlin protagonist. The family's reputation was fine. Years later, long after the UFO landing, I received additional supportive and culturally interesting data when the relative informed me that Mrs. Merriweather's agnostic husband had converted to his wife's Mormon religion, moved his family far away, and changed their whole lifestyle.

One more example might be as instructive as it was amusing. Several years ago my family was invited to my wife's niece's wedding in a Northern U.S. Plains state. Naturally, the family wanted me to go, but the pressures of my work, plus the anticipated drabness of the prairies, prevented my saying "yes" for my first trip there. After much badgering from my wife for a decision, since the deadline for reservations had come, I received a long-distance telephone call that night from Jerome Clark of Moorehead, Minnesota. Jerry, the famed Fortean explorer and UFO researcher, wanted to interview me for an article. In passing, he mentioned Dr. J. Allen Hynek's enigmatic "H" case (11) in a near-by state, which involved four witnesses and where one of them shot a landed ufonaut by his silo-shaped craft. Because of ethical considerations I could not invite myself into Dr. Hynek's case, and I had few clues about who this man "H" was, and where he lived. However, my curiosity was so thoroughly ignited that I immediately told my wife to make the plane reservations and to include me. I even took along my tape recorder and motion picture camera. At the wedding reception, after negative information from my wife's well-informed minister brother-in-law, I asked my nephew if he had ever heard of such-and-such a case. At first he said 'No,' but after more questioning he thought that the man I had in mind might be a fellow who was a member of his father's church and that he (my nephew) used to play baseball with him. Needless to say, things developed beyond my expectations: the needle in the haystack was found and we had a most productive interview. This well-studied UFO landing case involved intriguing presumed psychic healing examples, animal lore, and subsequent M.I.B.-like aspects.

The Simons, Merriweather, and "H" cases cannot indicate the emotional impact of other similar possible instances of synchronicity, including the Stickler (Chapter 4), Wilcox (Chapter 3), Trasco (Chapter 17), Woodstock Festival (Chapter 8), and Port Monmouth (Chapter 7) cases. By fortuitous coincidences, telepathy, or incredible luck, the cases were seemingly thrust upon me. They constituted some of the most unusual material I have studied. There must be some meaning to this. Sometimes the coincidences were so ridiculous that I could only laugh. However, if all the details were outlined the reader could easily become confused if not bored. As in reporting on telepathic episodes in psychiatric practice and every-day life, the best illustrations often cannot be used for these same reasons. Also, it is next to impossible in many instances to define a cut-off point. Although the reader can easily become lost in a maze of details that is part of the problem and should not be ignored — the facts still hang together.

★ ★ ★

After years of researching the psychodynamics of psychic phenomena and struggling to have my articles accepted in medical journals, I was at a standstill. The still wondrous nature of many psychic events which continued throughout these years no longer held the surprise and punch they did in the early years — for example, at the height of my researches of the nonagenarian paragnost Jacques Romano, and later Joseph Dunninger. My first publication on UFOs, which appeared in MEDICAL TIMES in 1968, was secretly destined to become my swan song. Enough is enough and I wanted a rest. However, in the meantime Pandora's box had opened, because synchronistic events intervened again in the Gary Wilcox case, which involved a New York State farmer who allegedly communicated telepathically with two entities in front of a landed UFO in his fields. This case had fallen into my lap. Also approximately at this time, I prepared a paper on "UFOs in New Jersey" for the *Journal of the Medical Society of New Jersey*. As I was consolidating this material with the intention of then calling it quits, and returning to a conventional and uninterrupted psychiatric practice, I received a call in 1968 from Paul Harvey, the eminent Chicago news commentator, asking me to appear in a TV documentary on UFOs.

Time and opinions change. What was thought to be unfeasible at a point can shift and later become more attractive. Harvey, who had invited several experts in UFO research, polled the participants near the end of the video taping. He asked if they felt that the source of UFOs was extraterrestrial. Everyone voted "yes" except Col. Lawrence Tacker (who had written one of the first serious books on UFOs) (12) and myself. I suppose that if the same group were polled today some of those who handily voted affirmatively for the extraterrestial hypothesis in the past might do so again, but they might pause, hedge their answers and give consideration to the vast complexities of the UFO-human interaction, the unconscious mind, and everything else about the human part of the equation, including the interface with possible psychic factors.

About this time the distinguished investigative reporter and authority on UFOs, John A. Keel, had seen my MEDICAL TIMES article and sent it to Charles Bowen, Editor of England's prestigious *Flying Saucer Review* (FSR) — the oldest scientific journal of its kind in the world — and Mr. Bowen responded by requesting permission to reprint my article. Furthermore, he was receptive to future UFO—psychiatric material. Through the years Charles Bowen, as had John Keel and the late Ivan Sanderson, became a good friend, and I learned much from our association and from reading his provocative editorials in FSR. In addition to having new worlds opened up to me through FSR I also came in contact with illuminating, mind-bending articles by such investigators as Gordon Creighton and Aime Michel. So, any weariness I had in trying to keep up with my UFO researches while also carrying on full-time psychiatric practice was throttled. I husbanded what time was available and culled my energies for the study of UFO landing cases, instances of alleged contact with entities, and various mental and physical effects. The material seemed to be pounding on my door and it hasn't ceased to this day.

In the midst of my early UFO studies, my physician father had died. Then exactly one year to the day of my father's death, my mother succumbed to a highly malignant brain tumor. These tragedies were compounded by my twelve-year-old daughter's developing juvenile diabetes mellitus. I renewed contacts with colleagues in other medical specialties and reviewed the literature on these conditions, for I desperately sought anything that would help my mother and daughter. Although they had excellent medical care, it was futile in the case of my mother, and there was no therapeutic breakthrough for my daughter. Despite the dubious advantages of being a physician myself, I was almost as helpless as anyone else in these situations. However, because of the gravity of their illnesses I paid particular heed to accounts of alleged UFO-mediated medical benefits, such as healing from cancer, Michel's (13) account of a physician's alleged sudden recovery from right hemiparesis of ten years' duration, and an inveterate war wound; a case where an old man grew new teeth; and also, not uncommon reports of UFOs causing such diverse physical states as temporary paralysis, blackouts, amnesia, burns, eye injuries, etc. (14) Furthermore, Creighton (15) and others had written about numerous instances of human-animal UFO biological effects, and Vallee (16) had detailed two well-documented fascinating cases of medical interest: the 450-year-old, non-decaying image of the Virgin of Guadalupe and the case of supposed instantaneous healing of a compound fracture of eight years' duration. If there was anyting of value here, or if there were any clues that could come from the study of UFO landing cases, I had to know and find out quickly. The field seemed to offer some appealing medical histories, but unfortunately, there were all too few modern critical studies by physicians or persons with backgrounds in biology.

Although UFO researches taught me something about the people involved in close encounters and perhaps provided a novel and deeper insight into the psychopathological-psychic interphase for dissociative states, I discovered nothing of any immediate benefit for those with various afflictions. However, this did not and does not discourage me, and there is no need to apologize, for this can be said for many new approaches. There was and is always the flickering hope that medical-psychiatric study of the people involved in close UFO encounters could some day lead to therapeutically useful hypotheses. Hope never dies as long as one always tries.

At the time of my mother's terminal illness and my daughter's developing diabetes I met Mrs. Stella Lansing of Palmer, Massachusetts. As already said, Stella, a middle-aged housewife and mother, claimed to have taken motion pictures of a UFO on the ground with purported entities in front of it (Chapter 21); in addition to showing me this film, she later projected many of her other motion pictures of flying saucers. Perhaps she felt comfortable meeting me at an APRO lecture (Chapter 17) because of my statement that many people could be driven into psychosis if they were not given respectful attention and if their accounts of contacts with UFO entities were not listened to. In any event, my first trip to Massachusetts to interview her was rewarded by my seeing and tape recording (while she filmed) an account of a UFO, or cat-and-mouse-like playful spook light, or whatever, on a mountain ridge, early on a cold winter morning. Then, a second trip shortly afterwards involved an unusual situation on a back country road, where we photographed pulsating, moving, changing lights until we suddenly were confronted with a strange automobile seemingly coming out of nowhere. The car parked about two hundred feet directly ahead of us while we were filming and taping, and it began flashing its headlights in code-like signals (Chapter 20). Of all the UFO people I have studied, Mrs. Lansing has been extraordinary, and whatever the explanation for UFOs and related phenomena, her filmic and audio tapes must be accounted for, and they seem applicable to the problem. Her evidence suggests that there is a strong dissociative state — paranormal component to her UFO experiences and perhaps, inferentially considered, to many others. For example, one of her motion picture films showed a somber color picture, overlapping a few frames, of a monk-like figure with a death agony expression (Chapter 22, Part 2). Later my family was involved with a presumed telekinetic literal flying saucer episode and Mrs. Lansing, which gave us much to wonder about. Although the studies with Mrs. Lansing were not quite so easy as they might sound, and were often reduced to a slow pace and tedious psychodynamic importunities, it has always been an honor, whatever the final interpretation of her data, to be associated with an honest, dedicated lady.

With these introductory notes, then, the reader might be encouraged to mull over these matters and decide for himself about the "people" part of the UFO equation, and the feasibility of undertaking experiments and studying the role of intertwining psychic elements and, for me at least, frequent interruptions of synchronicity.

REFERENCES

1. Fuller, C.G., Editor, et al: **Proceedings of the First International UFO Congress,** Warner Books, New York, 1980.
2. Arnold, K., and Palmer, R.: **The Coming of the Saucers,** Amherst Press, Amherst, Wis., 1952.
3. Fodor, N.: **Encyclopedia of Psychic Science,** University Books, Inc., New York, 1966.

4. Schwarz, B.E.: **Psychic-Nexus,** Van Nostrand Reinhold Col, New York, 1980.
5. —— **Psychic-Dynamics,** Pageant Press, New York, 1965; A Psychiatrist Looks at ESP, New American Library, New York, 1968, paperback.
6. Pollack, J.H.: **Croiset the Clairvoyant,** Doubleday & Co., Garden City, N.Y., 1964.
7. Huxley, A.: **The Devils of Loudun,** Harper & Bros., Publishers, New York, 1959.
8. Eisenbud, J.: The Mind-Matter Interface, address before the Institute on the Dissemination of Human Knowledge, University of Colorado, Boulder, Oct. 10, 1973.
9. Owen, A.R.G.: **Psychic Mysteries of the North,** Harper & Row, Publishers, New York, 1975.
10. Plank, R.: **The Emotional Significance of Imaginary Beings:** A Study of the Interaction Between Psychopathology, Literature, and Reality in the Modern World, Charles C. Thomas, Springfield, Ill., 1968.
11. Hynek, J.A., and Vallee, J.: **The Edge of Reality,** Regnery, Chicago, 1975.
12. Tacker, L.J.: **Flying Saucers and the U.S. Air Force,** Van Nostrand, Princeton, N.J., 1960.
13. Michel, Aime: The Strange Case of Dr. X, **Flying Saucer Review,** Special Issue No. 3 (Sept.): 3-16, 1969.
14. Schwarz, B.E.: Psychiatric and Parapsychiatric Dimensions of UFOs, in **UFO Phenomena and the Behavioral Scientist,** Edited by R.F. Haines, The Scarecrow Press, Inc., Metuchen, N.J., & London, 1979.
15. Creighton, G.: Healing from UFOs, Flying Saucer Review, Vol. 15 (No. 5): 20-23 (Sept.-Oct.), 1969.
16. —— A New F.S.R. Catalogue, The Effects of UFOs on Animals, Birds, and Smaller Creatures, Part I: Vol. 16 (No. 1): 26-28, Jan.-Feb., 1970; Part II: Vol. 16 (No. 2): 29, Mar. Apr., 1970; Part III, Vol. 16 (No. 3): 28-30, May-June, 1970.
17. Vallee, J.: **The Invisible College,** E.P. Dutton & Co., Inc., New York, 1975.

Part I:

Scope of the UFO Problem

Chapter 1

UFOs; Delusion or Dilemma?

Various press, popular, and crackpot accounts of UFOs (unidentified flying objects, "flying saucers") have ascribed their existence to aircraft, balloons, satellites, birds, meteors, marsh gas, quasi mystical or religious beliefs, malobservations, optical illusions, mass hysteria, hoaxes, hallucinations, or delusions. Despite the widespread interest in UFOs, little has appeared in the serious literature. Markowitz, a physicist (1), recently reported in *Science* that UFOs "cannot be under extraterrestrial control if the laws of physics are valid." He cited the U.S. Air Force UFO consultant, astrophysicist Allen Hynek's (2) studies of "several hundred reports (in my files) which are fine brain teasers and could easily be made the subject of profitable discussion among physical and social scientists alike." Although Markowitz alluded to Hynek's opinion, "There is a tendency in the 20th-century to forget that there will be a 21st-century, and indeed a 30th-century, science, from which vantage point our knowledge of the universe may appear quite different," he declared, "We, ourselves, look back on eras when many people believed in the existence of centaurs, mermaids, and fire-breathing dragons."

The Air Force, beset for years by charges that it considered reports of UFOs to have psychiatric, rather than an aerodynamic, basis, recently appointed and financed the distinguished physicist, Edmund U. Condon (3), as director of a no-strings UFO inquiry at the University of Colorado.

* * *

For the most part, psychopathological or parapsychological explanations for UFO phenomena are limited to those who are neither psychiatrists nor parapsychologists. An exception to this is Jung (4), who, in an article copyrighted in 1959, stated that, "the apparently physical nature of the UFOs create such insoluble puzzles for even the best brains, and on the other hand, has built up such an impressive legend, that one feels tempted to take them as a 99 percent psychic product and subject them accordingly to the usual psychological interpretation." Jung compared beliefs in UFOs to a God image. He felt that UFO sightings were understandable when related to man's eroded belief in God and his need for a redeeming supernatural event. "God in his omniscience, omnipotence, and omnipresence is a totality symbol par excellence, something round, complete and perfect." However, Jung later altered his position in a letter to the director of the National Investigations Committee on Aerial Phenomena (NICAP). Shortly before his death in 1961, he wrote that UFOs appeared to be space ships (5).

Benjamin Simon (6-7), a Boston psychiatrist, hypnotically treated an interracial couple who, among many other symptoms, had amnesia for an alleged harrowing two-hour experience aboard a UFO. While entranced, the couple related an encounter with humanoids aboard a UFO. Simon was less concerned with the objective existence of the UFO than with "the cumulative impact of past experiences and fantasies on their present experiences and responses." In reference to the validity of the material produced, he stated that "hypnosis is a pathway to the truth as it is felt and understood by the patient. The truth is what he believes to be the truth, and this may not be consonant with the ultimate non-personal truth."

In twelve years of private psychiatric practice, the author, who has never personally seen a UFO, has not found them or related phenomena to be part of any dereistic thinking for patients seen in consultation or psychotherapy. He has also confirmed this clinical impression by discussions with several colleagues in psychiatry. In four instances, however, patients revealed observations of possible UFOs at a great distance. In none of these cases was the patient's psychopathology related to the alleged UFOs, which were also witnessed by other people. On informal inquiry to the executives of two of the largest commercial airlines, the writer obtained confirmation of reports by pilots who had observed UFOs. Their accounts were entirely similar to NICAP's and other published reports (5, 8, 9).

It is the purpose of this report to give four accounts of people who had alleged first-hand experiences with UFOs and to relate them to their psychopathology and health. For each of the accounts the key participants were examined psychiatrically. In several instances other members of their families, friends, fellow employees, and attending physicians were also seen and questioned. Tape recordings were made of the descriptions and supplementary data were collected via telephone interviewing and correspondence. Hospital records were studied as described.

Case 1. Wanaque

The author, who had read newspaper accounts of UFO sightings in the Wanaque, New Jersey area, drove there to investigate by interviewing the town physician, local police officer, two reservoir officers, and a town service station proprietor. They all suggested that he see Sergeant

Benjamin Thompson of the Wanaque Reservoir Police Force.

Shortly afterward Sergeant Thompson was seen in his home and carefully studied in psychiatric examination. He was open, friendly, straightforward, and cooperative. Sergeant Thompson, a high school graduate, had been on the reservoir police force six years, and for twenty years previously he had been a security guard at an E.I. Dupont plant. Before that he had been in the U.S. Infantry, and in World War II had fought on the islands of Guam and Iwo Jima. The sergeant felt that he had been trained to observe things carefully — "Things and people. That's what we work with." He was familiar with various types of aircraft. He denied use of hard liquor or unprescribed drugs and had no history for emotional or psychosomatic illness. Nor was there any history for sociopathic behavior, brain syndrome, cultural-religious, dissociative, conversion, or other psychopathological reactions that could account for his UFO experience. The Sergeant's reputation for trustworthiness was confirmed on detailed questioning of some of his colleagues, a town police officer, a physician, and a garage proprietor.

Sergeant Thompson observed UFOs on four occasions. While on patrol car duty on the night of October 11, 1966, about 9:15 p.m., he received a radio message from a fellow police officer in a nearby community, reporting observation of a UFO. The sergeant drove to the area the UFO was approaching. In his own words: "It was diagonally 250 feet from me, out over the reservoir, as big as an automobile, or bigger. It was about 250 feet up in the air. When I got out of the police car, this thing was so bright that it blinded me so bad I couldn't find the car. It was all white, like looking into a bulb and trying to see the socket, which you can't do. I signed out of service [to the Ringwood Police] for twenty minutes because I couldn't see ... neither the fingers of my hands nor the lights on the jeep. I stood by the fence until it [vision] came back gradually. It made no sounds but left a heavy mist, as it went away; you could say it was a mist-like sort of fog. It really shook me up. When I got back into the car, switched on the red dome light and flasher, and then got out of the car and started walking toward it, it took off. It never made a sound. I would say I observed it about three minutes. I was totally blinded after the light. It took [away] my voice [no shouting] and I was hoarse for two weeks after that. I described the object as a basket-ball with a hole cut in it and a football set in it, so that maybe a quarter of the football was sticking out (see Fig. 1). When it flew over the water, it could make a square turn. It could shoot straight up in the air — nothing like an airplane."

On a subsequent interview, nine months later, all the salient details were reviewed with Sergeant Thompson. His account was exactly as

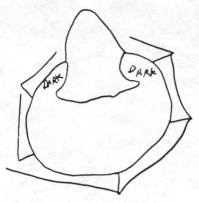

Fig. 1 Facsimile of Sgt. Benjamin Thompson's drawing of UFO.

noted earlier, and his experience was confirmed upon interviewing three fellow officers. Sergeant Thompson recalled that although he did not see a physician at the approximate time of his experience, he has been in excellent general health since then. Neither he nor his colleagues have had any other close experience with a UFO since the one reported here.

In addition to a fellow police officer and the Sergeant, this UFO episode was also witnessed by a woman who was driving near the reservoir at that time. She told her husband, who contacted the police. All the data were recorded in the police files.

The local area police checked with the Air Force: no planes were reported in the region of Wanaque Reservoir at the time of the UFO sighting.

Lloyd Mallan (10), a well known science writer, who had interviewed Sergeant Thompson, also attempted to determine if the overflights of many helicopters and high-performance aircraft within fifteen minutes of the UFO sighting were coincidental or were related to the UFO sighting. He checked with the "U.S. Air Force officers in the Pentagon and at Project Blue Book; with officers of the U.S. Navy at Lakehurst, New Jersey; [and with] Floyd Bennett, New York, and Willow Grove, Pennsylvania, Naval Air Stations; with the Bureau of Safety of the Civil Aeronautics Board (CAB), both at its Washington, D.C., headquarters and at its installation at JFK International Airport, New York; with the General Aviation District Office of the Federal Aviation Agency (FAA) at Teterboro, New Jersey, Airport; and with the U.S. Coast Guard. The results of all (my) inquiries were negative."

Case 2. Split Rock

Jerry H. Simons, a twenty-two-year-old forester of Newfoundland,

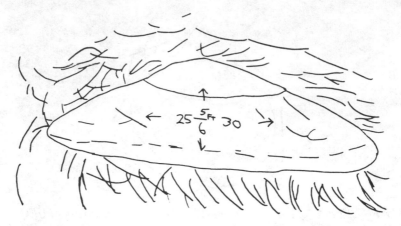

Fig. 2 Facsimile of Jerry H. Simons' drawing of UFO made shortly after his experience. Note similarity of Sgt. Thompson's drawing in Fig. 1.

New Jersey, revealed that on Saturday night, October 16, 1966, between 4:30 and 5:00 a.m., while camping and fishing at Split Rock Reservoir, in northern New Jersey, he had his first and only experience with a possible UFO. In an account, written the day after the experience, he stated: "I was travelling north on the road and noticed a very outstanding glow at the time I first noticed it. I tried putting my foot under the brake pedal and pulling it up. It was at this point that I became aware of the orange-red glow becoming brighter. I did not know what to think. In fact, I don't think it entered my thoughts [that it was] anything really out of the ordinary.

"I stopped the car and lowered my window. I stuck my head out to get a clear view of the rear of my car. What I saw took me completely unawares and scared the living hell out of me. I've never been so startled in my life. It was something I could not understand. At first glance it seems to be nothing but a huge glowing light, but then I noticed a very distinct outline of what appeared to be some sort of a solid body (see Fig. 2).

"I was in doubt of my sanity for a few seconds. I couldn't accept what my eyes were seeing, but it only took a few seconds for all doubt to leave my mind and for me to understand that what I was seeing was very real. It was then that I decided to get out on the main road as fast as I could get my car over the cow path. The object was directly in back and above me and followed my car along the road. Then my car began to act abnormally. All at once the power started dying out. Then the worst thing that could have happened in my frame of mind happened. Without

44

any warning, all the electrical equipment quit working. My headlights, dashlights and engine quit. I don't believe I have ever been so frustrated in all my life. I noticed this object was directly over the top of my car. Then it fell back and I could go on. Three times this happened, and three times my car refused to give any electrical response until this object either moved to the rear or to one side of the car. When it was right over the top of the car, all I could do was to lock my doors and hope. I cannot, will not, try to explain what or why. I was still aware it was with me because of the glow in the trees and on the ground to the right and left of the car. The only time the glow was very distinctive in front of the car was when everything went dead and then it was all around me.

"When I got to the Charlottesburg Road, I took a split-second look, glancing up and behind me to see if it was still with me. Even though the glow was still to be seen on either side of the car, I had to be sure that the glow on the ground was not my imagination; and it wasn't. The last good look I got of it was just before reaching the dam, when it was so bright in my mirror. Now I could not see anything in the sky. I did not waste any time looking for it because I was already running toward the house."

Simons, who was working for a meteorologist at the Weather Bureau, Newark Airport, at the time of his experience at Split Rock Reservoir, drove to the home of Thomas P. Byrnes, Superintendent of the Newark Water Shed, Newfoundland, New Jersey. Upon interviewing Mr. Byrnes, who has been well known to the writer for several years, I found that he fully confirmed the forester's experience. Mr. Byrnes recalled how he contacted the West Milford, New Jersey, police, and together with Simons they all drove to the site of the UFO experience. Nothing out of the ordinary was observed. Byrnes said, "He [Simons] woke my wife and was terribly excited, almost white." Further questioning of several of the forester's friends, fellow employees, and local police officers also confirmed Simon's experience and reputation for truthfulness.

The West Milford Township Police report by Officers A. Hooper and V. Meyer at 5:54 a.m., October 15, 1966, further confirmed Simon's account in all details.

In his original notes Simons had sketched the alleged UFO as being an estimated 25x30 ft., and at tree height. The object made no noise, and there was no odor or other sensation. He estimated that the auto motor was unresponsive for less than a minute, and then when the lights came back on he started the engine again. Although in all the excitement the total time of exposure was not noted, a conservative estimate, based on driving this rocky wood road during optimal daylight conditions, would be at least ten to fifteen minutes.

Simons parked his car at the Reservoir Office and went inside. But when he came out again, he and the man on duty, Martin Shauger, were startled to find that the car had apparently started spontaneously even though Simons thought the ignition key was in the off position. He switched the key back and forth between off and on, and the motor stopped. He later examined the motor and electrical system and found no explanation. A few weeks afterward, while Simons was driving his car, the motor exploded and was never right afterward. Simons, who had been a champion stock car racer and former employee of General Motors, was mystified.

A study of the forester's past life, gleaned in several interviews lasting many hours, led me to believe that he had never had any previous experience like this. He had never had any emotional illness. Although he tried to enlist in the U.S. Navy, he was not accepted because of a history of duodenal ulcer. He had formerly been an Eagle Scout (Troop 8, Kingsport, Tennessee). He was an experienced outdoorsman who had camped in many of the states of the United States for some years. He was a high school graduate and had had two additional years of industrial arts. Simons did not use drugs and although he had used beer in the past, he had not taken any at the time of his experience.

Review of the *Newark Evening News* files revealed three different sightings of UFO's in the vicinity of Split Rock Reservoir on October 15, 1966. The West Milford Police files for October 14, 15, and 16, 1966, yielded no UFO reports other than the Simons experience. An interview with the meteorologist who was formerly Simons' employer revealed that Simons mentioned the UFO experience shortly after it happened, and that although he was in good health at the time of the experience, he became ill shortly afterward.

Three months after the UFO incident (January 17, 1967), Simons was admitted to Montclair Community Hospital for a "fascinating" illness of three months' duration, characterized by fatigue, anorexia, generalized soreness, and weakness of the muscles, drowsiness, chills for three or four days, and a weight loss of thirty-five pounds. The symptoms had developed shortly after the UFO experience, and at that time the acute phase had lasted three to four days. A physician diagnosed the illness as "flu." However, the acute symptoms recurred every month (three attacks) until he was hospitalized, as noted above.

Although Simons told a second physician about his UFO experience, his statement was not recorded in the hospital charts. Instead, his illness was connected to an experience which occurred a month before the UFO episode and lasted an estimated several hours over a period of one week. This experience involved cleaning a room that had been occupied by cats. At the time, five other people, in addition to Simons, were bitten, were scratched, and had contact with cat faeces. DDT was sprayed in an enclosed area. Questioning of other people who were exposed revealed that no one, including Simons, developed any difficulty. It can be supposed that Simons was in excellent health because of his roughing it while camping out and fishing during the night and early morning of October 15, 1966 — the time of his UFO experience. Furthermore, a pre-employment physical examination on September 19, 1966 (after exposure to cats and before the UFO episode) revealed no mention of any recent illness. In fact, Simons was listed as having good physical health.

After "recovering" from his illness of three to four day's duration, Simons returned to work for six weeks. However, the recurrence of the soreness and weakness of his muscles and drowsiness necessitated hospitalization, and he was seen by his own physician and in consultation by a neurologist.

Physical examination revealed a young man who appeared chronically ill and who had "diffuse, moderate muscle weakness, more marked proximally and associated with cramps on contraction, and contraction fasciculations." A posterior-anterior chest X-ray revealed no pathology. Laboratory studies revealed no abnormalities. These included: hemoglobin 15.2 gms./100 ml.; haematocrit 45 per cent; white blood cell count of 8,500/cu. mm. with 51 per cent neutrophils and 49 per cent lymphocytes; erythrocyte sedimentation rate of 3 mm./hr.; LE clot test, negative; two urinalyses, negative. There was no evidence for myoglobinuria. The serum electrolyte concentrations were normal (sodium, 145 mEq/L, chlorides 107 mEq/L, carbon dioxide content, 29.8 mEq/L, calcium 5 mEq/L). The protein bound iodine was 3.3 microgm./100 ml.; the serum bilirubin 0.6 mgs. per cent; 2 hr. postprandial blood glucose 110 mgs. per cent; serum alkaline phosphatase 2.5 B.U., thymol turbidity 2.0 U./100 ml.; and the blood urea nitrogen 8.4 mgs. per cent. The cerebro-spinal fluid cell count was 2/cu. mm.; chloride, 122 mEq/L per cent; glucose, 73 mgs. per cent; colloidal gold curve negative; protein, 45 mgs. per cent; and culture showed no growth. the VDRL was non-reactive; lactic dehydrogenase 580 U., and the serum glutamic oxalacetic transaminase (SGOT) was 16KU, and serum glutamic pyruvic transaminase (SGPT) 16 U./ml.

Biopsy of three pieces of tissue from the biceps muscle, saphenous vein, and subcutaneous tissue, revealed no pathology. The patient had a provisional diagnosis of "diffuse inflammatory disease of the muscle." Because of the bizarre nature of his illness and the difficulty in relating his experiences with DDT and the cats, arrangements were made for his admission to the National Institute of Health for special study. He chose not to go. Gradually, over a period of several months, he made a complete recovery.

Although the family physician knew of the reputed UFO experience, he did not mention it to the neurologist. When the latter was told about it by the writer months later, he vividly recalled the salient details of Simons' illness as later corroborated in the hospital records, and then asked the writer (a psychiatrist), "Is he (Simons) schizophrenic?"

An electroencephalogram of the forester taken six months after hospitalization was normal. He had a good work record and was well thought of by his associates. Retrospectively, his bizarre illness did not conform to any readily identifiable pattern, including various psychosomatic reactions.

Although there is not sufficient supporting data, it is conceivable that Simon's overwhelming fear, associated with the strangeness of his UFO experience, could have precipitated a response similar to what is seen in animal hypnosis. Pavlov's statement might be germane: "Little has been done toward the elucidation of the class of negative inhibitory reflexes (instincts) which are evoked by any strong stimulus or even weak stimuli if unusual. Animal hypnosis, so-called, belong to this category (11)."

Case 3. Towanda

Earlier correspondence with Robert W. Martz, a 73-year-old retired Monroeton, Pennsylvania, electrical contractor, was followed by a later psychiatric interview in his home. From this it was established that at 8:15 p.m. on April 25, 1966, while driving with a friend, Charles Dayton, he noticed a "very awesome, huge, flaming body, which lit up a large area, visible for a few seconds. It had a red flame with a green and yellow tail. Then the second view was of a dark object. The huge flames went out like turning off an electric bulb for a few seconds. There was a dim light in four port holes, and then all darkness. It looked like it was 250 ft. in front of us and 250 ft. up, and it could go at a terrific speed. It was about 25 ft. in length and had a tail 35 ft. long (see Fig. 3).

The contractor did not detect any odor, but he recalled how warm he felt. He noted that the automobile engine stalled and the lights went out. He soon started the engine again. "I never saw such a sight. I was amazed and flabbergasted." He and his friend were concerned that the object would crash into the side of the mountain.

48

(a)   (b)

Fig. 3 Facsimile of Robert W. Martz's drawing of UFO. The first view (a) was "visible for a second — very awesome — a huge flaming body which lit up a large area (red flame, green and yellow tail.)" The second view (b) was a "dark object — huge flames went out like turning off a light bulb, a few seconds, then all darkness (dim light in ports)."

Messrs. Martz and Dayton are leading citizens in their community. The author has known Mr. Martz' daughter, Mrs. Evelyn Guldner, for ten years. She is a medical secretary and electroencephalographic technician. The contractor, who was celebrating his golden wedding anniversary at the time of this writing, has never had any emotional illness. He and his friend do not use liquor or unprescribed drugs. There was nothing in the contractor's history or behavior since the event to suggest dereistic thinking, sociopathic behavior, brain syndrome, and the like. It was interesting that the contractor had kept a daily weather log for the past twelve years in which he rarely mentioned anything else other than such data. However, on the date of the UFO experience he wrote in the log about the event. Written confirmation was offered by the *Daily Review of Towanda,* Pennsylvania, April 26, 1966, which had an article headlined, "Thousands Awed by Fiery Object Seen in Eastern Sky."

Case 4. Presque Isle

Shortly after dusk, Sunday, July 31, 1966, a hot clear day, four people and two infants drove to Beach Six at Presque Isle Peninsula Park north of Erie, Pennsylvania, for a picnic. Their car stuck in the sand, and one of them, Gerald La Belle, age twenty-six, went to Erie to seek help from friends. At 10:00 p.m., while on a routine check, Patrolmen Robert Loeb, Jr., and Ralph E. Clark, noted the mired auto and told the occupants they would return in a half hour to make sure the car had been freed. When the officers swung back at 10:30 p.m., they noticed that La Belle had not yet returned and they were told by Douglas J. Tibbetts, age eighteen, "There's something weird going on here." While the occupants were in the car, shortly after 10:00 p.m., they had suddenly seen a bright light shoot out of the skies from the north and land near Beach Seven, about 300 yards from their car. Tibbetts re-

49

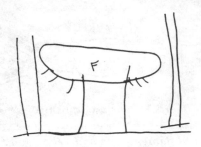

Fig. 4. Facsimile of Betty Klem's drawing of UFO on the ground as drawn, shortly after her experience, for (Erie) Morning News reporters.

membered the craft when it was "... hovering above the ground several hundred yards from the auto" (see Fig. 5). Betty Jean Klem, age sixteen, remembered the craft while it was on the ground. She described it as "mushroom shaped with a narrow base rising to an oval structure having three lights on the back" (see Fig. 4).

Later Miss Klem and Tibbetts drew a picture for the *Morning News* reporters of what they had seen earlier in the evening. Tibbetts' picture resembled a photograph of a UFO over a Lawrence County farm, unknowingly made by Joseph Yost, a New Castle, Pennsylvania, photographer for the *New Castle News*. When asked whether there had been any noise, Miss Klem said, "It sounded like the noise in a telephone receiver, only louder of course ... At first we couldn't believe it. We weren't scared at first. I kept saying, 'Doug, do you see it?' He said, 'Yes.' Then he would ask me if I saw it. We just couldn't believe it was really happening."

Miss Klem continued, "The ship was big. It came half way up between those trees, and when it came down and landed the car vibrated. We had the radio on ... No, it didn't make any interference on the radio ... Rays of light shone from the object. It lit up the whole woods along its path. It wasn't like a searchlight. There was a light along the ground, along its whole path. When the police car came up to the stuck vehicle, the UFO lights went out."

The patrolmen and Tibbetts set out for the UFO, but after going only about 300 yards they heard the stranded car's auto horn blaring frantically. Miss Klem, who was sitting in the driver's seat, and Mrs. Anita Haifley, age twenty-two, who was in the back seat with her two children, Sandra two years old and Sara, six months old, were terrified. Miss Klem was "hysterical," shaking and crying. She said she had seen, "a dark, apparently featureless creature, not human, maybe animal, which moved sluggishly back into the bush." She leaned on the horn,

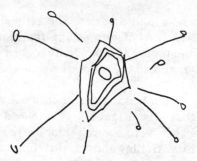

Fig. 5. Facsimile of Douglas Tibbetts' drawing of UFO as he recalled seeing it hovering above the ground, several hundred yards from where the auto was stuck in soft sand. This drawing was also made shortly after the experience, for (Erie) Morning News reporters.

having been frightened by the creature. Mrs. Haifley, according to what she told La Belle, the police, and a NICAP committee, also saw the creature. Terror-stricken, she threw her children from the seat to the floor of the car and huddled over them.

Miss Klem estimated the creature was in sight from one and one-half to two minutes. She sketched the "tall thing" (see Fig. 6). She re-

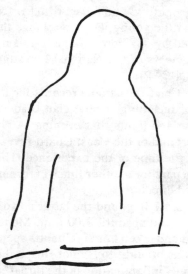

Fig. 6. Facsimile of the "creature" as drawn by eye witness Betty Klem for (Erie) Morning News reporters. "She described the creature as being upright, gorilla-shaped, about six feet tall, dark, and featureless."

called how it had no neck and no arms. She estimated the creature's height to be more than 6 ft. Before seeing the monster, they heard scratching noises on the roof of the car. Neither she nor the other occupants got out of the car, and all the windows were closed except the front side vents.

When the group were taken to the Administration Building, Patrolman Canfield noted that Miss Klem's "... forehead was covered with perspiration and her bangs were naturally stuck to her brow. I never saw anybody so scared." Mrs. Haifley and her two children were so disturbed that they were put in the first aid room.

Shorly after the episode, Miss Klem was seen and questioned by Park Police Chief Dan Dascanio and Larie Pintea, Editor of the (Erie) *Morning News*. The Chief said, "I'm convinced that the young people saw something. The girl was a credible person. Of the two individuals involved she was the most specific about what she saw — she made no attempt to fill in her story when she wasn't sure. She was one scared girl when I first saw her. Her hands were shaking, her face was trembling, her speech was more inarticulate, and she had difficulty maintaining her composure. Her eyes were red and she kept shaking her head from side to side."

Mr. Pintea wrote in the Erie *Morning News*, "Since we saw the condition of one of the witnesses [Betty Jean Klem] within one hour after the hair-lifting sighting, and talked with her for almost an hour, we have little doubt that the young lady saw things that night." The party was later interviewed by Air Force Major William S. Hall, of Youngstown, Ohio, and members of the National Investigations Committee on Aerial Phenomena (NICAP).

Study of Police Chief Dascanio's records for that day revealed that many other people, including a physician, had independently seen a strange aerial object and lights that evening. A check of the Port Erie International Airport and of the Coast Guard revealed that no craft had been in the area at the time of the experience. There were no bears or other animals in the park (or at other times in recent years) large enough to cause the reported effects.

Miss Klem, Mrs. Haifley, and the latter's two children remained at the Administration Building until 3:00 a.m. Monday, when they were picked up by friends and taken home. Tibbetts spent the night, and later in the morning he was brought to Hamot Hospital in Erie. Hospital records show that he had "inflammation of the throat" and a slightly elevated temperature. He was treated and released within one hour of admission. The only possible sequelae for the remaining occupants, according to La Belle, consisted of recurrent nightmares for Mrs. Haifley that

52

lasted for many weeks. She was, perhaps understandedly, reluctant to discuss her experience, and it was impossible to contact her (in 1968) for psychiatric interviews.

Two and a half weeks after the UFO experience when Miss Klem returned with La Belle to the site of the episode, she has sudden diffuse abdominal cramps, which were relieved shortly after she left the park. She had nothing like this previously or since.

At approximately 7:00 a.m. the day after the UFO experience, Patrolmen Paul H. Wilson and J. Robert Canfield went to the area where the craft had supposedly landed and discovered, "strange markings in the sand ... [two] triangularly shaped [impressions] about eight inches deep at the apex and then sloping upward to an area that was round and smooth. The lines of the impression were 'very distinctly made.' Going from there, moving toward where the car was stuck in the sand, the patrolmen found three other imprints ... These latter imprints formed a perfect triangle ... From where the first two imprints were found leading to within two feet of where the car was stuck, a pattern of conically shaped imprints was found. These imprints were also very sharply made and were about six inches deep, leading to the bottom of the cone-shaped impressions. They were staggered as if made by a walking creature. The patrolmen said the imprints were five to six feet apart. Later in the day, the same imprints were found leading to the water of the lake. The patrolmen were particularly intrigued by the markings on the imprints which appeared to be made by claws."

The State Police took plaster casts of the imprints, which formed a perfect triangle and of the "claw marks". All the information about the imprints was confirmed by review of Chief Dan Dascanio's records, as well as by interviews on January 6, 1968, of Chief Dascanio, Patrolman Albert J. Gagnon, Gerald La Belle, and a teenager who was living at the Presque Isle Lighthouse at the time of the reputed UFO experience.

An unidentified clear liquid substance found near the indentations, which was collected in five specimen bottles, was sent for analysis. The fluid was clear, colorless, and compared by Chief Dascanio to "silicone." Unlike water, soft drinks, and so forth, which quickly seep through the sand with little or no residue, the liquid spots lasted for several hours. Studies by Erie County Civil Defense workers revealed "no radioactivity from the area of the indentations in the same or where the drippings were found or the samples gathered by the Park Police."

However, Patrolman Albert J. Gagnon, who photographed the impressions and gathered the liquid samples at approximately 8:30 a.m., became suddenly and unexpectedly ill at home later (about 6:00 p.m.). His temperature rose to 102.6 at 8:30 p.m., according to his wife, a registered nurse. Gagnon took 10 gr. aspirin, and the fever and generalized malaise subsided within three hours. He had no previous or subsequent illness exactly like this. He was not exposed to anyone with a fever or recent history for influenza. He was in excellent condition before this sudden illness. He did not connect his possible illness to the "contamination" from the fluid samples until he was questioned (January 6, 1968).

A large, freshly gouged area of wood and bark (exact dimensions not recorded) was noted in the willow tree close to the picnic table. The bark was not found on the ground. The gouged area was recalled by La Belle and Patrolman Gagnon. It was also mentioned in the original NICAP records. A study of the area on January 6, 1968, revealed that the tree had been cut down and removed. This was apparently not the case with other trees in this immediate area.

The roof of Tibbett's car was alleged to have a dent on the right side. La Belle recalled that he helped Tibbetts wash and wax the car that afternoon before the UFO episode, and that there was no dent at that time.

On January 5 and 6, 1968, Miss Klem and La Belle were examined psychiatrically. Their accounts of the events and specific chronology were entirely similar to the many published reports and other records in Chief Dascanio's files. Miss Klem and La Belle, before the Presque Isle episode, had been "non-believers in UFOs," and neither of them has read more in the popular press than perhaps the average person. La-Belle recalled how he might have observed a widely reported possible UFO on September 7, 1965 [*Post Journal* (Jamestown, N.Y.): 'Something' in Sky Causes Furor; Believed Meteor]. Interrogation of three of Miss Klem's friends of several years' standing, as well as her husband [she was married in 1967], supported her reputation for truthfulness. Miss Klem seemed to be of above average intelligence. She answered questions in a straightforward, open way. She appeared to be healthy, her only defect being myopia, which was completely corrected with glasses. [She was wearing glasses at the time of the episode.] Although her family background had emotionally disruptive experiences, she herself had never suffered from any emotional, psychosomatic, or other serious disabling illness. There was no evidence for any past or present dereistic phenomena, sociopathic behavior, or neurotic character traits. In the presence of her husband, she was quickly induced into a hypnotic trance, and the salient details of the alleged UFO experience were fully confirmed. There were never any variations in her account.

Although not directly involved in the episode, La Belle, in some popular accounts of the UFO episode, was reputedly part of a fantastic hoax. However, it seems he was nowhere near the site of the alleged activity when everything happened at Presque Isle. At that time he was in Erie, getting a friend to bring him back to the park and to help tow the stranded car. He had no past emotional illness or penchant for pranks. He appeared to be an open, straightforward, if not rather serious, person. He supported the accounts of the others, and study of all the circumstances made the hypothesis for fraud seem most unlikely.

Unfortunately, it was not possible to interview Tibbetts and Mrs. Haifley. Their comments, however, as published in the *Morning News* and recorded in Chief Dan Dascanio's official records were entirely compatible with the other data furnished by Miss Klem and La Belle.

Miss Klem and La Belle recalled the social consequences of reporting their experiences, such as often derogatory implications of their lying or imagining things. Although the interpretation of the various reported facts is admittedly scientifically unsatisfactory and incomplete, it would seem that the group's experience was so unique and amply documented that despite the shortcomings it deserved study. It should be stressed that highly trained and experienced observers, such as Chief Dascanio and his patrolmen and Larie Pintea and his staff of the *Morning News*, carefully recorded all the data almost immediately after the UFO episode. All these circumstances make a hoax or fabrication very unlikely indeed.

The presence or absence of coexistent psychopathology is secondary to the purpose of this study in answering the question: Is it likely that the group had an objective, reality-bound, close experience with a UFO? Psychiatric evaluation suggests an affirmative answer.*

Comment and summary

Although the objective reality of the alleged UFO accounts can neither be proved nor disproved, the data are entirely similar to many published experiences and seem to be authentic. The behavior of the participants during psychiatric studies was consonant with truthfulness for the reported experiences. While psychopathology in one sphere does not *a priori* invalidate one's ability to report data accurately in other areas, it should be stressed that, unlike Simons' patients, in none of these examples was there any clinical evidence for current or past emotional illness or excessive phantasizing. Furthermore, the participants in each example were fully conscious of what was happening and

---

*Unfortunately, limitations of space preclude a more comprehensive presentation of the material at this time. The official Air Force release of the "evaluation on the sighting of July 31, 1966" consisted of five paragraphs that were, in the writer's opinion, insufficient for a scientific dialogue.

they recalled their experiences in a wakeful, alert state. There was no history for lying, dissociative reactions or possible drug effects. In the absence of permissiveness for lying in the history of the subject, or other members of his family, lying or unconscious fabrication becomes quite unlikely (12). There was nothing intrinsic about this possible UFO experiences, or in the histories of the participants, that suggested parapsychological aspects, such as purported telepathic communications, and so forth. Similarly, nothing in the study of the participants or their families suggested any unusual symbolical, mystical, or religious explanation.

The veracity of the UFO accounts is further supported because the participants did not seek notoriety from their experiences. Quite to the contrary, most were reticent about relating their experiences because of the fear of publicity and ridicule.

The objective reality of the UFO participants' reports of their unusual, traumatic experiences is also supported indirectly from clinical studies on various emotional illnesses. In his earliest researches on hysteria, Freud (13) discovered accounts of previous traumas. Although he originally believed his patients' accounts of the traumas, he later abandoned this position in the favor of the theory that the supposed past traumas were not objective facts but in the realm of fantasy and wish-fulfillment. However, Freud's earlier viewpoint of *actual* was subscribed to by Ferenczi (14) in an address given in 1932 (not published until 1949). Ferenczi's opinion that actual traumas took place as described was based on transference and counter-transference reactions with patients in therapy, rather than actual study of parent and child.

The Mayo Clinic (15-17) collaborative investigations of whole families by a team of highly skilled physicians has provided a major breakthrough to the question of trauma, fact versus fantasy. These up-to-date studies seem applicable to the problem of validity for the UFO experiences. For example, one such study of ninety-one patients and the relatives revealed that the majority of schizophrenic patients had actual traumatic assaults by parents or parental surrogates. It was clearly demonstrated how the first schizophrenic delusion represented in "a striking, specific manner the essence of a parental assault." By analogy and comparison to the first schizophrenic delusions, the UFO experiences of the healthy subjects — those who did not suffer from gross psychopathological distortions — take on even greater significance for objective reality. Fantasy and delusion versus objective reality is a complicated process, but for the skilled therapist experiences in collaborative psychotherapy dealing with both parent and child it is entirely possible to separate fact from fantasy. In a healthy person the task is that much easier. Therefore in the absence of psychodynamic motivation for conscious or unconscious fabrication it seems reasonable that the four UFO examples are factual and objectively accurate. The problem is the interpretation.

Although more UFO encounter data would be desirable, there is sufficient material for some speculation. For example, attention might be directed to various physical, physiological, and psychic effects, such as (1) the temporary blindness and hoarseness in Case Wanaque, (2) the development of severe muscular weakness and wasting in Case Split Rock, (3) the sensation of heat in Case Towanda, and (4) panic reactions following an encounter with an alleged "monster" in Case Presque Isle.

It is beyond the scope of this study to discuss the extraterrestrial hypothesis for UFOs, possibilities of electromagnetic effects, and the significance of a possible contactee encounter as in Case Presque Isle. Intriguing questions might be raised about the strange triangular impressions of "claw marks", and the fluid. All these points raise questions better left to the experts in other areas. For example, the biologist Ivan T. Sanderson, who has studied UFOs since 1929, has compiled some provocative data and has made some brilliant speculations that could be of particular interest to physicians (18).

Although many other eminent UFO authorities, both pro and con, could be quoted, we cite only Professor Hermann Oberth (19), "Father of Astronautics," who was originally trained as a physician and began his career "in a military hospital for three years, where [he] also had the care of mentally ill patients." On many occasions Professor Oberth stated his conviction that UFOs are piloted by superintelligent beings from another planet.

The data of first-hand UFO experiences should have practical value and interest to the physician who by training is in a unique position to make contributions to this problem. He is often the first to hear of such reports and is in a position to obtain all the facts and assess the human biological effects. While it is evident that the physician will undoubtedly come across some crackpot and irresponsible accounts, as a practitioner of an ancient art and science he should scrupulously avoid ridicule and keep an open mind lest he unwittingly discourage significant reports from those who might have had valid experiences, and thus inflict damage on them. A condemnatory attitude is as scientifically reprehensible as a gullible one. "We can now see, that in years past, patients were lost or driven into psychosis by our failure to believe them because of our conviction that much of their account must be fantasy (15)."

★ ★ ★

Four examples of allegedly close contact with UFOs are presented.

57

Possible physical, physiological, and psychic reactions are explored. The question of the validity of the data, and the evaluation of psychodynamic factors operating in fact versus fantasy, is discussed.

It is felt that the objective details of the reported UFO experiences are essentially real, and neither phantasied nor dereistic. By his training the physician is well suited for the task of interviewing and obtaining data from persons who might have had UFO experiences. Some of the medical implications of this challenging data are discussed.

REFERENCES

1. Markowitz, W.: The Physics and Metaphysics of Unidentified flying objects, Science, Vol. 157: Sept. 15, 1967, pp. 1274-1279.
2. Hynek, H.A.: Letters, Science, Vol. 154: 1966, p. 329.
3. Editorial: "Condon to Head UFO Study," **Science**, Vol. 154: 1966, p. 244.
4. Jung, C.G.: Cited in **The Flying Saucer Reader**, edited by David Jay, Signet Books, New American Library, Inc., New York, 1967, "UFO as a Psychological Projection," abridged from **Flying Saucers: A Modern Myth of Things Seen in the Skies,** copyrighted 1959 by C.G. Jung, translated by R.F.C. Hull, reprinted by permission of Harcourt, Brace & World, Inc.
5. Hall, R., Editor: The UFO Evidence, published by the National Investigations Committee on Aerial Phenomena (NICAP) 1536 Connecticut Ave., N.W., Washington 36, D.C., May 1964, p. 49 (for Jung), p. 184.
6. Fuller, J.: **The Interrupted Journey**, Dell Publishing Co., Inc., New York, 1967, p. 350.
7. Simon, B.: Hypnosis in the Treatment of Military Neuroses, **Psychiatric Opinion**, Vol. 4, October, 1967, pp. 24-29.
8. Edwards, F.: **Flying Saucers — Serious Business**, Bantam Books, New York, 1966, p. 184.
9. Valee, J.: **Anatomy of a Phenomenon**, Ace Star Books, New York, 1965, p. 255.
10. Mallan, L.: The Truth Behind the UFOs, in **The Official Guide to UFOs**, Science and Mechanics Publishing Co., New York, 1967, pp. 83-84.
11. Schwarz, B.E.: Electroencephalographic Changes in Animals under the Influence of Hypnosis, **Journal of Nervous and Mental Diseases,** Vol. 124, 1956, pp. 433-439.
12. Johnson, A.M., and Szurek, S.A.: The Genesis of Antisocial Acting Out in Children and Adults, **Psychoanalytic Quarterly,** Vol. 3, No. 21, 1952, pp. 323-343.
13. Jones, E.: **The Life and Work of Sigmund Freud**, Basic Books, Inc., New York, 1953, Vol. 1: pp. 262-265.
14. Ferenczi, S.: Confusion of Tongues Between Adults and the Child, **International Journal of Psychoanalysis,** Vol. 30, 1949, pp. 225-230.
15. Litin, E.M., Giffin, M.E., and Johnson, A.M.: Parental Influence in Unusual Sexual Behavior in Children, **Psychoanalytic Quarterly, Vol. 1,** No. 25, 1956, pp. 37-55.
16. Beckett, P.G.S., et al.: 1. The Significance of Exogenous Traumata in the

Genesis of Schizophrenia, **Psychiatry**, Vol. 2, No. 19, 1956, pp. 137-142.

17. Johnson, A.M. et al.: II Observations on Ego Functions in Schizophrenics, **Psychiatry**, Vol. 2, No. 19, 1956, pp. 143-148.

18. Sanderson, I.T.: **Uninvited Visitors: A Biologist Looks at UFOs,** a Cowles Book, New York, 1967, p. 244.

19. Oberth, H.: "Dr. Hermann Oberth Discusses UFOs," **Fate Magazine,** 15, No. 5, Issue 146, May, 1962, pp. 36-43.

Chapter 2

UFOs in New Jersey

Few subjects have aroused more controversy than unidentified flying objects. The atmospheric physicist, McDonald, (1) has called them "the greatest international scientific problem of our times." The recently released University of Colorado study (by the Condon Group) concluded that "... nothing has come from the study of UFOs in the past twenty-one years that has added to scientific knowledge ... and that further extensive study of UFOs probably cannot be justified (2)."

Hynek (3), professor of astronomy and chief scientific consultant to the Air Force on the subject, in a marked departure from his earlier skepticism, called for Congress to establish a board of inquiry for the specific purpose of an in-depth investigation of the UFO phenomenon.

The Aerial Phenomena Research Organization in its *APRO Bulletin* and the National Investigation Committee on Aerial Phenomena in its *The U.F.O. Investigator,* and other publications, have mentioned many possible UFO effects of interest to physicians, but there has been little in the medical literature. Meerloo (4,5), a pioneering psychiatrist in so many fields, gave an analysis of possible errors of observation, and Walker (6) "presented various procedures for establishing the credibility level for observers." Walker used a hypothetical case to illustrate his methods of combining different branches of medical knowledge.

A Brazilian physician, Olavo Fontes (7), studied an extraordinary alleged contactee case. In two recent reports (8,9) of close UFO encounters much of the relevant medical literature was mentioned. The first-hand studies showed how medicine could be useful (1) in evaluating possible UFO-induced biologic effects, and (2) in determining whether the alleged UFO episode was a reality, a delusion, an illusion, a hallucination, or a fabrication.

In thirteen years of private practice in which I have seen 3,391 patients in psychiatric examinations and have participated in thousands of hours of psychotherapy, I have never noted symptoms related to UFOs. A similar finding was confirmed on questioning Theodore A. Anderson, M.D., a senior psychiatrist, and Henry A. Davidson, M.D., (then Medical Director) of the Essex County Overbrook Hospital. Dr. Davidson recalled no patients with gross UFO symptoms out of three thousand in-patients, nor among all those presented to the staff while he was superintendent; nor of thirty thousand patients who had been hospitalized since the turn of the century. My own check of standard textbooks and journals in psychiatry, psychoanalysis, and neurology also confirmed this absence of UFO-like experiences in various "nervous" and mental diseases.

The physician can often be the first to obtain reports of possible UFOs and to uncover hidden cases because a patient will often turn to a family doctor as a trusted friend. With the kind assistance of colleagues and friends, I have learned of, and studied, numerous well-documented UFO sightings involving people from all walks of life, including professionally trained observers, such as physicians, engineers, psychologists, airline pilots, special police, and state troopers.

Let me present five close-range sightings which occurred under favorable conditions in northern New Jersey and which involved trustworthy witnesses. In each case, I undertook telephone, and later psychiatric, interviews in the homes or offices of the witnesses. In each case, I inspected the actual place where the UFO episode allegedly took place.

Case 1

Mrs. Janet Ahlers, age 32, of Oakland, New Jersey, is an artist-housewife and proprietress of an antique store. In excellent health, Mrs. Ahlers has had no serious previous illness or emotional disturbance. Excerpts from an interview with her follows.

"It was late spring, about 2:30 a.m., in 1957. I was expecting a baby and was up during the night. Our bedroom window faced east. I was lying in bed and was disturbed by a pulsating sensation in my head, like a sound that was too high-pitched to be heard. As it came closer it became a whining, pulsating, high-pitched sound. I tried to wake my husband but he didn't stir quickly enough. I got to the window just as the thing went over the house. I could see it clearly. It was close to the tree tops and it seemed to stir them. It was saucer-shaped and seemed to have a hard edge around the circumference where the lights were — the (port) holes. It had one light in the center on the bottom, and it was circled by six to eight other bright orange-red discs.

"It seemed to be a solid metallic object with holes on the bottom. The one in the center was larger and lighter in color. The UFO seemed to make everything reddish as it very slowly went over. I had to look up at it and could see under it (Figure 1). It just seemed to clear the knoll which was a few hundred feet from the house or so. It lasted less than a minute. This UFO was much larger than an automobile and wider than the house or a lot ... more than seventy-five feet. I woke my husband. I trembled for about two hours. There were no physical effects."

Shortly after this episode, Mrs. Ahlers told her mother about it and at a later time a circle of her friends, one of whom informed the author.

Case 2

John A. Collins of Glen Rock, New Jersey, age 49, has a responsible job in the world of banking. He is a lifelong outdoorsman, skilled in hunting and fishing. In his occupation he has flown all over the world and has dealt with many technically trained people, highly situated in the space-age industries. He is in excellent health and has never had any emotional disorder.

"It was one hour before sunset on July 8, 1958, the day of the All-Star game. I was fishing with a friend at Canistear Reservoir in northern New Jersey. It was bright and clear . . . cloudless. There was a slight surface wind (on the water). In the south, we saw in the sky what

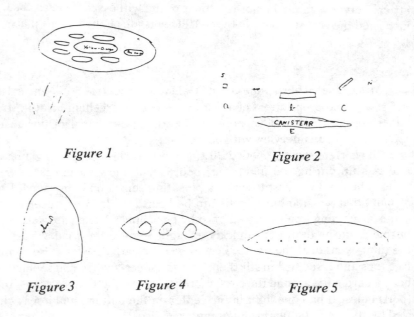

Figure 1

Figure 2

Figure 3

Figure 4

Figure 5

I thought was a shooting star, a big light. (Figure 2a). When we first looked at it, the size was that of two thumbnails of an outstretched upper extremity. We sat in the boat talking about it. 'Do you see what I see?' Instead of disappearing it kept coming along. As it got closer it was plainly visible. At first it looked like a bar of hot steel pressed in a rolling mill . . . about the size of a railroad tie and uniformly cherry red in color (Figure 2b). It was low in the sky and came directly toward us. It [UFO] moved slowly. I had a "Rollie" (camera) in the boat, but I was so scared I was afraid to take a picture. It was heading right for us and we didn't want to excite it. We watched for ten minutes and it was ever with us. It tilted 45 degrees, then (Figure 2c), leveled off, and took another 45 degree turn. It was turning from red to bluish-white to white as it went up. There was still no sound, no hum, no vibration, no odor, nor anything. It leveled off and took a 90 degree turn. It was still the same color, then it turned more than 90 degrees and was coming back toward us. When we faced the end of the bar, it was like looking into the firebox of a locomotive: cherry red in color. The rest of it was white, like two railroad ties attached end to end. We watched it for forty-five minutes in all. It was once less than 400 feet up and we were afraid it was going to land on the water. Then it went faster, rose quite steeply, and rode away. My fishing partner and I had nothing to drink. I have never seen anything like it before or since."

"When my partner got home and told his wife, she wouldn't listen. She was so scared. Once when I went to their home for dinner, about three months later, I thought I'd mention it as a conversation piece, but she wouldn't let met talk about it (confirmed by author's interview of the gentleman, whose wife interfered in the telephone conversation). Shortly after the event I told my wife, a close friend (a neighbor of the author), and a man that I do business with. Strangely enough, another friend of mine who was in the Catskills a hundred miles north of us, had noticed the thing the same day and at approximately the same time. I learned this one week after my experience."

Mr. Collins' trustworthiness was attested by three people who have known him for many years: the author's neighbor, the author's father, and the friend who had been in the Catskills.

Although there were no log-book fishing records going back to 1958, the time of Mr. Collins' experience, interviews with Officer Clyde Conway of the Canistear Reservoir Police, Mr. Conway's wife, his daughter, and his two sons revealed several sightings of possible UFOs in that area in the past three years. No member of Officer Conway's immediate family has had any emotional or psychosomatic illness.

Case 3

Mrs. Carol Vander Plate, age 27, a high school graduate, licensed practical nurse and housewife, lives on a mountain top in Hardyston, New Jersey, where her husband own and operates a radio station, WLVP. Her past life is free of any emotional or psychosomatic disease. It was on April 1, 1966 at 8:45 p.m., during a clear day, followed by moonlight: "Our two French poodles started barking and carrying on. They refused to obey and be quiet. They went crazy, running in circles and jumping over the furniture. There was a horrible rumbling sound. It sounded like a jet coming over and about to crash. I looked out the window and saw this thing sitting on top of the trees about four hundred feet from the house. I watched it for more than thirty seconds. It turned pink. It had three portholes that were black inside. The TV went off. When I turned on the porch light, the object seemed to turn off two big spotlights. It was white, then pink, then green; and then it took off like a streak of lightning. There was a trail of gaseous vapors. My husband announced it over 'open mike', and from then until midnight four lines were steady with calls on each line from others who had seen it. It was fantastic. It was twice the size of a jet. Much bigger than my house. There were no effects on the trees; I checked that the next day. But we've had no robins or cardinals in this particular area since then." (See Figure 4.)

This experience was confirmed upon questioning Mr. Louis Vander Plate and five other observers from the town and neighboring area. Mrs. Vander Plate uses no alcohol or drugs. She became pregnant two months after this experience and delivered a healthy baby. She and her husband estimate they have seen and/or heard of similar sounds seven to ten times since this initial episode. Many of these accounts have been verified by others in the vicinity. One year after this particular sighting, Mrs. Vander Plate developed an allergy to nickel and her husband a severe reaction to "foam rubber — as in earphones — I turn beet red: it swells." The possible allergic condition was never related to the UFO experience, but it is included should other similar observations be made.

The Vander Plates' experience might have been related to another sighting that occurred over the near-by Oak Ridge Reservoir that same night at approximately the same time. The Newark *Evening News* reported "a white light with red revolving lights under it. It was hovering over the reservoir. It remained stationary and then darted across the clear night sky and halted tantalizingly in midair." Many people telephoned in to the Milton Township police headquarters.*

Case 4

Mrs. Estelle Conway, age 51, a business-school graduate, housewife, and postal subclerk of Highland Lakes, New Jersey, looked out of her dining room window one fall day in 1966, at 7:30 p.m. She noticed a large "orange ball" with a dark vermilion border, suspended, or hover-

---

*As a clinical check on the veracity of the witnesses, the author first learned of this event from a nineteen-year-old boy who lives near Oak Ridge Reservoir. He, with his teen-age sister and brother, had seen UFOs at close range over the reservoir on two previous occasions.

ing by itself, over a pond a quarter of a mile away from her home. At that distance, she estimated the size to be that of a chicken coop, and guessed that it would have been much larger than an automobile. She couldn't makeout any other detail, but wondered if it was somebody's auto headlights shining on the trees in the woods. The lake is 1,100 feet above sea level and the hill about 1,400 feet; therefore, the object was estimated to be less than 300 feet above the water. The object didn't change color or shape; it had no sound; and it did not influence the radio or electrical devices in the home. The object was some 700 feet from high-tension wires.

Mrs. Conway was embarrassed because people would not believe her when she told them what she saw. She does not use drugs, and only occasionally does she have a cocktail. She told her husband and other members of her family about the episode. The husband told a neighbor, who was a state policeman. Her experience was confirmed on a telephone interview of the trooper. Mrs. Conway had no past history of any emotional disorder or other illness. When she looked for the object, approximately fifteen minutes after first seeing it, it was no longer there. (See Figure 3.)

At the same time of Mrs. Conway's experience, Mr. Guy F. Adams, age 46, an electrical engineer, of Glenwood, N.J., while driving on the road and approaching the Conway's home, had the "surprise of my life" when he noted, "a big, opalescent-like neon-green ball, 500 to 600 yards out. Not on a ballistic course, but gliding — not enough speed to maintain flight itself. It slowly went across the road — tree-top to tree-top — for an estimated six to eight seconds. It was a ball, straight ahead, right across the road. I have good depth perception. It was aquamarine in opalescence. However, it kept perfect geometry all the time. (It did not shimmer.) It passed over the mountaintop store. There were no effects in the car. If it had been a ballistic trajectory, it would have had to crash into the lake (in the valley).

"I stopped the car near the store and jumped out to see. I went down to the point where it had crossed and where I thought it should have crashed. But it had by then disappeared. There was still good light out. The sun was setting. Obviously the light of the object had to be greater than the light of the sun to be seen. I was very excited and wondered how could a thing appear to have no weight and "fly" across the road at such a very low speed. It traveled in an east-to-west direction. The estimated size was 50 to 55 feet across — approximately the size of a dime on the windshield — roughly half the size of a B-17 bomber. I was a U.S. Army Air Force gunner in World War II, and saw active duty. I'm a student pilot and have designed beacons for space probes, and such, but have never come across anything like this in my life."

Mr. Adams told his wife and a state trooper at the time. The locale of the Conway-Adams sighting is only a few miles from radio station WLVP-FM. Aside from two weeks of a "nervous breakdown" in 1944 (when in the Service) he has had excellent health. Following the "breakdown" he returned to active duty in the Air Force, and served six more years as a career man. He does not use drugs unless prescribed and has had excellent emotional health.

The Newark *Evening News* contained several articles of similar sightings in northern New Jersey during the fall of 1966.

Case 5

Frank Scanlon, age 56, has been a United Parcel Service driver for 37 years. He is a union steward. He has had a northern New Jersey route for twelve years. As a U.S. Air Force veteran or World War II (Fifth Air Force, ground crew in Japan) he is familiar with aircraft. He is respected by his boss and fellow employees. He neither smokes nor drinks. He enjoys excellent health. Psychiatric interview revealed no evidence of emotional illness. Although he could not recall the exact date of his alleged UFO experience, at that time he told his immediate family, his boss, many fellow workers, and several people. Interviews with his wife, two of his children, and four other people, including a police officer, confirmed Scanlon's excellent reputation and his report of the experience shortly after it happened. It was stressed how excited and frightened he was.

"It was November, 1967. It was bare and there were no leaves on the trees. It was on Rudeville Road on the way to Great Gorge (within a mile of the Vander Plates' radio station) at twelve noon, on a clear day. I went to the back of the truck and heard this terrific pounding noise. As I went to the front, I stepped away from the truck as I thought the noise was from the well digger across the street. But he had dived into the hole. At tree height, I saw a cylindrical object, like a dirigible, more than twice the size of the von Hindenberg. It was big enough for several Mack trucks to get into it. It had no cabins or propellers, no markings of any kind. It was a duller grey than aluminum. There was no smoke, heat, or exhaust. There was no effect on my truck motor. It was unbelievable. It had roundish windows that looked black inside. There was no reflection on them. It took off with such force toward Newton that it disappeared in an estimated two minutes.

"I never saw such a burst of speed after hovering. I was amazed.

There were no exhaust fumes. I wondered what could defy gravity and hover there. It was gigantic." (See Figure 5).

Comment

Single-witness UFO examples, and, in some cases, lack of specific dates, have drawbacks. However, the favorable close-range circumstances support the validity of the experiences. The witnesses were healthy and trustworthy. They had no gross defects of vision or hearing. They had ample time to observe the UFOs. There was nothing suggestive of malobservations, behavioral aberrations, mass hypnosis, contrived posthypnotic suggestion or fraud. The unique characteristics of the episodes and the backgrounds of the witnesses excluded such explanations as satellites, airplanes, balloons, helicopters, or birds, although very atypical ball lightning could have been a possibility for Case 4. There was nothing suggestive of a parapsychologic explanation in any of the examples. Most of the witnesses were frightened and had a vivid memory of their unique experiences. In Case 3, it was possible to see how easily mass panic could have developed. The physician, by having an awareness of UFOs, can help to avert mass hysteria.

Five hidden reports of UFOs from a relatively circumscribed area in northern New Jersey are but a small sample of the thousands of documented accounts from all over the world. UFOs indeed, do seem to be real. Physicians are in an excellent position to uncover "hidden reports" of UFOs and help to establish the reliability of the witnesses. By study of the possible emotional and physiologic effects of the UFOs, and of the witnesses themselves, the physician can go beyond merely establishing the event and contribute to the more meaningful questions of (1) what UFOs are (2) where they come from, and (3) what is their purpose.

Bibliography
1. McDonald, J.E.: Paper on UFOs presented at the Canadian Aeronautics and Space Symposium in Montreal, March 12, 1968.
2. Boffey, Philip, M.: **Science** (News and Comment) 163:260 (January 17, 1969)
3. Hynek, J. Allen: Hearings before the Committee on Science and Astronautics, U.S. House of Representatives, July 29, 1968, pp. 2 to 17.
4. Meerloo, J.A.M.: Le Syndrome des Soucoupes Volantes, **Med. Hyg.**, 25:992, 1967.
5. Meerloo, J.A.M.: **JAMA**, 203:1079 (1968)
6. Walker, Sydney: Hearing before the Committee on Science and Astronautics, U.S. House of Representatives Ninetieth Congress, Appendix 2:152 and 2:185 (July 29, 1968)
7. Fontes, Olavo, Martins, Joao (Irene Granchi, translator): Report on the Vil-

las-Boas Incident, February 22, 1958. In Lorenzen, Coral and Jim: **Flying Saucer Occupants,** Chapter III, 42 to 72, Signet Book, New York, 1967, pp. 215.

8. Schwarz, B.E.: UFOs: Delusion or Dilemma, **Medical Times,** 96, 10:967 (1968)

9. Schwarz, B.E.: UFO Occupants, Fact or Fantasy? In publication.

Chapter 3

Gary Wilcox and the Ufonauts

Psychiatric study of witnesses to close-range UFO sightings is useful in establishing the reliability of the witness in obtaining data of medical significance, and in understanding the event.

Unfortunately, of all the episodes involving possible UFO occupants, there are very few published studies by physicians (1-4). The writings in the popular press and, in particular, the detailed, documented accounts by Charles Bowen et al. (5), and the provocative data collected by John A. Keel (6-12), raise many questions in the answering of which psychiatric techniques might have value. Such problems as psychosis versus health, paranoid state versus the alleged reality of bizarre "men-in-black" persecutions, such paranormal phenomena as prophecy, hauntings, telekinesis, and sightings of supposed monsters have come to light.

The author first learned of the extraordinary experience of Gary Wilcox, Newark Valley, New York while studying many UFO sightings in the vicinity of Towanda, Pennsylvania. His informant, Mrs. Aileen Isbell of Luther's Mills, whom he had studied and found trustworthy, mentioned her brother-in-law, Arthur Frederick, Jr., who formerly rented an apartment next to Gary Wilcox's farm. Mr. Frederick, a computer programmer, who had worked on the Apollo simulator project, vouchsafed for Mr. Wilcox's veracity.* The author then recalled Olga Hotchkiss's story (13) of the Wilcox experience, and also paperback reports (14-16) which at the time seemed rather farfetched, and which might have been based on Binghamton, New York, newspaper accounts. After the author had studied Mrs. Isbell, however, the Gary Wilcox UFO encounter seemed most intriguing. Therefore, on October 18, 1968, Gary Wilcox was psychiatrically examined in his home. His wife was also interviewed.

These studies were supplemented by several telephone interviews with the Wilcoxs and face-to-face interviews with Mr. Wilcox's younger brother Floyd, of Newark Valley, and Sheriff Paul J. Taylor of Tioga County, Owego, New York. Mr. Wilcox's mother and his second oldest brother, Barry were questioned on the telephone. A neighboring farmer and steelworker, Vic Kobylarz, whose daughter

---

*A telephone interview with Mrs. Arthur Frederick, Jr., fully confirmed this opinion.

was a schoolmate of Gary Wilcox, was also interviewed on the telephone and through letters. Mr. Kobylarz is a relative by marriage of Mrs. Theresa Krajewski and also thĕ uncle of her closest, lifelong friend. Mrs. Krajewski is a close friend of the author. Mr. Kobylarz talked with Gary Wilcox shortly after the UFO event. Mrs. Winifred Martz, Monroeton, Pennsylvania, mother of the author's EEG technician, Mrs. Evelyn Guldner, also contacted one of her close friends, Mrs. Pauline Beale, of Newark Valley, New York, whose son Philip had been a classmate of Gary Wilcox. Strangely enough, Mrs. Martz's lifelong best friend, Mrs. Adriana Gutowski, of Glen Rock, New Jersey, is a good friend of the author's family and, in fact, the godmother of his first cousin.

Miss Priscilla J. Baldwin, a former neighbor of Gary Wilcox, who is a legal secretary and who was a radar technician during World War II, kindly supplied much crucial information through correspondence and on the telephone. She contacted friends of neighbors of Gary Wilcox, Mrs. Helen MacPherson and Walter Stevens, who supplied additional information. It was due to Miss Baldwin's initiative that this extraordinary case came to the attention of the Binghamton, New York, newspapers and to Sheriff Paul J. Taylor of Tioga County, New York.

I — MISS BALDWIN'S ROLE

The following notes were recorded by Miss Baldwin, age 37, on April 28, 1964, after talking with Gary Wilcox, age 26, about "the space ship" that landed on his property on April 24, 1964.

"Some questions and answers I received:

Q. When did you notice object?

A. About 10 a.m. I was spreading manure in lower field above my house and barn. Noticed a white (or shiny) object above the field, just on inside edge of woods. I was curious and drove tractor (and manure spreader) up to edge of woods and stopped. Got closer look at object and thought it to be a fuselage (or fuel tank) from a plane.

Q. What did you do?

A. I thumped it and kicked it. Felt the metallic canvas.

Q. Then what?

A. Two men appeared from under the object. These men were holding what seemed to be a metal tray (approx. 1 ft. square) filled with alfalfa, with roots, soil, leaves and brush. The men were attired in what seemed to be white or some kind of metallic suits, with no part of their body showing.

Q. Were you frightened?

A. I sure was. I didn't say much for the first few minutes, but thought it was some kind of a trick being pulled on me.

70

Q. What were the first words spoken?

A. They said 'do not be alarmed.' They asked what I was doing, what the tractor, manure spreader, and manure was. I told them I was spreading manure. I talked and answered their questions for two hours and learned they had been watching me for quite a while. They were very interested in organic substances, such as soil, as Mars is made up of rocky substances, not fit for growing. Was told that in the future, Mars and Earth will be trading environments, due to the rockets, missiles, and miscellaneous objects ejected into space from Earth.

I asked them if I could go back with them. Was told I could not, due to the thinness of atmosphere. They also said it was impossible for them to land in congested areas. The fumes of traffic were too dense.

They also mentioned that Astronauts Glenn and Grissom (?) and the two astronauts from Russia would die within a year, due to exposure of space.

They seemed interested in learning the art of farming and growing. After learning that fertiliser would enrich this art, they wanted to know more about it. They did not seem to know what cows were either.

I told them I could get a bag of fertilizer for them, but they did not wait.

They said they usually did not appear after dark, as their metallic ship would be too obvious. It made swishing noise only, and in daylight the ship is not easily observed.

I watched them take off, after being advised not to mention the incident. After a burring and swishing sound, they disappeared to the north. Only marks remaining that I could detect were a kind of red dust (evidently from propulsion) where vehicle rested. I could not tell if it actually was resting on the ground or whether it was hovering in mid-air. It seemed to be larger than an auto, approximately 20ft. long and 14ft. wide, and shaped like an egg.

The voices seemed to come from what might be the chest of the men and they had an eerie sound.

Later that same afternoon, I returned to the spot where this took place, and left a 75-lb. bag of ferlitizer near a small tree. On returning to the scene, Saturday morning, April 25, 1964, I found the fertilizer was gone." (End of personal talk with Gary.)

"On April 29, 1964, I went up to Gary's and asked if he would take me to the spot on his tractor. After finishing his afternoon chores, he took me up (in the rain) on the back of his tractor and he also spread some fertiliser on the way. I had a camera with me and took a couple of shots. With the rainy weather, it is doubtful if they are good. I also picked up some rocks and leaves that were lying where the red dust had

Figure 1. Miss Priscilla J. Baldwin's photo of site of UFO landing

accumulated. However, after the rain, there was no evidence of dust.

"That same day, on my return home, I contacted Sheriff Paul Taylor by telephone, and told him of this incident. He had not heard of it before. He said he could not come to Newark Valley that day, but would when there was time.

"After not hearing if the Sheriff had been up or not, I made another call to his office on Friday, May 1, 1964. I was informed he had not, but would soon. About 1½ hours later an officer from the Sheriff's office, George Williams, drove in my driveway. He asked if I was the one that made the 'complaint' to his office. I said 'yes.' I asked him if he had been up to Gary's farm and he said he had, but found no one there. I told him I thought he would be doing chores at that time and I offered to go back up with him, which I did. We found Gary in the barn and after the officer questioned him for a short time, he (the officer) wanted to go up to the place where the incident occurred. Gary did not want to interrupt his chores, but said I could show him the exact place. I agreed to go with him and after trying the hill with the Sheriff's car, decided to walk, as the ground was very muddy. We walked up and I showed him just what Gary had shown me and pointed out where the red dust had been and also where he had left the fertiliser. After inspecting the surrounding areas, we came back down. The officer asked me if I thought Gary would be willing to come to the Sheriff's office to make a statement and I told him I thought he would. On returning to the barn, the officer entered the barn again and asked Gary if he would. Gary agreed to be at the office in Owego at 7:00 p.m. that night.

"On bringing me back to my home, the officer questioned my being so interested in this. I told him that Gary had told several people, but, like the majority, very few believed his story, and he was going to do nothing further about it. I had asked him prior to my telephone call to the Sheriff if he cared if I did. He said he didn't and that he would just tell them the same he had everyone else.

"I told the officer I had written down notes after I had talked to Gary the first time. The officer took these notes with him and said he would return them to me after talking to Gary. They evidently were used in cross-checking his story.

"Thursday night, May 7, 1964, I stopped in the Sheriff's office with a friend, and picked up my notes. They had been retained in a sealed envelope.   (Signed) P.J. Baldwin"

On November 24, 1968, Miss Baldwin wrote the author and enclosed newspaper clippings of the event. She also sent "some very brittle leaves and pieces of stone that I picked up at the scene (of the UFO landing). Your are welcome to them if they could be of any significance. It was raining the day I rode up the hill with Gary on his tractor. The leaves and stones were wet. . .I picked them up right on the spot where 'the red dust' was supposed to be. After I had been on the hill, I did read that samples had been taken on the spot* for researches, so I

---

*Check for radioactivity of appropriate samples was arranged by Sheriff Taylor shortly after his investigation. The results were negative. On December 17, 1968, Philip M. Johnson, M.D., Associate Professor of Radiology at Columbia University College of Physicians and Surgeons, and Director of Nuclear Medicine, Presbyterian Hospital, New York City, reported that the specimens collected by Miss Baldwin were not "radioactive in so far as my instrumentation can determine. Each sample was exposed to a 2 in. scintillation crystal with flat field collimator and pulse height analyzer. By varying the setting on the analyzer, the crystal was made sensitive to gamma photons in the energy range of 30 Kevs to one Mev. No activity above background levels was observed. I did not test for alpha-particle radiation nor for low-energy beta radiation since I do not have the proper equipment."

always thought the 'samples' I had taken were of more value, seeing I had been at the scene before anyone else had. I am also enclosing two very dim pictures taken the day I was there. You may not be able to decipher same, but the one picture does show broken branches on the trees where this object appeared (see Figure 1)."

Miss Baldwin continued, "I have known Gary since he was a boy and knowing what a quiet, shy fellow [he has always been], I have never had any doubts as to what he saw. There are people who would revel in causing this kind of excitement, but I truly believe Gary would have been the last person who would have wanted this type of notoriety. . .I was in the Air Force for three years and my career field was A.C.&W. (radar). In my work I plotted 'UFO blips' (as they were called at that time) on the radar screen in the control center. Many times blips were not identified. The speed in most cases was unbelievable. However, I don't know if any of that was ever the reason for my interest or not, but I do believe it had a lot to do with it."

II — SHERIFF TAYLOR'S REPORT

Miss Baldwin contacted the Sheriff's office, Tioga County, Owego, New York, on April 29, 1964, and on May 1 Gary Wilcox was visited by officer George Williams. He reported:

"Travelled to Newark Valley and contacted Priscilla Baldwin on matter pertinent to this complaint. We drove to farm of Gary Wilcox. His farm is off the Wilson Creek Road, the second place on the left side on the Davis Hollow Road. Gary was milking his cows at the time of our arrival, which was about 4:15 p.m. He stated that he milks some of his heavy milkers three times a day. This, of course would cause him to lose some sleep. The text of his statment concerning the unidentified object is contained in statement which is made a part of this file. He admitted that he drank a little but that he was not drinking at the time of this reported incident. He also stated that he had some marital difficulty, but this did not encourage him to drink any more than he had been accustomed. This man does not appear to be unstable or mentally disturbed in any way. His eyes are slightly different in appearance from the average person, but it is believed that it is more of a physical characteristic than it is a mental affliction. He is a hard worker. The complainant in this case says that she has no reason to doubt him. We (complainant and myself) walked to the top of the hill where this 'space ship' was reported to have landed or hovered. This hill is northeast of the farm buildings, and there is an old, abandoned refrigerator on top of the hill, which was reported to be physically situated about 20 feet from where the 'space ship' had been. We checked the area, particularly for the red-colored dust and impressions in the ground. This was about a week after the reported incident and there had been considerable rain during this time. The only thing unusual noted at this time was that the ground where this 'ship' was reportedly hovering was damp. This could have been caused by a spring or ground formation. The ground surrounding this area was comparatively dry. There was no evidence of red dust. This would have been washed away anyway. Did not look too close for any evidence of digging at this time as we were not advised until later that the individuals of questionable origin had been holding trays of sod. This, Gary believed, had been samples of his soil. He stated that the sod had grass or vegetation on top. In event that samples had been removed from his property in this area, it would be comparatively simple to locate the place of digging. Even at this late date, it might be possible to locate evidence of digging in the grassy area on top of this hill. We continued to look around for a while and then returned to the barn."

Officer Williams then incorporated Miss Baldwin's notes into the official record, as reported above. His next entry was as follows:

"*May 1, 1964.* Upon checking the area with complainant (Priscilla Baldwin), it was noted that there was one (1) set of tractor tracks near the scene of reported incident. Gary stated that the first time he went up the hill he stopped the tractor about 100 yards from the top of hill where ship was reportedly parked, and then he dismounted and walked the remainder of hill (to top). Gary then stated that he returned later that day and dropped off a bag of fertiliser at site. He then stated that he again drove the tractor to top with complainant Priscilla Baldwin to show her the spot this incident reportedly occurred. If this was the case, there should be two sets of tractor tracks near the site. One set when he brought the bag of fertiliser to the spot and one set when he transported the complainant to the site. There was only one (1) set of tracks noted. It isn't likely that the tractor could get to this area without making some tracks even if the ground were dry because the incline is great."

The following statement and diagrams by Mr. Wilcox (see Figure 2) were obtained by Sheriff Taylor and Officer Williams on May 1, 1964.

"I, Gary Thelbert Wilcox, say that I am 28 years of age the 7th day of this month, having been born May 7, 1936, at Endicott, New York. I live at R.D. No. 1, Newark Valley, New York, with my wife, Judith Lynda. I am self-employed as a dairy farmer. I graduated from Newark Valley Central School in 1954.

"At about 10:00 o'clock in the morning last Friday the 24th of April, 1964, I was spreading manure with my manure spreader on one of my fields located east of my house. My house is the second house on the left on Davis Hollow Road which runs off the Wilson Creek Road out of

Figure 2. Gary Wilcox's sketch of occupants and UFO

Newark Valley. The weather was clear and the sun was shining. The ground was dry. I glanced up the hill from the field I was working and noticed a shiny object on top of the hill. I thought at the time that it was the abandoned refrigerator that I knew was up there. After again glancing I noticed that the object did not seem to be the refrigerator, but that it was something else. Then I started driving the tractor with the manure spreader up the hill, toward the object. The distance from the bottom of the hill where I first noticed the object to the top of the hill where it appeared is about 800 yards. While I was driving up the hill toward the object and about 100 yards from it, this is when I thought it was a wing fuel tank from an airplane. I wasn't scared or anything. I parked the tractor at this point and walked the remaining 100 yards to the object. The first thing I noticed was that it was off the ground, it was a little bigger than a car in length. It was an oblong shape something like an egg. There were no seams, rivets or anything like that. It was completely smooth. It was aluminum color, I touched the thing and the metal was harder than aluminum and it did not move. I don't know whether it was on legs or hovering in the air. It was about 20 ft. in length, 4 ft. high and 15 or 16 ft. wide. While (I was) feeling it there was no vibration or sound and it was not hot or anything. While I was touching it, two (2) small men about 4ft. high came out from under the tank object. I don't know where they came from. Each of them was carrying a tray about a foot square. The tray looked like it was made of the same stuff the ship (tank) was made of. Inside the tray was what appeared to be sod. I was standing about a foot away from the ship. I will refer to this object as a ship from now on. I first thought it to be a tank. The two little men started walking toward me from under the ship. They stopped about one (1) yard away from me. then it sounded like one of them spoke and said 'Don't be alarmed, we have spoken to people before.' Their voices did not sound like a voice I could describe. I could understand what was said but cannot tell whether they were speaking English or not. One of the men was standing in rear of the other. I could see that both of these 4-foot-high men had arms and legs the same as us. I couldn't tell whether they had feet or hands the same as us. They were quite broad for such short persons (or individuals). I could not distinguish whether they had shoulders or not; they seemed to just go straight down. They had no face, such as eyes, ears, nose, mouth, or hair. The voice seemed to be coming from about them rather than from either of them. There was a voice, but I don't know where it was coming from insofar as their body was concerned. They seemed to have a sort of suit on that covered where the head would normally be located all the way down. When they raised their arms, you could see a wrinkle where our elbow would be located. The color of this completely smooth cover-all-type suit was whitish-aluminum-tint color. There was no evidence of hair. The only thing I noticed was the wrinkle when they moved their arms at the elbow.

They said, 'We are from what you know as the planet Mars.' They then asked me what I was doing. I told them what I was doing was spreading manure. They asked me to explain what this was in more or less detail. They seemed interested in what this manure did. After I told them what it was and where it came from, they asked what else I made stuff grow with. That's when I told them about the lime and fertiliser. They did not say anything about the lime but were interested in the fertiliser. I told them it was made of bones from dead animals. During the time I was explaining to them the function of fertiliser, they asked if they could have some. I told them that I would have to go down to my barn and get some. Then one spoke up and said that they were travelling this hemisphere. I don't know which one it was as I have said before. The voice seemed to come from the front one, the one closest to me. I then asked them if I could go. They then said that they could only come here (earth) every two years. Their conversation seemed to shift rapidly from one subject to another. They mentioned that we should not send people out into space. They said that they have watched us. They said that we could not survive there at Mars and that they could not survive here on Earth. They also said that they got stuff out of the air to live on and that they were here to see what they could learn about our organic material because they felt that the earth and Mars, plus some other planets, might be changed around. They said there was a difference in the gravity pull and that there was a change taking place. They said they did not fly near cities because the fumes or stuff in the air affected the flight of their ship. That they tried to stay where the air was pure. They seemed to know more about planets, air, and all that kind of stuff, but they did not seem to know much about our agriculture. They also said that our people that had entered into space would not survive over a year. They then walked back under the ship and disappeared. They ducked a little bit when they went under it. The ship then seemed to hover. I heard a noise that sounded like a car motor idling. It was not loud. Then it just took off slowly forward above the ground in a gliding manner and flew over the valley in the direction of Sokoloski's barn and disappeared into the air after it was about 150 ft. away. There was no heat, blasting, wind, dust, noise (other than the idling sound), light, or anything else left behind when the ship took off.

"They did not try to harm me in any way and there was nothing with them that looked like a weapon. They did not raise or lower their voice. It was the same throughout the conversation. They did most of the talking.

"After they left, I drove back home and called my mother on the phone. I told her the highlights of seeing this object. I then milked the cows and did some other chores. I went back up the hill with a load of manure about 4:30 p.m. and put a bag of fertiliser on the spreader. When I got back to the top of the hill where the ship had been, I dropped the bag of fertiliser to the ground and left it. The next morning, I went back up the hill and noticed that the bag of fertiliser was gone.

"I have read this statement and it is true. I realize that the incident described above is unusual, but I do certify that it is a true and accurate account of what actually happened."

(signed) Gary T. Wilcox
(witness) George E. Williams
(witness) Paul J. Taylor

III — PSYCHIATRIC STUDY

On October 18, 1968, psychiatric examination of Gary Wilcox (in his home) corroborated all the salient features mentioned in Miss Baldwin's and Sheriff Taylor's reports. At the time of the psychiatric study Mr. Wilcox was no longer a farmer but a highly skilled mechanic. He was respected by his employer and had received several promotions. He had never had any UFO, psychic, or other very unusual experiences before, nor has he since. Although he could not recall any details, he mentioned that a neighbor told him about a close-range UFO experience at the approximate time of his episode.*

Mr. Wilcox's attitude was open and cooperative, and produced no material that conflicted with the previous reports. He spoke in a polite, refined manner, and his answers had a literalness about them. There was no tendency toward expansiveness or embellishment. He was quite reserved. He was sure that he had seen only two occupants of the UFO, and that at one time he was approximately 10ft. distant from one of them. He felt he could judge their height quite accurately because he is 6 ft. tall. When asked about his initial reaction to the supposed ufonauts, he said, "I was laughing. I thought it was the Candid Camera — you know, somebody pulling a gag, or something."

Wilcox had no past history for neonatal disturbances, serious illness in the formative years, neurotic character traits, dissociative or amnestic experiences, fugues, sociopathic behaviour, school problems, head injury, encephalopathy, surgery, or any kind of aberrant behaviour. He had never been hospitalized, and he did not have a family physician. Review of all his bodily systems revealed no disease stigmata. He was a

---

*Although this could not be confirmed via correspondence with the deceased neighbor's wife, she reported that a respected gentleman of Berkshire, New York, was "out in his field that day and saw something that was unexplainable." Also, in a letter to the author, Walter Stevens recalled that he and a friend saw a possible UFO that "almost blinded us for a moment," on April 18, 1964, on Highway 38. Also, Mr. Kobylarz remembered how "one or two people saw something [UFOs] near Gary Wilcox's farm that day."

good student in school† and had one semester in college. He spent three years in the Army, being stationed in Germany.* He was a sergeant in the Engineers and received an honorable discharge.

The oldest of four siblings, Gary Wilcox has a sister, Sandra, who is two years younger, and two brothers, Barry and Floyd, who are four and seven years younger. There was no family history for mental illness, sociopathic behavior (such as lying, stealing, cheating, truancy, fire setting, delinquency, drug usage, alcoholism, etc.), or difficulties with the law. He is of old American stock and his family has an excellent reputation in the community. Gary Wilcox has always enjoyed good health and has rarely consulted physicians. He seldom dreamed and could not recall any particular dream, including one about his UFO experience.

Direct examination revealed him to be a tall, handsome, intelligent-appearing man (see figure 3) who became restless and fidgety when describing his encounter with the alleged UFO occupants. There was no evidence for any undue preoccupations, trends of thought, pathological thinking, or inappropriate affect. "Within one hour" after the UFO experience Wilcox telephoned his mother, and then the other members of his family quickly learned about it. Direct and telephone interviews with his mother and his two brothers confirmed this.† No one in his family had ever experienced anything like this before. Wilcox had no previous particular interest in UFOs or any other kind of exotic subject. His reading was limited to newspaper and magazines like *Look, Life* and the *Reader's Digest.* Wilcox and the other members of his family gave no history for any unusual paranormal phenomena before or after this

---

†This was verified by the parents of two former schoolmates and longtime friends. Mr. Kobylarz said, "A well-liked kid, modest, and never a braggart — of a reliable and hardworking family — he knew it wasn't a mirage because he had his hand on it (UFO). They are very fine people. My brother has known his people for forty years." Mrs. Beale wrote: "Philip [her son] knows him . . . was in his grade in school . . . and says he is an honest person and wouldn't concoct a cock-and-bull story just to get publicity."

*When Mr. Kobylarz talked with Gary Wilcox, he asked if the UFO occupants were Russian. Wilcox said they were not and they had no accent. He was familiar with many foreign accents from his Army service in Germany.

†Gary Wilcox had no knowledge of Sergeant Lonnie Zamora's UFO-occupant experience (17) until shortly before May 11, 1964, when he brought an undated news-clipping (from his father) to Sheriff Paul Taylor. "Dad told me about it — came up to the house with it (clipping) about a week or so later (after Newark Valley UFO episode)." It is of interest that many features of the Newark Valley and Socorro experiences are similar.

episode. He gave no history for unusual harassment since the episode. Wilcox had never been hypnotised. However, he was annoyed by various eccentrics and curiosity seekers who sought him out or ridiculed him. He was particularly irritated by one newspaper article that falsely stated he was being treated in a hospital in New York City for radiation burns. Although hardly affluent, Wilcox, according to his brother Floyd, turned down a considerable sum of money offered by a leading national magazine for the publication rights to his story. He also refused payments for lectures about his experience. He graciously consented to psychiatric study and freely gave permission for publication of this story in a scientific journal with the understanding that his current address would not be revealed.

In an interview Gary Wilcox's second wife (married for two years, and after UFO episode) confirmed the foregoing UFO information. She described her husband as a quiet, family man, "conscientious and doesn't easily lose his temper. . .yet he has a sense of humor." He did not use alcohol or tobacco and has always enjoyed excellent health.* He occasionally attends the Baptist church. Questions pertaining to Gary Wilcox's past life and the personal nuances of his marriages† elicited no evidence for any disrupting psychopathology, psychosomatic reactions, dishonesty, or proclivity for playing practical jokes or hoaxes. Mr. Wilcox was characterized as a serious, truthful, hard-working man who had little time for frivolity. There was never any suggestion of jealousy or unfounded suspiciousness. His chief pleasure seemed to be playing with his children (two by his second wife and four adoptive children from his second wife's first marriage).

Study of Gary Wilcox's (and his wife's) answers to the Cornell Medical Index Health Questionnaire, Rotter Incomplete Sentences Test, and the computer automated Minnesota Multiphasic Pesonality Inventory (MMPI) revealed answers consistent with physical and emotional health. On the MMPI "a configural search for positive traits and strengths showed correlations for describing the subject as compliant, methodical, orderly, socially reserved, and sincere."

DISCUSSION AND SUMMARY

Although single-witness UFO experiences have obvious drawbacks, Gary Wilcox's report is exceptional because of his unusually healthy

---

*At the time of the UFO incident he had not been under the influence of alcohol. During his farming years he used alcohol only infrequently and sparingly.

†His first marriage, which lasted only a short time, was terminated under amiable conditions because of lack of harmony of interests.

PAUSE IN WORK — Gary T. Wilcox, 28, of Davis Hollow Road, Newark Valley, works in the barn on his 300-acre farm unperturbed by interest he roused with a report of talking April 24 with two Martians who, he said, landed in a spacecraft at a secluded spot a mile from his barn.

Figure 3. Gary Wilcox, from the "Press",
Binghamton, N.Y., May 9, 1964

background, during and after the purported incident, the rarity of such close-range UFO-occupant encounters, and the difficulty and need for recording all data that might contribute to this multi-faceted problem. Despite some explainable discrepancies, such as Officer Williams' observation that there was only one set of tractor tracks instead of two, Wilcox's account was essentially unchanged. It should again be stressed that Gary Wilcox told his mother (and other members of his family) shortly after the incident, and that it was not until several days later that he learned of the Socorro, New Mexico, episode involving Officer Lonnie Zamora. It is odd that the widely reported and studied account of Lonnie Zamora occurred on the same day, and approximately eight hours earlier than Gary Wilcox had his experience. Recently the Newark Valley incident has received renewed attention (18). The independent studies of Walter N. Webb, NICAP adviser, and his associates (and the NICAP file on the Newark Valley case (19) provided detailed data that supplement and coincide with the material reported here. Should future investigations confirm the "reality" of such experiences: for what actually seemed to happen or for some new and strange kind of mental or psychic influence, or the converse — the discovery of some new and hitherto unrecognized type of psychopathology, the psychiatric studies would still have significance.

Study of the UFO-occupant problem is still at an early, explorative-qualitative stage. Had circumstances permitted, it would have been desirable to have had additional procedures, such as physical and neurological examination, an electroencephalogram, polygraphic studies, hypnotic trance, laboratory and some complete psychometric evaluations. It is unfortunate that it was not possible, at the time of this report (1969) to have traced out more completely the various collateral leads as suggested by the situations of Kobylarz, Stevens, and MacPherson.

As has been pointed out by Keel (10, 11) who has had much experience with alleged contactees, the interpretation of what was supposed to have happened is an entirely open question. For example, that the occupants said they came from Mars does not mean that they did come from Mars.* Everything that the contactees (or ufonauts) reputedly said should be critically analysed from many points of view: truthfulness, purposely implanted lies, distorted propaganda, material that could be communicated and understood only by one of Gary Wilcox's psychodynamic make-up, possibility of telepathy, and so forth. Unfortunately, the facts do not justify much speculation in this regard.

*It should be noted that Peter Gilman called attention to the unusual compatibility between what the Martians told Gary Wilcox and what Dr. Immanuel Velikowsky has theorized (20).

It would be most unusual, however, for Gary Wilcox to concoct such a fantastic story without some clues for this from his psychiatric examination or from interviews with his friends, acquaintances, and family. It should be stressed that as a down-to-earth person, a highly skilled machinist, with a rather literal frame of mind, Wilcox never showed any unusual interest in UFOs or space. He had no undue preoccupation with abstruse, esoteric matters, quasi-religious cults, or offbeat stories, before or since the episode.

The ufonauts' prophecy of the death, in space, of some astronauts was not completely fulfilled as stated; however, it is of interest that Virgil A. Grissom (along with Edward H. White and Roger B. Chafee) died in the tragic Apollo capsule fire on January 27, 1967. Although not specifically named by the ufonauts, Russian astronauts Vladimir M. Komarov* was the first man known to have been killed in actual space

---

*On October 12, 1964, Komarov was scheduled to orbit for at least five days, but according to London newspaperman Bruce Sandham (**Daily Gleaner,** Jamaica, Monday, February 26, 1968), he returned to earth after twenty-four hours. "Recording of radio transmissions . . . indicates that the spacecraft's crew had seen something strange and inexplicable in orbit — something that terrified them so much that they made a hasty and unscheduled descent from space." It may be proper to mention here that Komarov, through an interpreter, told the world-famous telepathist Joseph Dunninger, during a banquet at the Benjamin Franklin Hotel at the Seattle World's Fair in 1962, that he (Komarov) had observed during space flight "strange phantasms . . . odd things that appeared before his eyes. He was sure his mind was not playing tricks on him, and that it was not an illusion." Dunninger was impressed with Komarov's openness. Although there was a language barrier, Dunninger recalled how he also tried a telepathic stunt with Komarov: "I never got an analysis of what I drew on my pad . . . something that I saw in my mind's mirror." However, according to Komarov's reaction and that of the interpreter, Dunninger succeeded. The author clearly recalled this unusual interview because Dunninger had given him an autographed photograph of Komarov and Dunninger in May, 1965.

It might also be noted here that the reporter, Sandham, quoted observations of strange space objects by American astronauts: (1) the NBC-monitored space flight of Gordon Cooper (May 15, 1963); of (2) Edward White and James McDivitt (June, 1965); and of (3) James Lovell and Frank Borman (December, 1965). Another astronaut sighting, according to the **UFO Investigator** (Vol. IV, No. 9, January, 1969), is that of Charles Conrad, September, 1966.

It would be of interest, since many contactee experiences allege telepathic communication, to have a proven, eminent telepathist work with them and study what "impressions" (telepathic thoughts) might be received. It is not far-fetched that someone like Dunninger, who has amazed the world for more than fifty years with his extraordinary mental abilities and who has also successfully used his talents to aid the police in the solution of crimes, and physicians in the treatment of diseases, might be able to "recall" (amnestic) material "forgotten" (repressed) by the contactee. Such repressed data, accessible to paragnost, might provide further clues in the study of such cases.

flight when his capsule plunged to earth under unopened parachutes (April 24, 1967), exactly three years after the prophecy. Keel has documented some unusual instances of successful prophecy in connection with UFOs (9).

As described elsewhere (4), nothing in the medical aspects of a possible human-UFO-occupant experience is applicable to the situation of Gary Wilcox. As in the examples of Miss Stichler and Mrs. Carow, Wilcox also had no mental disturbance, no history of being hypnotized, no suggestion of paranoid thinking, no hints of specific psychopathology, and no cultural-religious-like determinants that could account for his experience. Although inexplicable, there is much in Gary Wilcox's encounter with the UFO and its occupants that sounds like data obtained from other worldwide sources (5). There might be considerable value in psychiatric study of many more contactee experiences. It is ironic that billions are spent to put men on the moon in order to probe the secrets of space, yet apparently little attention is paid to the possibility that forms of life — ufonauts — from somewhere in the universe, possibly outer space, may have already landed on earth.

In summary, Gary Wilcox, almost twenty-eight years old and a farmer of Newark Valley, New York, claimed he had a close-range experience with a UFO and two of its occupants. From psychiatric evaluation of Wilcox and interviews with various members of his family, neighbors, and friends, it would seem that he is a truthful person with no emotional illness and that his experience was "real" even though the interpretation of his encounter is a complicated and uncertain matter.

★ ★ ★

ACKNOWLEDGEMENTS

The author thanks Gary T. Wilcox and the many other people, mentioned and unmentioned, in this study for their indispensible help.

REFERENCES

1. Fontes, Olavo (Gordon Creighton, translator). "Even More Amazing." **Flying Saucer Review,** Part I, II, III: Vol. 12, Nos. 4, 5 and 6 (July/ August, September /October and November/December), 1966. Part IV: Vol. 13, No. 1 (January/February), 1967. Part V, Comments by Dr. Olavo Fontes and by Gordon Creighton, Vol. 13, No. 3 (May/June), 1967. Part VI, The Medical Report, Vol. 14, No. 1 (January/February), 1968, pp. 18-20.
2. Simon, B., quoted in Fuller, J. **The Interrupted Journey.** Dell Publishing Co., Inc., New York, 1967, 350 pp.
3. Schwarz, B.E. "UFOs: Delusion or Dilemma?" **Medical Times,** 96, 10: 967-981, 1968. (Reprinted in **Flying Saucer Review** Special Issue No. 2, BEYOND CONDON . . . , June, 1969.)

4   Schwarz, B.E. "UFO Occupants: Fact or Fantasy?" **Flying Saucer Review,** accepted for publication.

5. Bowen, Charles, Editor. THE HUMANOIDS. **Flying Saucer Review** Special Issue No. 1, London, England, October/November, 1966, 77 pp.

6. Keel, John A. "An Unusual Contact Claim from Ohio." **Flying Saucer Review,** Vol. 14 (No. 1), 25-26, January/February 1968.

7. Keel, John A. "The Little Man of Gaffney." **Flying Saucer Review,** Vol. 14 (No. 4), 17-19, March/April, 1968.

8. Keel, John A. "A New Approach to UFO Witnesses." **Flying Saucer Review,** Vol. 14 (No. 4), 23-24, May/June, 1968.

9. Keel, John A. "West Virginia's Enigmatic 'Bird'." **Flying Saucer Review,** Vol. 14 (No. 4), 7-14, July/August, 1968.

10. Keel, John A. "Behind the UFO's Undercover Flying Saucer Investigation." **Men,** Vol 17 (No. 10), 24-25, 74-77, October, 1968.

11. Keel, John A. "UFO 'Agents' of Terror." **Saga Annual,** Vol. 1 (No. 1), 17-19, 91-100, 1969.

12. Keel, John A. "Savage Little Men from Outer Space." **Saga,** Vol. 37 (No. 6), 40-41, 82, 84, 86, March, 1969.

13. Hotchkiss, Olga M. "New York UFO and Its 'Little People'." **Fate Magazine,** pp. 38-42, September, 1964.

14. Trench, le Poer, B. **The Flying Saucer Story,** pp. 53-55, Ace Books, Inc., New York, 1966, 190 pp.

15. Lorenzen, Coral and Jim, **Flying Saucer Occupants.** Pp. 131-132, Signet Books, New York, 1967, 215 pp.

16. Green, G., and Smith, W. **Let's Face the Facts About Flying Saucers.** Chapter entitled "The Farmer Who Talked with Saucer Pilots," pp. 38-40, Popular Library, New York, 1967, 127 pp.

17. Lorenzen, Coral, "UFO Lands in New Mexico." **Fate Magazine.** Pp. 27-38, August, 1964.

18. Keyhoe, D.E., and Lore, Jr., G.I.R. Editors. **UFOs, a New Look.** P. 31, published by The National Investigations Committee on Aerial Phenomena, Washington, D.C., 1969, 46pp.

19. Bloecher, Ted. Private communication (2-14-69) of Walter N. Webb's interview with witnesses (November 8, 1964); and Xerox copies of NICAP files on Newark Valley Incident.

20. Gilman, Peter. "Do the Cherubim Come From Mars? **Flying Saucer Review,** Vol. 13 (No. 5), pp. 19-21, 29, September/October, 1967.

Chapter 4

UFO Occupants: Fact or Fantasy?

A psychiatric study of two possible cases

Across the world there have been many reports of possible UFO occupants (1). With few exceptions (2), however, little attention has been given to this matter by physicians.

The eminent psychiatrist, Joost A.M. Meerloo (3,4), discussed various medical aspects of UFO reports. In a proposed method of medical investigation of a hypothetical UFO witness, Walker (5) enumerated various tests and procedures. In a recent report (6) of actual close UFO encounters, much of the relevant medical literature was mentioned. That study stressed (1) how medicine could be useful in determining the possible human biological effects of exposure to a UFO, and (2) how listing all the data connected with a possible UFO experience might aid in determining if the event was a reality or, in fact, the product of mental illness, a delusion, an illusion, an hallucination, or a fabrication. It was noted that an attitude of *a priori* condemnation or *a posteriori* ridicule of possible UFO witnesses was potentially destructive to their health and obstructive to the scientific purpose of obtaining all factual information on UFOs and their purported occupants.

Psychiatric evaluation of persons who have claimed close contacts with UFOs and their occupants might have value. The following accounts are therefore presented.

Farm Lady Sees UFO and
Occupant at Close Range

At approximately 6:00 a.m., just before sunrise, on a clear day in late May, 1957, Miss Frances Stichler, age 62, of Route 6, near Milford, Pennsylvania, saw at close range a UFO and its occupant. A detailed account by J. Edson Myer, of Milford, was published in the *Pike County Dispatch*, Thursday, December 19, 1957. Mr. Myer, together with his wife, are leading citizens of Milford. Mr. Myer has known Miss Stichler from high school days before 1914. The Myers made a careful, onsite investigation. (They had formerly lived and worked in Washington, D.C., for many years. Before retirement they had had responsible and sensitive positions in the Federal Government. They were trained to state facts in careful English and, when possible, use careful measurements.) Their report follows, in part:

"As Miss Stichler was about to enter the barn to feed the chickens, a soft whirring or spinning sound caused her to hesitate and look upward. A rather flat, bowl-shaped object with a broad rim soared into view over the barn, only about 15 ft. above the roof. About 50 ft. away and up about 35 ft. from the ground, the saucer came to a stop in a somewhat tilted position and remained poised for nearly a minute. Then, spinning around, it sailed in a large, nearly horizontal arc to the southeast and disappeared over the wooded hill.

"The detailed observations which Miss Stichler made of the object are fascinating. A man in a light gray, tight-fitting helmet and loose-fitting, shiny suit of the same color was sitting on the broad rim with his feet and legs in the lower portion of the saucer. The man sat on the rim on the far side of the saucer, facing directly toward Miss Stichler, the saucer being tilted so that his body could be seen down to his knees. No detail, however, could be made out much below his waist because of the lack of good light and the angle of the saucer. The man, of average size, had deep-set eyes and a rather long face with a calm to quizzical expression. His skin was suntanned. Miss Stichler reported that the man may have been wondering what she was thinking about and if she would scream or run.

"At no time did she think of speaking to the occupant of the saucer. The two looked at each other for the entire time. Miss Stichler was at first too surprised to be uneasy. Then as the man continued to gaze at her, she began to feel disturbed and wondered what his next move might be and what she should do. About that time the whirring sound began to increase and the saucer took off.

"Miss Stichler, with a great sense of relief, then went back to the house and wondered for some time to whom she might phone. she thought about phoning the police, since if it were a Russian spy it should be reported. But because there was no material evidence of any kind to exhibit, she felt that she could not present a logical case. Miss Stichler did report this happening to a few friends shortly thereafter; but it was always taken lightly and they never failed to ask what she had been drinking. (Miss Stichler is not a drinking person.) For this reason no attempt was made to report a detailed account. A short previous account of this experience was reported in Mrs. Emilie Case's column in a recent issue of the *Pike County Dispatch*, but it was felt that a more detailed story would be of interest to many readers.

"The rational thoughts about this episode which occupied Miss Stichler's mind during the sighting and afterward are quite convincing evidence that this was anything but an hallucination.

"The saucer with the flange was estimated to be about 20ft. in total diameter with the flange 3 to 4 ft. wide. No bubble cover over the top of the shiny, aluminum-colored saucer was visible.

"As the saucer disappeared, the bottom came into view and gave the impression of being a shallow hemisphere. The impression also of something spinning was again evident although nothing was observed to be spinning, nor were there any noticeable air currents which disturbed the ground cover. The spinning or vibrating sound which the saucer emitted made Miss Stichler feel that it was mechanically operated. Because of the relatively small size of the device it was felt that the saucer was based nearby."

Psychiatric examination

After preliminary telephone interviews with Miss Stichler and her cousin, Mrs. Viola Weiser, with whom she lives, and with Mr. Myer, arrangements were made for psychiatric examination of Miss Stichler, which took place on December 7, 1968. Miss Stichler was an open, friendly, cooperative woman who vividly recalled all the details as described in Mr. Myer's account. In response to questions, she produced these following additional points:

1. "[UFO] seemed to be aluminum. . .over the top of it it had a clear plastic. . .it was circular. . .no blades. . .stood there without noise. . .I don't know what made it go. . .[estimated time of observation] not more than 3 to 4 minutes.

2. "[Occupant] looked like a slim, 18-year-old boy. . .had a uniform like a mechanic wears. . .helmet over head to protect him, no goggles. . . face open. . .no hair showing. . .face looked like normal person. . . white. . .eyes and eyebrows. . .hands like anybody else's hands. . .had gloves on. [No buttons, seams, or zippers seen.]

3. "He was as surprised as I was. We looked at each other for a few minutes, and I wasn't frightened. He just stood there, and then I got frightened. [No discernible effects on chickens or birds.]

4. "It had no [steering] wheel (as in an auto) but had things you would pull [levers].

5. "The thing seemed to die down [vibrations]. . .you didn't hear any engine. It was standing still. . .he [occupant] wasn't doing anything while he was looking at me.

6. "He started off and went at right angles to where he had come from before. It seemed to be like a puff of steam out of the back as it flew off. . .went faster and faster. . .seemed to get louder as it went ahead. . . at a distance all you noticed was the plastic covering. I had looked for that [identification] but didn't see anything like that. [No odor or dust.]"

7. Beyond Mr. and Mrs. Myer's first-hand investigation (and the author's), no one has studied Miss Stichler.

Miss Stichler's past medical history revealed no previous emotional or psychosomatic illness. This viewpoint was also confirmed after questioning of Mrs. Viola Weiser, her cousin (who is older than Miss Stichler and whom she has known all her life), and Mr. and Mrs. Myer, acquaintances for many years. There was no suggestion of any lying, dishonesty, or proclivity for being a practical joker or hoaxer. Although Miss Stichler, as a practicing Christian Scientist, seldom called on a physician, she had seen Jack S. Bullock, M.D., on occasion. A telephone interview with Dr. Bullock revealed that his patient was a truthful person, and at the time of the episode she had no illness. Years after the alleged episode, he treated her for essential hypertension, and at that time, in other respects, she was in good general health and had no evidence of gross disturbances of seeing, hearing, or mentation.

After graduation from high school, Miss Stichler taught school for a short time, and then she helped her parents in the management of their farm for more than fifty years. Miss Stichler, an only child, came to the Milford region near the turn of the century. Aside from occasional head colds and minimal deafness in one ear, she always enjoyed good health.

At the time of the psychiatric study, more than ten years after the purported episode, Miss Stichler spoke in a brisk, logical, coherent manner and reacted appropriately to all the nuances of her story and other significant events in her life. She related warmly and appeared to have a good sense of humor. There was no suggestion of any dereistic thinking, undue preoccupations, and so forth. It was the author's impression that she had above-average intelligence. She was correct in all her responses on formal testing in the mental status examination. Her seeing and hearing were grossly intact. She did not wear eyeglasses. She was not colorblind on testing with the pseudoisochromatic plates.

II. Two Tiny "Men" In Uniform at Conashaugh

On the last day of the deer-(doe)-hunting season [December 17], 1956, Mrs. Marie Carow, age 68, had an estraordinary experience with "two little men." At that time Mrs. Carow lived in a very isolated region, Conashaugh, in Pennsylvania (between Milford and Dingman's Ferry). Because of the initial derisive reaction of her neighbors and family, Mrs. Carow's experience was not presented to the public until April 17, 1958 *(Pike County Dispatch).*

After Mr. Myer's article about Miss Stichler, Mrs. Carow wrote about her experience. She sympathised with Miss Stichler because of the "ribbing" she felt Miss Stichler might have experienced. Her letter

90

was forwarded to Mr. Myer who, with his wife, visited Mrs. Carow and conducted an on-the-spot interrogation. Excerpts from his account follow.

"The estate on which Mrs. D.* lives is rather secluded, with a large lawn and garden area to the rear of the house. Beyond this area is an open field flanked by woods, which are roughly 400 ft. from the house. A second field farther away lies behind a big old barn and cannot be seen from the house. As a nature lover, Mrs. D. derives great pleasure from watching the deer which come out of the woods into the field and on to the lawn both during the day and at night. They are observed at night by spotting them with a strong flashlight.

"During the last day of hunting season, 1956, there had been a great deal of shooting in the woods beyond the fields, and Mrs. D. was concerned whether there would be any deer left. About 9 o'clock that night Mrs. D. decided to take her flashlight and see if she could spot any deer. Stepping a few paces from the house, she immediately located objects with her flashlight which she recognized to be two men standing on the lawn, close together, with their arms at their sides and facing her a short 150 ft. away. They were standing a few feet from garden stakes used to hold up raspberry bushes, so that their height could be judged quite accurately. One figure was estimated to be 3½ft. tall and the other 3ft. tall. [Mrs. Carow is 5ft. tall] Mrs. D. played the flashlight beam on and off the men for about three minutes. At no time did they move but stood perfectly still.

"Both men were dressed alike in snugly fitting suits made of shiny silvery material which glistened in the light. Each wore a snugly fitting helmet leaving the face visible. Both men had fair complexions. They were well-proportioned and had good muscular development.

"As Mrs. D. continued to play the light back and forth across the men, she hoped that they would depart. However, as they remained motionless, she began to get excited. Finally, she retreated to the house, hurried inside, and bolted the door. She then ran to her husband who was watching television in the living room and very excitedly, with her knees shaking, told him that two little men in shiny suits were on the back lawn. She said that she didn't know what they were and begged him to come out with her and look at them. Mr. D., however, was so interested in his TV program and at the same time somewhat skeptical of the presence of the two little men that he didn't go out.

"About 15 minutes later Mrs. D. had calmed down and became so anxious about the men that she again went out by herself to see if the

---

Mrs. D. was the pseudonym chosen for Mrs. Marie Carow.

men were still there, but they were nowhere to be seen. During this 15-minute interval, Mrs. D. became impressed with the idea that these little men with their well-formed bodies and shiny uniforms were possibly from outer space and probably had their space vehicle parked behind the old barn.

"About two weeks later Mrs. D. related this account to friends living a few miles away on a hill back of Dingman's Ferry. The friends, a mother and daughter [a Mrs. Johnson and her daughter], said that about two weeks previously, at about 9 o'clock in the evening, they had seen a large luminous object in the sky speeding in a westerly direction. They expressed the opinion that this may have been the space vehicle of the two little men."

Psychiatric interview

After two telephone conversations, a psychiatric interview of Mrs. Carow was undertaken on December 7, 1968. Mrs. Carow, who was seen in her daughter's apartment, was a sincere-appearing, elderly lady, alert, serious, and open. She clearly recalled all the details mentioned in Mr. Myer's article and supplied additional information.

1. "The little one was stocky but the other was slender. They were both perfect in proportion. They were miniature men — perfectly dressed." When asked if they resembled the dwarfs she had heard about in Bavaria as a child, she said 'No.'

2. "It [uniform] looked like aluminum foil, shiny. They had gloves and shoes." [She could not tell if they had seams, pockets, zippers, buckles, or belts.]

3. During the time of the episode (as is true most of the time), there were no automobiles around and there was complete silence.

4. The next morning Mrs. Carow found an area, "in back of the garage" (close to where she had seen the men), where there "was squashed-down grass — but it could have been from the cattle that went through in the afternoon."

5. Mrs. Carow illustrated her comments about the episode with photographs of her former home and surrounding property.

6. In addition to telling her husband at the time of the possible UFO-occupant experience, Mrs. Carow also told her daughter shortly afterward and three of her neighbors. This was confirmed on careful questioning of the daughter (December 7, 1968). At the time of the event the daughter recalled how, "Mother was excited, said no one believed her, but she was staunch in what she believed she saw."

7. Because of her fear from the episode, Mrs. Carow was reluctant to go out at night for approximately six months thereafter, unless she

was accompanied by her husband. She never had experienced anything remotely like this event in her past, nor has she since. Prior to her experience, Mrs. Carow, like Miss Stichler, had no more than a most casual interest in "flying saucers."

As was true in Miss Stichler's experience, it should be stressed that Mrs. Carow at that time of her life enjoyed superb health and had good vision (no spectacles) and hearing. She was a housewife and her husband worked as a bartender. Mrs. Carow was certain that she saw two tiny men, because she had a "five-battery, focusing (magnifying glass) flashlight" which she had bought for the specific purpose of observing deer and other wild life on her property. Although there was no moon, it was a clear night and there were many stars.

Mrs. Carow denied any past history of emotional, psychosomatic, or debilitating illness. She did not use alcohol, tobacco, or unprescribed drugs. She seemed to be of above-average intelligence and was quick and crisp in her answers to questions. She did not hedge in her account and was not reluctant to say "No" when called for. Despite her advanced age, at the time of her interview, her mental-status examination was correct in all areas. With the exception of old-age vision corrected with eyeglasses and suspected mild "old age" diabetes successfully treated with diet (negative urine tests) she enjoyed excellent health.

Mrs. Carow, the youngest of seven children, was born and raised in Germany. She was educated by the Dominican nuns for seven years and then came to America in 1902. She was married the first time in 1907, and her only child was born in 1909. After the death of her first husband she remarried in 1921.

Study of the family history revealed no mental illness, alcoholism, or sociopathic behavior (lying, stealing, apprehension by authorities, and so forth). On the contrary, Mrs. Carow presented evidence that many of her ancestors were notable for long and healthy lives. She illustrated this with appropriate photographs.

Mrs. Carow seemed to be a completely truthful person. This observation was supported by questioning of Mrs. Carow's daughter. It was also confirmed by discussions with Mr. and Mrs. Myer and with the people who bought Mrs. Carow's former home.

Jack S. Bullock, M.D., for many years Mrs. Carow's family physician, stated that at the time of the possible UFO-occupant episode [which he was not told about] his patient was in good general health. She had no impairment of vision or hearing and had no unusual changes in her state of awareness. She had an excellent reputation for truthfulness;

she was one who did not exaggerate. She had never suffered from illusions, nor had she become involved in cultist activities.

Discussion and Summary

Single-witness reports based on purported happenings of more than 10 years ago have obvious shortcomings. However, the rarity of such alleged experiences, the surrounding circumstances in these examples, the probity of the witnesses, their excellent past health records, and current data learned on direct psychiatric examination justify such a report.

Hoax, as a possible explanation in both instances, would appear to be unlikely because of the prevailing circumstances. There was no motivation for either Miss Stichler or Mrs. Carow to perpetrate a hoax, or reason why they should be the victims of such a trick. Neither lady had in her long life ever shown any need to seek notoriety, to play practical jokes, or to tell fish stores. They both lived in very remote areas. There were no close neighbors.

Lying or fabrication is most unlikely without a past history of such behavior. This is almost unthinkable without clues for such conscience defects of the ladies or of their families (7). It is not common for one to change his character or alter the entire course of his lifetime in the manner described: i.e., one bizarre, outlandish incident that only brought sniggers or ridicule to the witnesses when they told others.

A false confession, as an explanation for these two instances, is far-fetched without a past history of such repeated conduct and a psychodynamic reason for its existence. Careful study of the past lives of the two ladies revealed no overwhelming emotional problems, guilt complexes, or need for confession.

There was no suggestion of delusion, hallucination, or severely disturbed state of undue suspiciousness. Both ladies had stable and down-to-earth personalities. In the opinion of their peers and the family physician they were incapable of lying or indulging in a flight of fancy.

There was no clinical evidence indicating how their purported experiences could be products of a brain syndrome, head injury, temporal lobe epilepsy, metabolic disease (viz., diabetes mellitus, uraemia, etc.) or ophthalmological condition. There was no history of alcohol, hallucinogens, other toxic agents, or psychosis.

In neither of these cases was there any build-up of various experiential, cultural, or religious factors that could have culminated in the experience. There was no acute precipitating event, as one would expect in various acute behavioral reactions. A psychiatric diagnosis, like an opinion in other medical specialities, is a positive one. It depends on a concatenation of highly specific events and reactions. There is, almost always, a pre-existent history of faulty reactions to various life situations, premorbid personality traits, neurotic character traits, and so forth. A psychiatric diagnosis is not made by exclusion: everything else being ruled out; therefore it must be of an emotional etiology.

Illusion as a possible explanation of Mrs. Carow's experience can not be excluded. However, the questions to ask would be (1) if her "little men" were illusory, why did they occur precisely when they did? (2) why would they not have occurred under similar circumstances at other times before or after this experience? and (3) would not such an illusion be most unusual without a history of an appropriate psychopathology, possible drug reactions, and other toxic-delirious states, and so forth? If the little men in uniform were in fact children, where in such an isolated area as Conashaugh would the children have come from, at that time, and in that way? None of the other myriad of possible explanations seem applicable here.

A possible parapsychological causation should also be considered. One who is acquainted, from first-hand study, with gifted paragnosts and telepathists (or good magicians, for that matter!), is well aware how easily one can see what isn't there and yet solemnly swear to the validity of his experience. There are examples involving multiple witnesses to alleged ghostly apparitions, and examples of telepathically projected visual hallucinations and illusions. In the lives of both of these ladies there was nothing remotely like such spontaneous psychic examples.

In both instances the difficulty is in the interpretation of what Miss Stichler and Mrs. Carow separately experienced at different times and in isolated places, unknown to each other. It would appear they were frightened from what they observed and *not* that they were first frightened because of some other reason and then developed the event as the product of their minds.

A psychiatric opinion can only assist in assessing the reliability of the observers and the interpretation of their experiences. What the ultimate reality is (or was) is another problem.

Psychiatric study of two witnesses who had alleged close contacts with (1) a UFO and its occupant, and (2) two "little men" (occupants) revealed the witnesses to be stable, healthy women. There was no apparent psychiatric explanation for the experiences. Medical-psychiatric techniques can be of value in assessing the reliability of the witness, eliciting data, and evaluating their experiences.

REFERENCES

1. Bowen, Charles, Editor, **The Humanoids,** FSR Special Issue, London, England, October/November 1966, 72 pages. (Now published in enlarged form, August 1969, by Neville Spearman Ltd., London, 256 pages — EDITOR.)
2. Fontes, Olavo; Martins, Joao (Granchi, Irene, translator). Report on the Villas Boas Incident, February 22, 1958.
   Lorenzen, Coral and Jim: **Flying Saucer Occupants,** Chapter III, 42-72, Signet Book, N.Y., 1967, pp. 215. (See also Gordon Creighton's complete translation in **The Humanoids**, Neville Spearman Ltd., 1969 — EDITOR).
3. Meerloo, J.A.M.: **Le Syndrome des Soucoupes Volantes,** Med. Hyg., 25:992, 1967.
4. Meerloo, J.A.M.: **The Flying Saucer Syndrome and the Need for Miracles,** J.A.M.A., 203:1074, 1968.
5. Walker, Sydney: **The Applied Assessment of Central Nervous System Integrity: A Method for Establishing the Creditability of Eye Witnesses and Other Observers.** Symposium on UFOs, Hearings Before the Committee on Science and Astronautics, U.S. House of Representatives, Ninetieth Congress, July 29, 1968, pp. 152-176, 185-189.
6. Schwarz, B.E.: **UFOs: Delusion or Dilemma,** MEDICAL TIMES, 96, 10:967-981, 1968. (See also BEYOND CONDON ... FSR Special Issue No. 2, June, 1969 — EDITOR).
7. Johnson, Adelaide M., and Szurek, S.A.: **Etiology of Antisocial Behavior in Delinquents and Psychopaths,** J.A.M.A., 154:814-817, 1954.

Chapter 5

Possible UFO-Induced Temporary Paralysis

A state of temporary paralysis, presumably caused by UFOs, has often been reported (1,2,3). This report explores various aspects of this baffling condition, as well as other purported UFO—associated physiological and psychic effects.

I
The Setting

On a field trip to study a family that had reported many terrorising UFO sightings, bizarre poltergeist manifestations, etc., the author travelled to a small Catskill Mountain community (in west-central New York State). When he stopped in a gift store to purchase some postal cards and make inquiries about the locale, a neatly groomed, pleasant, middle-aged woman customer told him about the strange UFO experience of temporary paralysis that happened to her lifelong friend, Mr. O.*.

II
The Experience

It was late in August, 1968, between 8:00 and 9:00 p.m., on a pitch-black night. Mr. M. O., age 58, a self-employed garage mechanic, a bachelor, and an elementary-school graduate, was alone on his farm in an isolated area of the Catskill Mountains of New York. As was his custom, he went outside with his French poodle to feed his horse some bread and honey. The dog was about five feet in front of him, and he had milk in his hand for the cat, who was then in the garage.

Suddenly, "I heard a shrill sound — a whining, like a dynamo. I could not move. I looked at the dog and he was standing motionless. The horse (Morgan gelding) was at the fence, standing still with his head in the air, turned toward the side of the hill. I lost all sense of time — it might have lasted seconds or five to ten minutes. I realized I wasn't moving, but I felt my body from the head down to my hips. It was pins and needles, like when you get a cold. I shook. I could not move — only my head. I could only watch, turning my head a bit, but I couldn't take a step. All of a sudden the noise stopped, and I could move. When I looked

---

*The names and addresses of the witness, and of the other people interviewed, are on file with **Flying Saucer Review** — EDITOR.

Sketch map of New York; location of the Catskill mountains

around, the horse and the dog were also moving. I looked up the valley and saw nothing, but over the barn there were two holes in the sky, as white as snow. It was like looking into a barrel. They were perfectly round, automobile-tire size and about three feet apart. They stayed still and didn't move for ten to fifteen minutes — then disappeared. The next morning I discovered that the cat didn't drink the milk I had put out for him the night before, and this was unusual. There was no effect on the household electric lights, clock (battery-powered), or radio, but there was something odd — the telephone didn't work when I went to make a call that night. It was all right the next day."

Shortly after arising in the morning, Mr. O. noted dysuria: "Burning urine, like a red-hot poker. Ten minutes later it was all right." Several hours after this symptom, he developed red streaks on the glans penis (uncircumcised). This disappeared in one day. There was no ostensible reason for these complaints, such as cystitis, prostatitis, or various venereal diseases. There was no change in his sexual function before or following this experience.

Mr. O.'s general health was good, and he prided himself on his near-perfect work record of forty years. However, six months prior to this episode, he had had pain in the right sacrosciatic notch radiating along the sciatic nerve to his heel. Chiropractic manipulations were ineffective. However, the day after his nocturnal experience he was completely relieved of pain and he has been well until the present time (December, 1970).

Two weeks after his experience, Mr. O. suddenly "remembered the spot I had noticed in the field [one week before the episode] where the hay was flat in a round area about six feet in diameter. I noticed this when I was mowing. At the time I didn't associate this to anything, but later [after the episode] when I got out to the spot, I found that the grass was only four to five inches tall. I was amazed to see that the area was as dry as the floor and with all fine little stones — not cobbles as there are surrounding the area — unusual for this place."

Six telephone interviews with the subject and psychiatric and neurological examinations at Mr. O.'s place of business on March 3, 1970, and December 2, 1970, confirmed his general good health. There was no discernible reason, psychopathologically or neurologically, for his strange experience. There was no impairment of orientation, nor of various intellectual and memory functions. There was no objective evidence for a ruptured intervertebral disc. There was nothing to suggest untruthfulness or fabrication as an explanation. There was a past history for a healed duodenal ulcer** that had prevented military service. In previous years he had had migraine: "I'm a great one to keep stuff inside of me." The overall picture of good health was supported by Mr. O.'s answers on the Cornell Medical Index Questionnaire and computerized Minnesota Multiphasic Personality Inventory.

Shortly after the episode, Mr. O. told several neighbors and friends about his experience. On the telephone, the physician interviewed a distinguished actor and his wife; a lady acquaintance since Mr. O.'s boyhood (the author's original informant); a veterinarian and her secretary; and a close lady friend who is a medical technologist; plus several other people. They remembered hearing about the experience and had confidence in Mr. O.'s veracity.

The actor recalled Mr. O.'s peculiar genito-urinary history and sciatic pain. The actor's home, also on the same Catskill mountain ridge, was approximately 150 yards away from Mr. O.'s. The actor, too, saw the round flattened area, and noted that the affected grass was very green and stunted. Once last year (one year after the episode) the actor telephoned Mr. O. to see if his outside spotlights were turned off (they were) because there was "a greenish, glowing light around your place." No further significance was attached to this event other than its uniqueness. It had not been noted in the past. Until the interview it was not related to the previous happenings. However, since then it has been observed on a few occasions and attributed to the stars by Mr. O. (?).

It might be noted that during the playbacksessions of hypnotic interviews, Barney Hill's duodenal ulcers flared up. (Fuller, J.G.: **The Interrupted Journey, Dell Books, New York, 1967, pp. 312, 325.)

The actor has had a distinguished career and is known and vouchsafed for by the author's friend, Joseph Dunninger.

Interview of the medical technologist on September 9, 1970, also confirmed all the history, including Mr. O.'s physical data. The technologist's mother was a highly regarded private duty nurse at Mountainside Hospital, Montclair, New Jersey, where the author was on the staff for ten years.

When the veterinarian and her assistant were contacted, they corroborated Mr. O.'s narrative, and also recalled the odd effects on the animals. They knew of no similar effects on other animals in their professional experience.*

From the study of Mr. O., as well as the opinions of these five people, it was evident that Mr. O. had no previous experience or consuming interest in UFOs, science fiction, psychics, and the like. He was described as a hard-working, warm-hearted, extroverted auto mechanic

---

* Gordon Creighton has recently catalogued "The Effects of UFOs on Animals, Birds, and Smaller Creatures" (FSR, Vol. 16, Nos. 1, 2, 3, and 4, 1970). In another study (Delphieux, M., translated by Gordon Creighton: "Nearlanding in Herault", FSR, Vol. 16, No. 1, January/February, 1970, pp. 13-14) it was noted that a herd of goats following exposure to a UFO came in heat at closer intervals and that an excellent male goat for breeding purposes ... was no longer doing his job. O., who was raised on a farm, did not observe any sexual changes in his animals. Close UFO sightings involving dogs, investigated by the author are:

(a) In a widely publicized case of Wednesday, November 13, 1957, Mrs. John Trasco of rural New Jersey, a nurse's aide, said, "One creature (little, small green man) came out and wanted the dog — had a glowing from each finger tip. They (UFO and two occupants) landed by the outhouse, which we don't use. The dog (a six-year-old partially blind, charcoal-colored Belgian shepherd) howled, and was very frightened. (**Delaware Valley News,** November 15, 1957.)

(b) A close, tree-height sighting happened over an outdoor pool at White Rock Lake, New Jersey, on March 31, 1966, at 8:05 p.m. ([Dover] **Daily Advance,** Friday, April 1, 1966, p. 1), and Mrs. Connie Bateman's dog "howled and my sister's dog whined and tried to get into the house through a window."

(c) On April 1, 1966, at 8:45 p.m. (UPI, April 4, 1966), Mrs. Carol Vander Plate, while in her home on a mountain-top at WLVP-FM, Hardyston Township (which is close to White Rock Lake), New Jersey, noted a UFO at tree height, and " ... All of a sudden my two French poodles started barking and carrying on. They refused to obey. They went crazy, running in circles, and jumping over the furniture." ("UFOs in New Jersey", The **Journal** of the Medical Society of New Jersey, Vol. 66, No. 8, pp. 460-464, August, 1969.)

(d) A close sighting lasted for one hour, beginning at 10:10 p.m. on a Wednesday in April, 1967, at Hackettstown, New Jersey, directly over the houses at tree-height and over the fish hatchery, where Mrs. Lawrence Robinson's springer spaniel puppy "sat still on the ground, howling, and wouldn' move."

and outdoorsman, without literary inclinations.

Although Mr. O.'s past experiences included some psychic phenomena, there was no more than is apparent in many case histories. There were no associated psychic events or harassments with, or after, his experience. Mr. O. has had no previous dissociative states, time lapses, blackouts, seizures, hypnotic trances, head injuries, encephalopathies of any cause, injudicious use of alcohol, or drugs. He had taken no alcohol at the time of his episode. He could recall no dreams.

Careful scrutiny of the family history and of other significant people in Mr. O.'s background yielded no material for remotely similar UFO-related experiences.

III
Possible Mechanisms
(a) Paraesthesias

Descriptively, it would seem that Mr. O., his horse, and his dog had catalepsy that correlated with the duration of a strange dynamo sound. Such UFO-related sounds are not uncommon, and the author has reports of similar sounds from investigations of the Split Rock and Wanaque Reservoir areas of northern New Jersey. Mr. O's paraesthesia, or tingling pins-and-needles sensation, is a common symptom seen in medical practice, and is usually associated with an anxiety state. The anxiety causes unconscious overbreathing, which in turn, leads to alkalosis and latent tetany, or the physiological effects on the perpheral nerves: typically, paresthesias of the fingers, toes, and so forth. In many instances, the patient is aware of the cause-and-effect relationships — the overbreathing induced by anxiety, causing tingling.*

Mr. O.'s paresthesia could have been a physiological reaction to his overwhelming anxiety.

(b) Catalepsy

As noted, UFO-associated temporary paralysis (catalepsy) and other neuromuscular effects are not uncommon. The rigid, immobile posture is a way of reacting to overwhelming, emotional stimuli: fear, bereavement, catastrophe. It results when more active measures: i.e., fight, flight, would be too difficult. In some cases the catalepsy is associated with an alleged "ray" from the UFO. In one well-documented case of close exposure to a UFO, the subject, who did not have catalepsy, developed profound reversible muscular weakness and wasting and was hospitalized (4).

---

*Unfortunately, the demonstration of this relationship is seldom therapeutic, because of the deeper problems having to do with the patient's unconscious life.

(c) Question of Amnesia

Although Mr. O., apparently did not have amnesia from his experience, the uncertainty of the time lapse suggests the need for further investigation by hypnosis, psychotherapy, and electroencephalography (5). In acute brain syndromes, toxic confusion-states of various causes, and states of heightened anxiety, etc., the loss of the sense of time is often the first symptom.

(d) Psychical Seizures

Psychical seizures (6) (temporal lobe epilepsy) have some symptoms similar to Mr. O.'s experience: (1) disorientation, (2) behavioral response, (3) sometimes relatively prolonged episodes (unusual for psychical seizures) and (4) rapid onset and termination. However, the nature of Mr. O.'s "attack" and the fact that he had only one such experience in his life, plus the involvement of the animals, and so on, makes a solitary psychical seizure very unlikely.

(3) Sleep Paralysis

"Sleep paralysis" (7) (cataplexy), which has been known in folklore throughout history as being caused by a nightly visitation of devils and demons, is characterized by a state where the subject feels awake and is aware of his surroundings, but is incapable of voluntary movement. The attack usually lasts from several seconds to several minutes and is accompanied by terror, with or without hallucinations (see case report that follows). Cataplexy, however, would not explain the simultaneous animal effects in Mr. O.'s experience. Patients with sleep paralysis usually have many attacks, and unlike Mr. O., a definite psychopathological history.

(f) Genitourinary Effects

The dysuria and penile lesions would seem to be a complication of Mr. O.'s experience. Although there is only Mr. O.'s report of them, and no record from a trained observer, the "red streaks" were most unusual (8). By description they were not psychosomatic or factitial (self induced). This opinion was supported by George R. Read, M.D., urologist, who felt that the specific reported events, dysuria and lesions, were unlike those seen in practice.

Dr. Benjamin Simon (9) noted how in his treatment of the Hills, Barney had an inflammation of the small circle of warts that had developed in an almost geometrically perfect circle around his groin. Barney wondered if the warts were psychosomatic or if they were caused by the examination and instruments aboard the UFO (ibid., pp. 283-284).

102

Barney also recalled the cool sensation in his groin while being examined aboard the UFO, and Betty (his wife) had a bizarre "pregnancy test" in which a long needle was injected into her navel. Keel (10) described a spectacular contactee case involving a prominent Brazilian lawyer who allegedly went on a UFO trip during which he noted he felt pain and cold in his genitals.

These examples, with the sexual motif, in addition to the extraordinary Villas Boas (1) case, and others,† raise the question of reality *vs.* delusions, hallucinations, and illusions. It is well known that in some emotional disorders there are often numerous sexual symptoms. The symptoms usually are the result of the (interpersonal) anxiety rather than the cause of it. Mr. O.'s rash and dysuria were not typical for an emotional or psychosomatic reaction. Moreover, there was a lack of any previous concatenation of events or a crisis leading up to his once-in-a-lifetime experience. There was neither a build up of tension nor a previous sexual problem. The UFO-effect hypothesis remains.

Mention should be made of the dramatic relief of Mr. O.'s sacrosciatic notch and sciatic nerve pain, following the nocturnal experience. From his past history, and upon direct examination, Mr. O. seemed to have a high pain threshold and he was not hyper-suggestible. Since his occupation called for rugged physical health and strong back, his backache was a serious threat to his livelihood. There was nothing to suggest any "purpose" (e.g., secondary gain, disability benefits, etc.) for such a backache. Manipulation of his back for months had been ineffective. Conversion was a most unlikely explanation because of the anatomical distribution of the pain, and because of the absence of previous similar episodes. Perhaps Mr. O.'s unusual therapeutic result is similar to a case reported by Finch (11), in which a toothache was relieved following a UFO experience.

Keel described a widely publicized incident in which a Texas deputy sheriff's left index finger, painful, swollen, and bleeding from an alligator bite, was almost immediately relieved and healed following close exposure to a "great rectangular glob of purple light, about fifty feet in height" (*ibid.*, p. 254).‡

---

†In a New Jersey presumed-UFO-landing case of July 3, 1970, near Sandy Hook, with many extraordinary features, one of the witnesses, a young mother, following a nocturnal "smell of death" episode, had a terrifying dream of faceless forms trying to break into her house. She awoke with severe right sacrosciatic notch pain. At the time, the woman wondered if she had a needle puncture in the gluteal region. She told several members of her family and consulted her physician, who confirmed this history to the author.

Possible Radiation

Although specific supporting data are lacking, it can be speculated that high-frequency electromagnetic (radar) waves, microwaves, or infrasound could have conceivably been causative factors. All of these modalities can produce a variety of physical effects. When told about Mr. O.'s case, Karl Olsson, an electrical engineer, conjectured that Mr. O.'s reaction was due to high-frequency radar combined with infrared (for directing the energy) from a twin-engine turboprop airplane. A particular U.S. experimental military reconnaissance aircraft can fly as slow as an estimated 50 m.p.h., and because of the turbines, makes a whining sound. The twin white lights over the barn could have been due to cabin lights from the plane reflected off the revolving propellers.

This explanation, although superficially attractive, is incomplete. For example, why would such an experimental aircraft, fifty miles from the nearest military base, be in this isolated area of the Catskills at that particular time, and be visibly stationary for ten to fifteen minutes? And if the purported effects were random, why were they not more widespread, or why was there not other physical evidence? Furthermore, how could such an explanation be reconciled with (1) the appearance of the circular, flattened-out area in the field, at the approximate time of Mr. O.'s experience and (2) the strange, green, luminescent effect around Mr. O.'s house one year after the event?

Consultation with Keith Keeler, M.D., physiatrist, and Hector Giancarlo, M.D., otologist, yielded no conclusive explanations for either the microwave or infra-sound hypotheses. There were the same objections as with the hypothetical radar effect: how such an effect, as in Mr. O.'s case, could have been so selectively, and reversibly produced: e.g. without permanent thermal or hemorrhagic tissue damage, with resultant tinnitus and deafness, etc. Thus, if there was radiation, what was it? What was its source? Some experimental military craft, other sophisticated weaponry, or UFO? And then, how did the supposed radiation mediate the particular non-injurious biological effects?

Psychic Red Herrings?

Another possible way that these effects could have been induced in Mr. O. and his animals may have been telepathic. For example, the following highly compressed vignettes, specific for Mr. O., illustrate

‡ Gordon Creighton has recently summarized this and several other UFO healing cases (FSR, Vol. 15, No. 5, September/October, 1969, pp. 20-23) and Aime Michel has documented an extraordinary case involving a French doctor and his infant son (FSR, Special Issue, No. 3, September, 1969, pp. 3-16). It is hoped that many more examples can be collected.

this complex relationship.

1. A young woman patient, who was seen in psycho-therapy for depression, came one day for her session, terrified. She stated that on Sunday, at 9:30 a.m., while home in bed: "I suddenly tried, desperately, to get up but *I couldn't move.* It was very weird. I became panicky. I thought I was going to scream. You (physician) appeared like a vision. It came on through gauze — instead of projecting onto a screen, it came in backwards, like a camera behind the screen. It had a floating effect. It was a moving, floating face — ethereal. Only, it had just your head; nothing was said. It appeared out of nowhere, like those crazy horror stories or in seances where a head appears out of nowhere. Boom! That's the only way I can describe it."

At the time of this woman's experience, and unknown to her, the physician in his home, miles away from the patient, was visiting with Mr. Clement Tamburreno, psychic healer. He was discussing two specific points of urgent interest at that time (1) the UFO temporary paralysis of Mr. O., and his animals, and (2) materialization of UFOs, apparitions, etc. I wondered if Mr. Tamburreno, who lectures widely to interested groups, would know of someone who might have had similar experiences. The woman patient, who was *en rapport* with her therapist, had specific reasons to be upset at that time; for his part, the physician was keyed up about traumatic events in his own life, and sought some clues from his researches that might have a practical medical application. The conscious and unconscious needs of patient and physician telepathically served each other.†

As the patient related her presumed telepathic hallucinatory experience, the physician made a note on his pad of other similar examples. He jotted down the name of another patient, who had telepathically hallucinated a coffin (12). Hardly had he finished than this patient telephoned long distance for an appointment. She had not been seen in many months. It was learned that she had no pressing problems at this time. It was speculated that she telepathically reacted to the possible use of her highly charged life example (of which she was unaware): e.g., unconscious competition with the other lady patient.*

---

†In the course of her psychotherapy there were numerous other presumed telepathic episodes.

*The element of cut-off in some of these possible telepathic examples can extend to absurd lengths. For example, when the author was preparing the final draft of this report and wondering if the patient would make her next session, since she had travelled three hundred miles away for the week-end, a lady friend of hers 'phoned to say that the woman had just called her and asked that she confirm the appointment.

Telepathy is not directly linked to Mr. O.'s temporary paralysis. However, telepathic claims are not at all infrequent in some UFO cases, and they could be capable of mediating all kinds of effects (telesomatic reactions) (13). It is difficult, if not impossible, as in Mr. O.'s case, to collect all the relevant data; but these examples show that what can and does happen in psychotherapy can also (and does?) happen in UFO cases. Since UFO experiences are often associated with terror and take place in awesome and emotionally splitting situations — the same substrates that seem to be prerequisites for many telepathic experiences — some or much of their (UFO) content could come from the unconscious minds of others (telepathic suggestion). Ehrenwald (14) has shown how such unconscious bias or telepathic leakage might be a factor of considerable significance in psychotherapy. By analogy, this could also be highly inportant to UFO investigations. To try to be objective without taking into account the subjective (i.e., one's unconscious bias) can fool the investigator of the best intentions. The following example of a possible telepathic linkage involving Mr. O. further illustrates this.

2. On Thursday, June 18, 1970, the physician was upset by serious illness in his family, and, perhaps as an escape from such grimness, he phantasied about the unusual O. case, and its interesting medical implications. He yearned to return to the Catskill Mountains to obtain more data. While he was thus musing, the friend who had originally invited him to the Catskills (where O. and the other case described in the beginning of this chapter were located) telephoned, and again extended an invitation. This friend knew nothing of the physician's own pressing events and the invitation had to be declined. The frustration was aggravated by the physician's accidentally coming across for the first time, a large newspaper advertisement of the hit play in which Mr. O.'s neighbor was the leading actor. Hardly had these emotionally charged thoughts of desiring to see Mr. O. crystallized, than O. himself telephoned for the first and only time in our association. Thus, it can be supposed that telepathic linkages can account in this way for many of the strange "coincidences" or serendipity that one seems to find in ufology.

It may be asked: (1) can the awesome tracer-laden UFO events — as in Mr. O.'s case — account for the awareness of telepathy (and other psychic phenomena) or actually generate its happenings; or (2) could the hypothesized intelligent force behind the UFOs directly cause the telepathic and other psychic events, as is claimed in many instances; or (3) is it a phantasmogoria: a combination of both: i.e., an original telepathic stimulus setting up a chain reaction of psychic and other events that are colored by psychopathological, experiential, cultural factors, and so forth?

106

Autographed photograph of Joseph Dunninger and Vladimir Komorov, cosmonaut, who died April 24, 1967, when descending to earth and his space capsule parachute failed to open.

Since it is often the "forgotten" (Mr. O's confusion of time during the episode) that is accessible to the telepathist, possibly the gifted paragnost can make worthwhile contributions to ufology in this area. In the attempt to decipher this mystery, Joseph Dunninger, America's greatest telepathist, whose formal career has extended world-wide for over fifty years, graciously volunteered his skills. Dunninger is also a much-honored magician, inventor of illusions,‡ revealer of fradulent seances, participant and witness to numerous unexplainable, extraordinary, presumed psychic events in and out of seances. After meeting Mr. O., on December 2, 1970, Dunninger felt that he was an honest man, and that his experiences involved no trick or illusion. Dunninger, whose highly developed and documented telepathic talents were occasionally used for the solution of crimes and the treatment of patients in medical school settings, received no telepathic impressions from Mr. O., but felt that from his experience Mr. O.'s case was unique and worthy of intensive scientific study.

In summary, temporary paralysis, among other causes, can also be a UFO-associated condition with many ramifications which can be studied from a variety of viewpoints.

---

‡Dunninger, who invented many of his friend Houdini's best illusions, had also developed, during World War II, a means of making a battleship invisible. He showed the author his correspondence with the U.S. Navy Department.

REFERENCES

1. Bowen, Charles, Editor, **The Humanoids,** Neville Spearman Ltd., London, 1969, and Henry Regnery Co., Chicago.
2. Lore, Gordon, Chief Researcher and Writer: "Strange Effects from UFOs". A NICAP Special Report, National Investigations Committee on Aerial Phenomena, Washington, D.C., 1969.
3. Vallee, Jacques, **Passport to Magonia,** Henry Regnery Co., Chicago, 1969.
4. Schwarz, Berthold Eric: "UFOs: Delusion or Dilemma?" **Medical Times,** Vol. 96, No. 10, pp. 967-981, October 1968.
5. Thorp, Barry R.:' The Electroencephalogram in Transient Global Amnesia", **EEG and Clinical Neurophysiology,** Vol. 26, pp. 96-99, 1969.
6. Whitten, J.R.:"Psychical Seizures," **American Journal of Psychiatry,,** Vol. 126, pp. 560-565, October 1969.
7. Liddon, Sim C.: "Sleep Paralysis, Psychosis and Death", **Amer. Journal of Psychiatry,** Vol. 126, pp. 1027-1031, January, 1970.
8. Fiumara, Nicholas, J.: "A Guide to Lesions of the Penis", **Hospital Medicine,** Vol. 6, No. 3, pp. 22-34, March, 1970.
9. Fuller, John G.: **The Interrupted Journey,** Dial Press, New York, 1966.
10. Keel, John A.: **UFOs: Operation Trojan Horse,** G.P. Putnam's Sons, New York, 1970.
11 Finch, Bernard E.: "Physiological Effects on Witness at Hook", FSR, Vol. 13, No. 6 (November/December), pp. 7, 27, 1967.
12. Schwarz, Berthold Eric: "Prerecognition and Psychic Nexus", **Journal** of The American Society of Psychosomatic Dentistry and Medicine, Part I, Vol. 18 (No. 2): 52-59, 1971; Part II, Vol. 18 (No. 3): 83-93, 1971.
13. Schwarz, Berthold Eric: "Possible Telesomatic Reactions", **The Journal** of The Medical Society of New Jersey, Vol. 64, No. 11, pp. 600-603, November, 1967.
14 Ehrenwald, Jan.: "The Telepathy Hypothesis and Doctrinal Compliance in Psychotherapy", **American Journal of Psychotherapy,** Vol XI, No. 2, pp. 359-379, April, 1957.

Chapter 6

Beauty of the Night

While researching a complex silent contactee, Mr. X (1) of northern New Jersey, I stumbled upon some interesting tangential data when referred to two of her former acquaintances from the late 1950s. These men, now in middle age, recounted to me their UFO experiences in northern New Jersey and the Pocono Mountains of eastern Pennsylvania.

B.C., a fifty-three-year-old salesman, who had university training in engineering and business adminstration, was very active in ufology for a six-to-nine-month period in 1958. During that time he was involved with a highly publicized northern New Jersey contactee, some of whose claimed UFO experiences were, in B.C.'s opinion, frankly spurious, and others inexplicable. B.C. independently witnessed some purported associated UFO events. He vividly recalled four distinct episodes. It facilitated this study to learn that he was formerly from my home town, Montclair, and was currently living in a neighboring community.

Three psychiatric interviews in my office and several extended telephone conversations with B.C., his wife, and other members of the family revealed him to be intelligent, truthful, and free of any relevant psychopathology. Although he currently had mild diabetes, which is being successfully treated with diet and oral medication, his UFO experiences occurred when he was in good general health. He has always had excellent vision and hearing. The following experiences are presented chronologically.

I — The radio
"My wife and I heard a WOR radio news bulletin which interrupted the regular program for a few minutes, but which no one else heard. We were driving from Montclair to Pluckemin, New Jersey, where a meeting on saucers was held every week. While I was listening to the regular program, an announcer cut in and said, 'It's been reported that the British have communicated with a saucer in England and have made arrangements with the occupants.'

"I turned to my wife and was stunned. When I asked her, 'Will you

---

● The title "Beauty of the Night" is quoted from "God's World," a poem by C.B. Brailey, in **Secret of the Flying Saucers from Outer Space,** by Howard Menger, Pyramid Publications, Inc., New York City, 1959.

tell me what was just said on the radio?', she gave it to me just the way I had heard it.

"I inquired about this when we arrived at Pluckemin, and although the people there were also listening to that particular radio show, they hadn't heard what we did! I could hardly believe what I had heard. I never had an experience like that before or since. A hoax would have been very unlikely."

II — The death light

B.C now moved on to the second incident:

"The contactee's son, aged twelve, was dying of brain cancer. The parents had given up on doctors and were using advice from the 'spacemen.' The boy was close to the end. My friend Rob* and I went up there to see if there was anything we could do.

"We were sitting in the kitchen and the boy was in the other room with the nurse, who was on twenty-four hour duty. The sick boy then called urgently. His mother rushed into the room and we followed. The nurse took his pulse; it was very slow. The boy had a convulsion and a light started to show up above his bed. It began as a light blue, and was about eight inches from the wall but not casting any light on the wall. It was like a bar of light. It pulsated and grew whiter, and then it faded. The whole manifestation lasted about one and a half minutes.

"The nurse left to call the doctor. Rob and I were alarmed. When the boy relaxed the light was white. By the time the doctor came there was no light and the boy was all right. When I saw the light, I turned my head sideways to make sure that it was not an optical illusion which would travel with me, but it was still there. I asked Rob what he had seen in the last several minutes and he described it to me the same way.

"The night of the column of light, I saw four men in luminous uniforms. They were about three hundred feet away on a hill-top in the pasture. They stood in front of a dark grove of trees behind a fence. It was a moon-lit night. They were on the edge of the rise and walking and glowing. If they were stooges, it would have been a very strange hoax. The sick boy's mother was with us: the other children were too young and too small to fake this. The [contactee] father was in the house, as was everyone else whom we had met when we first came. The father might have been grieving over his very ill son and flipped,† but this would be hard to accept. It was not very cold that night."

This incident was independently confirmed by Rob and the same light over the dying boy was seen under similar conditions at several

---

*This experience was independently and spontaneously confirmed by Rob and his wife.

111

different times by Mr. and Mrs. X, who independently volunteered this information, and were quite mystified by it.

The Xs recalled how, before the boy was completely blind (i.e., couldn't distinguish light from dark) and disfigured from the brain tumor, he could 'see' many people around him when the others claimed they saw the columns of light. The boy said, "they (the hallucinated phantoms?) are from the planet Orion and are coming to take me away." The mother and Mr. and Mrs. X had no idea where the boy received this information since the father and the rest of the family were unfamilar with Orion and such concepts.

All who visited the boy were impressed with his composure in the face of death and with his intellectual brilliance. Although only twelve years old and blind, he could talk on a variety of subjects, and many people came from afar to see him, including, on one occasion a high-ranking Jesuit from Washington, D.C., who interviewed the boy in private and at length.

The account of Mr. and Mrs. X was fully corroborated by a three-hour psychiatric interview of the boy's mother. Her narrative and experiences included the episode with luminous entities that "could almost be seen though — and that seemed to hop around like the astronauts (whose Apollo XVI moonwalk was on television during the interview). There were no discrepancies between the mother's comments and the versions given by B.C., Rob, and the Xs.

The mother expatiated on other personal UFO and UFO-related experiences. She appeared to be an open, honest, cooperative, intelligent, middle-aged woman who was free of any gross psychopathology. From the interviews of her and others, it would seem reasonable to suppose that the elements of later fraud and presumed serious psychopathy involving her husband, the publicized contactee, were an entirely different matter and a tragic story in themselves.

It is of interest that despite some dreadful life experiences, the woman's children have all done well in the world. The mother handled the truth and reality of the valid, early, family UFO experiences in a fac-

†H.W., who was a high school friend of the sick boy, recalled how the contactee father once brought the sick boy out into the pasture "to meet the spacemen and receive help. The boy, who was blind from the brain tumor, couldn't see the spacemen, and the father screamed and smacked his son." Because of this, H.W. felt that the father was a hoaxer. However, even superficial scrutiny of this unfortunate episode reveals other alternative and perhaps more plausible hypotheses: (1) the father had hallucinations and delusions of spacemen; (2) the father actually saw something and was furious and frustrated that his son couldn't share his experience either in reality or in an induced psychosis, folie a deux.

112

tual way — even though she had no explanation. The later alleged UFO material involving her husband alone, which she believed was fraudulent, she also handled on a reality plane. It can be conjectured that if she had not assumed such a course, her children (and she herself) would not have survived without serious emotional decompensation.

None of the people involved in the light experiences were spiritualists, adepts in psychic phenomena, or in any way accustomed to such events.

On telephone interview, the sick boy's physician claimed no knowledge of the light episode. Perhaps because his wife was flagrantly deceived by the publicized contactee's egregious stories, the physician dismissed everything and everybody associated with these alleged UFO-associated events as "bunk".

Karlis Osis (2), the parapsychologist, has carefully analyzed many deathbed experiences, some of which are possibly analogous to this. In his examples, the dying person had the vision, which was only rarely shared by others. Not one of his examples had multiple visions by observers on different occasions. However, Osis cited an amusing experiment by the Cambridge Society for Psychical Research: A Mr. Cornell once masqueraded as a ghost by wearing a white garment and then walked in a lighted churchyard "in view of a street with much traffic." He next walked across a screen during a performance in a crowded movie theatre, and still later, using luminous cloth, he masqueraded at a garden party. Thirty-two percent of the theatre audience did not notice him at all, and of those who did, he was not interpreted as an apparition. Of the sixteen observers at the garden party, only the bartender (and he might have been under the influence of alcohol) took Mr. Cornell for an apparition.

The applicability of this experiment both to UFO data and in particular to the UFO-associated multiple-witness experiences of seeing luminous figures with peculiar astronaut-like gaits, as well as the columns of light, is evident. The framework of negative expectancy, which would tend to minimize or deny such experiences, would tend to make any residue that is reported more significant. Therefore, because UFO experients are often ridiculed for reporting "such nonsense", it is likely that there are as many cases understated as there are overstated — even to the extent of the grievous omission of bizarre data.

Although there is nothing is Osis' accounts that are remotely reminiscent of UFOs, one might wonder about a possible UFO-parapsychological linkage. How does one find out unless he thinks of the possibility and has asked?

III — The ravine+

B.C. next recalled a personal sighting:

"This event happened late one winter night about six weeks after the death-light experience. It was snowing. We were near the Mt. Airy Lodge in an isolated area of the Pocono Mountains in eastern Pennsylvania. A group of us were in a cabin with a fire going and decided to experiment by having one of the fellows hypnotized. When entranced, he said that there would be [UFO] action in the region that night and that we should go to a ravine. Nobody, however, gave us a direct route. Rob, several other men, a few wives and I went to a ravine. It was snowing. The (publicized) contactee was not with us and knew nothing of what we were doing or what we had planned on the spur of the moment. We stood on a ridge, looking down into the gulley while Rob (§) and the hotel desk clerk went down to see what was there. When they were about twelve feet into the clear area at the bottom of the ravine, a man's voice, seemingly from the brush on the side, said, 'Who's with

---

+My hour telephone interview of an anonymous physicist (Ph.D., Princeton; currently professor and chairman of a university department of physics) years later confirmed his similar experience of seeing a noiseless disc 3 feet in diameter, in a rural New Jersey ravine (near the home of the publicized contactee). The disc changed in color for approximately 15 to 20 minutes and was observed at a distance of 6 to 8 feet. The physicist was unable to offer a plausible explanation, although he was aware of such hypotheses as Wood's light (ultraviolet) on fluorescent painted discs, etc. While a hoax seemed unlikely because of the intelligence of the people involved, the cost, and the technical difficulties, it was impossible to rule it out entirely. As a matter of fact, the physicist credited this experience with a significant influence on his life and career. It aroused his curiosity; but even though through the years he has interviewed many people who have had UFO experiences, few of his colleagues know of his personal UFO involvement.

The episode in the ravine was also witnessed by the young man H.W. (see footnote†), the friend of the publicized contactee's dying son. Direct interviews of H.W., of his father-in-law (a newspaper reporter) and of his mother-in-law, both of whom were thoroughly familiar with the whole bizarre publicized contactee's story, confirmed the physicist's account, allowing for some omissions (e.g., H.W. offered more details: ". . . a little light came out of the disc and circled around"). The reporter and his wife were high school classmates of my (B.E.S.) former college room-mate and friends of his parents, a psychiatrist and housewife, who were also well known to me. Mr. and Mrs. X and the contactee's former wife all recalled the essentials of this event and they also did not see how it could have been faked since the contactee did not have sufficient skills, electrical knowledge, finances, or friends suitably qualified to perpetrate such a hoax. According to these people (and even some state police officers whom I once interviewed on another matter), this contactee's later hoaxes were easily discovered and were quite crude.

§This experience was independently and spontaneously confirmed by Rob.

114

you, Rob? Don't be afraid.' Rob and the desk clerk ran back in panic. Rob was all shook up. Then the light business started.

" A light sprung out of the ground and shot up vertically, with a point at the top. It was about 12 to 15 feet high. The point then dropped and became an elliptical white light (Figure 1, a and b). It suddenly went back to the vertical shaft and then went out. It was amazing. I have never seen anything like it. If this was a hoax, it would have cost thousands of dollars. The next morning, Rob and several other fellows went down to look for footprints and found nothing but some deer tracks. There was a stream running through the bottom of the ravine, the ground was soft, and there was some snow. It had stopped snowing before the light business started. The men also reported that the tree tops were broken and the bark on the lower limbs was scraped off. Something must have risen."

IV — Archbald Ufographs

This is the last of the four incidents recounted by B.C.:

"These pictures (Figure 2, the four pictures from left to right) represent what I saw near Archbald, Pennsylvania, in 1958. Rob, the photographer, some others, and I were cruising around in our car late at night. Somebody said we should go to Archbald because that was where the action was. It is an isolated open-pit mining area with lunar-like craters — a grotesque place at night. There was no lake around. An

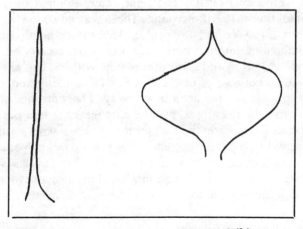

Figure 1 (a)   Figure 1 (b)

(It has proved difficult to fit the author's copious footnotes, so some of these will be found on pages following the indicating signs — EDITOR.)

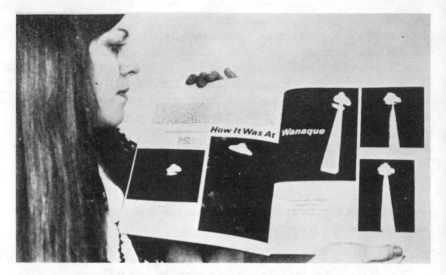

Figure 2: Erroneous attribution of B.C.'s UFO photographs to the Wanaque flap. The fifth photograph (lower right) was not taken by B.C.

unknown amateur photographer from a local town took pictures. He had no tripod.

"The craft came out of nowhere. I only saw the outline and light beam which swept back and forth like a pendulum and then withdrew. The lights were never on us. The light beam stopped in mid-air and never went all the way to the ground. There was no sound, and it lasted only a few minutes. We had no warning. There were no physical effects. It occurred about midnight. There was no snow on the ground.

"My friend Rob ** and a few others were with me and saw the same event. Rob and I got a set of prints a year and a half later and immediately recognized what we had seen in actuality. The word got out that the FBI¶ came after the negatives, but the photographer had put them in a safe-deposit box. He later issued prints to those who wanted them. Unfortunately, I have no details about the exact date, camera, the film, the timing, etc. This is the only time in my life that I ever saw UFOs at such close range. Once, years ago in Montclair, I saw several star-like objects which moved rapidly and performed unusual zigzag maneuvers."

B.C.'s photos were submitted to the ufographer August C. Roberts, who has a collection of more than 15,000 UFO and UFO-related pictures — both real and spurious. Roberts recognized B.C.'s four ufographs as being previously published. The photos were "erroneously associated

Figure 3: The fifth photograph in full.

with the UFO flap over the Wanaque Reservoir" (3) (New Jersey) in 1966, and the four such pictures were published elsewhere in 1967 (4) (see Figure 2). At that later time they were linked to the then recent Wanaque sightings. Only part of the fifth picture of the series is published (Figure 3, ufograph at lower right-hand margin). The complete fifth picture hitherto unpublished, is from the files of August C. Roberts (Figure 3). Note the round white area (artifact? UFO?) to the right of the beam of light.

According to Roberts, the five alleged ufographs were presented to the editor of the special UFO publication by the original photographer, who insisted on anonymity. After much detective work, Roberts tracked down the Wanaque alleged photographer but he was unable to prove conclusively that this man had taken any or all of the pictures. At first the mystery photographer refused to acknowledge his photographs because two of his former employees (one of whom had also seen the

---

**Rob was visibly shocked at the time I interviewed him and he examined the silent contactee X's photographs of an alleged UFO with a changing and cut off beam of light. Although Rob had never before seen X's pictures, they resembled what he had seen in actuality when he was with B.C., near Archbald, Pennsylvania, in 1958 and his own set of photographs. Rob's account of various UFO experiences at that time was unusual. For example, he stated that on several occasions he received nocturnal "telepathic impressions to get up, dress, drive to an unanticipated location" where he met several other men who had similar alleged telepathic experiences. Then on one occasion, within a short time lapse, they all saw a tree-height UFO with flashing lights. He said that at other times he was telepathically directed to various places where he discovered alleged dehydrated (?) vegetables, fruits, and nuts, which when rehydrated soon had the appearance and taste of fresh foods. This was long before dehydrated or freeze-dried vegetables were commercially available.

Although reluctant to let his name be used or even to be interviewed because of the effect of any possible adverse publicity on his business, he and his wife told quite a story. As another odd coincidence, Rob, who came from a distance away in New Jersey, was the brother-in-law of my wife's friend's neighbor at our summer cottage. It was through her that this interview was arranged.

Cursory psychiatric screening of Rob and his wife revealed no UFO-relevant psychopathology. He is a successful and respected businessman in his community. It would be desirable, however, in this instance, as well as in many other UFO-related witness claims, to have prolonged psychiatric study. Any additional data might throw light on the validity of the claims and the possible tie-in with psychodynamic and paranormal factors. Either way — acceptance or rejection — the potential information could be crucial. It is a much more complex problem than can be "solved" in a hit and miss fashion with short-term hypnotic interviews, sessions with a lie detector, or telephone interviews. Clinical psychotherapeutic practice verifies this assumption: the more time spent the more valid the impression.

118

Figure 4

beam of light hit the water) had lost their jobs.

Roberts, a professional photographer and pioneer ufographer, could not see how the UFO beam of light, which can be seen through, could easily be duplicated by technical means. The fifth ufograph (shown in entirety in Figure 3) probably was taken over the Wanaque Reservoir because, according to Roberts, the mountain in the background and the water matched the actual locale. This is unlike the other four pictures. Furthermore, Roberts wondered if these particular ufographs were similar to the UFO reported from nearby Lake Hoptacong, New Jersey, a syndicated drawing of which was published by Otto Binder (see Figure 4) in 1966.

Since B.C., Rob, their wives, and others, owned the same set of four photos from the late 1950s, and these ufographs were obtained directly from the amateur photographer who accompanied them when they actually saw the UFOs, it is quite possible that four of the alleged Wanaque ufographs are actually not Wanaque at all, but the earlier

---

¶Another example that I studied, and that involved films of UFOs which were allegedly confiscated by the FBI, happened early Thursday morning on September 20, 1962 (Passaic-Herald, 9/21/62, and subsequent editions), and again on Friday, at 3:45 a.m. William Stocks, a watchman at Braen's Quarry, Hawthorne, New Jersey, saw a brightly-lit object in the sky for approximately twenty-five minutes. The latter episode was corroborated by four policemen.

On several subsequent occasions a multi-colored lighted object was again seen at the quarry by Stocks and many other people early in the morning. A photographer shot about eighteen feet of color motion picture film of the colored object, and, as he later told the watchman, the film was confiscated by people who claimed they were from the FBI. Mr. Stocks said, "The object hung in space, made no noise, lit up the whole area, moved quickly from side to side, and up and down, and out of the jeep's headlight beams. There were thousands of red particles that were drawn up through the machine from the quarry. For a day and a half following this, everything I went near, or touched, I'd get sparks from (static electricity?). I didn't see a physician." This experience was obtained by telephone interview of William Stocks on January 14, 1971; direct interview of his former Lodi, New Jersey, neighbor; telephone interview of his former employer's son; and the reading of several contemporary accounts kindly supplied by the employer's son. Mr. Stocks currently holds a position of trust and responsibility. On psychiatric screening he gave no evidence for past or current emotional illness.

In his lecture, "Common Features of 160 UFO Reports," to the Eastern UFO Symposium, Baltimore, Maryland, January 3, 1971 (Proceedings published in 1971 by Aerial Phenomena Research Organization, 3910 East Kleindale Road, Tucson, Arizona 85712), Thomas Olsen reported a UFO episode five years after the Hawthorne UFO hovering, in Springdale, Ohio, on October 9 1956: ". . . with red objects, swarming like birds, flying straight, flopping over and over."

Pocono series. The text of the Wanque article (4) stated that the photographer was concerned about the confiscation of his negatives and since this account coincides with B.C.'s and Rob's independently given versions, one wonders about various hypotheses: the photographer might have been over-awed by his experience and then felt threatened by whatever the sources are that sought to purloin his photographs; however, after a safe period of several years had elapsed, he might have capitalized on his earlier ufographs by either selling them directly to the magazine as coming from the highly publicized and timely Wanaque flap, or he might have acted indirectly and dealt through a local intermediary (perhaps the ufographer of the intriguing fifth picture) for the ring of greater authenticity, possible profit for both, and increased anonymity for himself.

It is unfortuate but understandable that so many people are reluctant to give first-hand accounts of their UFO experiences, that some who are easily intimidated, or succumb to ridicule, risk losing their jobs, etc., but this is part of the problem and such sticky nuts-and-bolts sleuthing cannot be ducked if one aims to grapple with the often inexplicable, paradoxical, "mind polluting (?)" aspects of ufology.

Although final answers, as in this case, are not forthcoming, the spectacular nature of the evidence, even with its many admitted shortcomings, would seem to justify the preparation of some kind of a report. Perhaps this case illustrates the wealth of material that is hidden on somebody's closet shelf or in a desk drawer. Although much of the data in such instances cannot be accepted on face value, it is a folly to ignore and a challenge to explore.

REFERENCES

1. Campione, M.J.: **UFO's, 20th Century's Greatest Mystery,** Cinnaminson, N.J., 1968. Chapter 12, "Other Unusual Individuals, Mr. X of Norhtern New Jersey," p. 61.
2. Osis, Karlis: **Deathbed Observations by Physicians and Nurses,** Parapsychology Foundation, Inc., New York, 1961, pp/ 82-83.
3. Steiger, Brad, and Roberts, August C.: **Enemies from Outer Space: The Flying Saucer Menace; with 90 Astonishing Photographs,** Award Books, New York, 1967, p. 24.
4. Freedman, Carmena (Editor): "How It Was at Wanaque," **Flying Saucers UFO Report No. 2,** Dell Publications, New York, October, 1967, pp. 58.59.

Part II:

Psychiatric Dimensions to The UFO Syndrome

Chapter 7

The Port Monmouth Landing

Port Monmouth, New Jersey, is a small residential community on the Raritan Bay, and about ten miles from New York City. It is closely surrounded by numerous installations. Throughout recent years the newspapers have reported many UFO sightings in this area.

In an article in the July 18, 1970, issue of *The Courier* of Middletown, New Jersey, Mr. Walter Garner described a UFO hovering over the meadows for approximately one hour. Mr. Garner, who visited the scene as late as two weeks after the incidents, said the grass was "still flattened" in the reported areas as well as in a smaller section several feet away. The grass, "still living, would not stand erect, yet grass flattened by footsteps quickly bounced back (Photographs 1 and 2)." The family who witnessed the incident did not wish any notoriety and therefore was not identified, but the following is an account of their experiences.

On Saturday, July 4, 1970, at 3:00 a.m., Mrs. D.J., a 33-year-old housewife, suddenly woke up for no apparent reason and looked out of her open second-floor cottage bedroom window. Hovering over the meadows, across the street, she saw "a big round ball. It had an eerie white glow, and was bouncing back and forth across the meadows. I propped myself up on the pillow and watched it for approximately 15 minutes. I shook my husband but he wouldn't wake up. I had gotten in bed at two in the morning, and had dozed off again before waking. We had been out but had no liquor.

"It was something spectacular. The light was flashing in order as in the back tail-lights of modern cars — flashing red in a series across the middle. I could only see half the thing (see Fig. 1). It was the size of our garage (approximately 20-25 ft. in combined width and height). There was no sound. The street light had gone out for 15 to 20 minutes and then came on.

"When I woke up again at 5:00 a.m., the fog was rolling in (it was clear before) and I couldn't see anything. I told my husband but he wasn't impressed. The kids were excited and wondered why I hadn't called them. A little later they called me, and my son said, 'Mom, you should see the big spots in the meadows.' There were areas where the grass was mashed down."

*Name and address on file with FSR — EDITOR

Photograph 1 — Mr. Walter Garner — "Something strange is leaving marks on the Port Monmouth meadows. " (The Courier, July 16, 1970.)

Interviews with Mrs. D.J.'s son Billy, age 15, and her brother-in-law, D.R., age 22, revealed that, "There were three imprints that made a perfect triangle. They were about 30-40 ft. apart and about 18 in. square. There was a large circle (in the grass) between 15 and 20 ft. in diameter, and a smaller circle about 50 ft. away, which was about half the size of the larger one.

"Then we saw tracks going to the creek like they had dragged some small round thing into the ditch. (On the periphery of the large circular flattened area) there were about two sets of a dozen imprints which were about 2 ft. apart. They were curved like raindrops (see Fig. 2). It was very visible, the grass was all crushed down, there was mud on the banks of the creek, and there were signs of the tracks in the mud."

One week to the day, at 4:00 a.m., Mrs. D.J. suddenly woke and pounded her husband in an attempt to arouse him, "for I felt that something was going to happen. It was a funny feeling — I was scared half to death. I told him. Then the street light went out. We sat there for about five minutes and out of the sky came a round ball of light. It went from the tower (across the field) behind the trees. It was glowing, yellowish-white. I called the police. They came with their guns drawn."

While this was going on, Billy was sleeping on the front porch. He

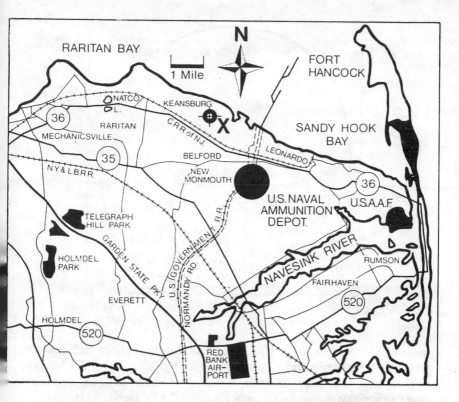

The Raritan Bay, N.J. area. "X" shows the position of Port Monmouth; the crossed-O symbol indicates the approximate location of the UFO sightings.

noted, "There were three colored — red patches of lights. They went around the disc in about one to two seconds. The outer part was greyish in color (see Fig. 3). The noise it made was like an airplane in the distance. The noise became louder as it picked up speed. Just as soon as it was out of sight I didn't hear it any more. I would guess it was going very slowly, as it came up from the ground.

"The police were starting to go upstairs to my parents and look out of their bedroom window when the disc came up from the ground (across the street — approximately 60 ft. away) and I saw it for a half minute. The disc was hidden in the grass (about 10 ft. tall) and was the size of an Oldsmobile. I yelled, 'Look, Look!' but nobody heard me. I watched it as far as I could and again yelled, 'Mom, look!' I was wide awake, and don't often see things like that (Photograph 3)"*

As far as the family could tell, there were no physical changes in the

125

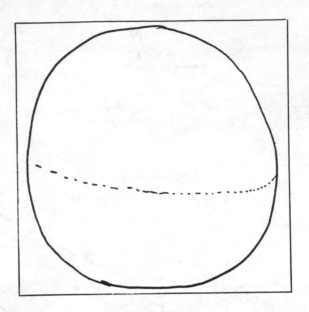

Figure 1. Mrs. D.J.'s drawing of the UFO

meadows across the street after this close sighting. However, from then on the television set, which had worked well previously, no longer functioned. Mrs. D.J. said, "Although the tubes were changed, and it was taken to a repair man, the TV only flickered." The family were unable to use it for many weeks, and had to borrow the grandfather's TV set, which worked all right in their house. When they took the broken TV set to the grandfather's home and tried it there, it still didn't work. "Also the ignition in my husband's car was ruined. It conked out five times in the middle of the road, although it had not given trouble before. Even though we had a mechanic work on it and had a new ignition put in, it still gave this trouble.† There was no effect on other household appliances. I cannot remember if the electric (battery) clock stopped working. I phoned Army Intelligence. The guy pumped me. He pooh-poohed it and implied it was all baloney, and I was nuts."

Although Mrs. D.J. has un unlisted telephone number, she received two to ten calls a day between 9:00 a.m. and 10:00 p.m. for four days following the sightings. When the phone receiver was picked up, there was no one on the other end. This had seldom happened in the past, and never in the exact manner recorded after the sighting.

Mrs. D.J., her older children, her husband, and her brother-in-law recalled several other possible sightings that occurred throughout the remainder of the summer. These generally happened when they were

Photograph 2 — Mr. Garner, standing in an area of "flattened grass, approximately 25 ft. in diameter beneath the spot where the UFO reportedly hovered for an hour." He is pointing to the D.J.'s house and the second-story window, on the right from which Mrs. D.J. made her observations (Courtesy of The Courier).

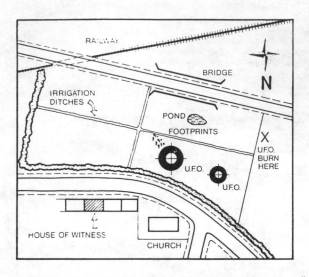

Figure 2. Billy's sketch of the landing sites and "footprints" was the basis for our artist's version.

driving on the highway to get the children ice cream. As an example, Mrs. D.J. recalled such a sighting when, "My ten-year-old said, 'Look at the bright star.' We looked up and (I knew) I'd seen this before. 'That's no star — it's moving. It's not a plane, because it stopped.' We were all eyes then, as it moved across the highway. It came so close, it was like a big light, but with no form behind it ... yellowish-white. It seemed to follow the car. When we were halfway down the highway it veered off to the left and went over the bay. This happened on about ten occasions ... usually on Fridays. It scared us."

Approximately two months after the first sighting, the D.J.'s had a very strange experience. Mrs. D.J. said, "When I came upstairs there was a smell in the bedroom: rotten, like death: I never noticed this before, or since. I woke up my husband. The smell was not from the meadows. It made me want to vomit. I went downstairs to check on the kids and I closed the windows. I went back to bed and felt as though I slept in a coma. I had no energy and my husband couldn't arouse me. I finally got up at 9:30 (a.m.) whereas I usually get up at six. I had no contact with the flu or anything like that. Everyone at home was fine. My husband noticed the odor also. We had lived in the house a long time (house 90 years old).

"While in the 'coma' I had a dream. I was at home (Colonial Spy House by the beach) and my father was there. The UFO landed in the meadows and there was water all around and everybody was screaming.

128

Photograph 3 — Billy on the spot where the craft hovered. Photograph taken October 21, 1970.

I got all the kids upstairs and locked the windows and doors. In the bathroom I could see (indistinct) forms but no faces [Mrs. D.J. was too upset to draw them]; they were trying to get in. There was fire, and I saw my father breathing hard, and having a heart attack. These things were coming in and hurting me.

"The next day I thought I had needle [points to the gluteal region] in me. I looked to see if there was anything wrong. I had trouble bending the right knee, and pain [along the sciatic nerve] down the back of the heel, like when I had a blood clot on the left, following the birth of the twins. Because of the pain, I went to the doctor, who examined me and found no reason for it."§ Also my 11-year-old son acted strangely and talked foolishly and I don't know why."

When asked about her associations to this dream,‡ Mrs. D.J. said, "I had a feeling that something was wrong, like when I saw a werewolf movie as a child, when they would say, 'They're calling you.' That's the

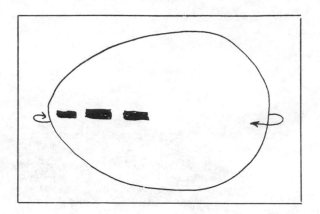

Figure 3. Billy's sketch of the UFO. The dark areas were red lights, and the outer area was greyish.

feeling I had. I did not have any alcohol, and I only have an occasional Scotch when we go out. I was not taking any drugs, and I have never been hypnotized."

Mrs. D.J. then described some highly personal possible prerecognitive experiences that pertained to the death of her baby years ago, an episode where she unexpectedly received a minor windfall of money, and several childhood episodes when she lived in her maternal grandmother's haunted house.

The possible UFO landings were explored by interviews with Mr. and Mrs. D.J., and their two older sons, ages 15 and 14, their oldest daughter, age 10, Mrs. D.J.'s sister and brother-in-law, Mrs. Marie S., a lifelong friend of Mrs. D.J., the Chief of Police of Middletown, New Jersey, and Officer Chick Wilson, who was on the switchboard the night Mrs. D.J. phoned the police, and Mr. Walter Garner, business manager of the *Courier.*

Although Mr. D.J. was interviewed only on the telephone, he confirmed the essentials of the events and seemed quite disturbed and puzzled over the experiences. He said, "I hope it never happens again."

The essential facts of the D.J. case were also checked out later by an interview with Mr. Garner on September 16, 1970. He recalled a similar UFO sighting, which was reported in the *Courier* two years ago. He remembered how the D.J.'s experience was relayed to the Army on a Saturday morning and that helicopters flew over and examined the meadows shortly after that time. He mentioned a private citizen, who works for one of the adjoining government installations, and who checked for

130

radiation one week after the sighting. Nothing, allegedly, was found. Arrangements were made to have an article about the incident published in a national weekly, of wide circulation, but nothing appeared. Similarly, nothing was carried in any of the larger New Jersey newspapers.

An interview with the Middletown Chief of Police and several of his officers on September 16, 1970, revealed that there had been many UFO reports over the past 18 years. On one occasion a few years ago, an officer chased a light. The police knew Mrs. D.J.'s family for many years, and they clearly recalled how frightened Mrs. D.J. was when she telephoned. They recalled how the street light was unaccountably out (and came back on after the UFO went away). Mrs. D.J. had never called the police before, nor has she since for such a complaint. Confidential material that the police told the physician about Mrs. D.J. was independently volunteered by her. In two different accounts there were no discrepancies or apparent attempts to withhold details. This particular background material was not relevant to the presumed sighting.

The family doctor was contacted on the telphone and he recalled seeing Mrs. D.J. on September 15, 1970, for pain in the right sacro-sciatic notch with radiation down the sciatic nerve. He had no record of any rash or puncture mark. He knew nothing about his patient's possible past UFO experiences, and felt that as the mother of eight children she was kept very busy. Although Mrs. D.J. frequently sought medical help for her family, and was often upset and had multiple complaints, these events did not seem to have any direct bearing on the possible UFO sighting. The physician's records indicated that Mrs. D.J. had had previous occasional sciatic notch pains since 1968. + Physical examination revealed that Mrs. D.J. could do straight leg raising without any difficulty. There was no history for the injudicious use of drugs or alcohol.

Indirect check with the commanding officer of the nearby Sandy Hook U.S. Coast Guard Station revealed that the men there were unaware of any UFO reports at the time of Mrs. D.J.'s sighting. However, the Commander did not rule out their possibility. Because of some unique circumstances, it was possible to ascribe a high degree of credibility to the Commander's appraisal.

An interview with Mrs. D.J.'s father, aged 70, who is custodian and lives in a "Colonial Spy House (built in 1667)," confirmed his daughter's experience. He recalled how, when he was a little boy in Little Rock, Arkansas, he had an experience: "It was a big round ball that sailed overhead in the sky, just over the tree tops. I saw it for several minutes and it affected me all my life. I was a salesman for 44 years and travelled in all the states, but I never saw anything like it before." The father told

Photograph 4
Colonial Spy House

his experience to his daughter only after she had her sighting. The father's past history was healthy. He is descended from Parnell, the famous Irish statesman on his father's side, and on his mother's side is a Sioux Indian. Mrs. D.J.'s mother, age 50, who lives in California and is divorced from Mrs. D.J.'s father, heard about the UFO experience from other members of the family. She had no previous knowledge or interest in UFOs.

The Colonial Spy House overlooks Raritan Bay and is close to Mrs. D.J.'s home. The father has never noted UFOs since his boyhood.¶ The Colonial Spy House is supposed to be haunted, and is a museum where different artifacts which have been found there are displayed (Photograph 4).

Mr. William A. Roventine, Radiological Physicist, St. Barnabas Medical Center, Livingston, New Jersey, kindly performed an analysis for gross gamma activity on various specimens of marsh grass and soil taken on September 29 and October 21, 1970, from the landing sites, track areas, creek, and from control areas that were presumably not affected. The general appearance of the landing sites at these times was essentially similar to the earlier *Courier* observations and photographs. Mr. Roventine reported: "No activity above background levels was observed. In addition, a cursory examination for high energy alpha or beta radiation was negative."

Psychiatric study on three separate occasions (September 29, October 21, and November 5, 1970) and several phone calls to Mrs. D.J., two of her sisters, her brother-in-law, and two older boys failed to reveal any UFO-relevant psychopathology. There was no past history for neurotic character traits. Mrs. D.J. is left-handed. She has had relatively good health in the past, with excellent vision and hearing. With her eight children, she had little free time for reading or television. She did not classify herself as a UFO "believer". Although she was most cooperative and open for the purposes of this study, she assiduously avoided any publicity about her experience.

Mrs. D.J. was the oldest of four surviving sisters. She spent most of her life in New Jersey, and was mostly of old American stock. She had a former marriage that was at times stormy and terminated in divorce. Her account of these life situations was in accord with what was learned from other sources, and there was no apparent motivation or evidence for dishonesty. She could have omitted several aspects of her life that might have raised questions about her social adjustments, but she chose not to do so. In all, her accounts of her UFO experiences seemed to be truthful.

She recalled a life dream of "A bronze man laying naked by a small lake. I'm in the attic. There are bars in the window and I see out. I'm a child. The attic door isn't locked but I never think of turning the knob and going out. This dream means that I want to get down to that bronze man [Oedipal dream of half-Indian father?]"

On November 5, 1970, Mrs. D.J. and her children were studied by Joseph Dunninger, the famous telepathist.@ Although Dunninger could not remember any experience quite like hers from his more than half a century career,‡ he felt that she was reporting the truth as she saw it, and that something very frightening had happened to her. He could think of nothing along the lines of a hoax or distortion of everyday natural phenomena that could account for this. Mrs. D.J. related several psychic experiences that had happened to her during her life and which in the opinion of Dunninger (as well as the physician) were not in themselves unheard of: viz., *if* one asks about such data, they are not at all rare, even though often extraordinary and unexplainable.

Mr. Dunninger did not receive any telepathic impressions from the D.J. family that could throw any light on their experience. We checked the house, the rooms from which the phenomena were witnessed, the meadows across the street, and the surrounding areas.

***

The Port Monmouth UFO landing might constitute a hidden case. There might be several obvious and also less apparent reasons about why this was not widely reported in the press: e.g., military security, tie-up of highways, unanswerable questions asked of the authorities, etc. This part, as well as different segments of this report, might be profitably explored by sociologists and others. Stress is placed in this report on the psychiatric and possible paranormal aspects.

From the personal experience, perusal of the psychiatric literature, and discussion with colleagues, the writer suspects that such UFO events as reported here seldom, if ever, come to the attention of the psychiatrist. As in some other critically important but neglected areas (1) that do not ordinarily come to the psychiatrist, it is necessary for the psychiatrist to go out and conduct first-hand studies. In the Port Monmouth case the persons involved were obviously not psychotic or suffering from delusions or hallucination, and did not have a pre-existent relevant psychopathology. Then what happened?

Certainly, it would be desirable to have many more details about the family before, during, and after the event, than are reported here. The technique of collaborative research has been very useful in elucidating a variety of hitherto vaguely defined conditions (2). In this technique a team of highly skilled psychiatrists study separately each member of a family over a period of time, compare notes, and then piece together the

134

detailed chronology of events and, in particular, all the subtle conscious and unconscious communications within the family.

Collaborative research might be most useful in evaluating what happened in Port Monmouth and possibly in eliciting other significant data that might otherwise have been overlooked. For example, one would be curious about the grandfather's possible UFO experience in Arkansas years ago, the 15-year-old Billy's 1961 Florida sighting with friends, and the events involving the family in 1970. Could there be hypothecated psychosomatic factors as a common denominator for three generations of the family? Or, assuming the accounts are valid, as claimed, is the family "selected" for some particular reason? The confusing, often contradictory, bizarre, and tragic experiences of various contactees and their families have been investigated by Keel (3).

If, after collaborative study, the family UFO experiences are substantiated — even allowing for some discrepancies and inaccuracies of memory, cryptomnesia, etc. — we would still be left with questions of how to explain the apparent physical evidence of the landing in the meadows, the "monster" tracks, possible electromagnetic or telekinetic phenomena, odd phone calls, odor of sulphur, and possibly Mrs. D.J.'s nightmare and its sequelae.

It is an admitted shortcoming that Mrs. D.J.'s paranormal experiences are anecdotal. However, they should not be dismissed from consideration because of this. Although intensive psychiatric study might show how the paranormal events might be interrelated with the psychodynamic *Anlage*, the connection with the UFO experiences is tenuous and mostly speculative. Mrs. D.J.'s past history for psychic events is in itself not unusual for many families. Her premonitory feeling of dread and then her awakening to see the UFO might best be explained as a response to the subliminal stimuli. However, this type of specific UFO experience, of which I have collected several examples, might also be telepathic. Under such awesome circumstances, telepathy serves the purpose of maintaining communication or equilibrium. As in applying the telepathic hypothesis to the psychopathology of everyday life, where one is confronted with the paradox of being both cautious yet audacious, in the attempt to grapple with the relationship of the paranormal to ufology one has a tiger by the tail.

Thus, in the instance of the D.J. family one might ask, as in other examples that involve psychic matters and UFOs: (1) how firmly established is the alleged UFO-psychic relationship and in what precise ways are the two phenomena linked? (2) could the anxiety and splitting in the awesome UFO situation have opened the way to telepathy? (3) was the pre-existent experiential awareness to telepathy evoked by the unusual

UFO circumstances, and then psychopathologically colored in such a way as to make it *seem* as though it came from the UFOs or the intelligence behind them [many alleged spiritist communications are probably mediated in this manner]? (4), or, did the telepathic notions come directly from the intelligence behind the UFOs?

The last possibility, although espoused in many sensational contactee claims, is the most difficult one to document with solid facts. Yet the matter should not be written off as completely hopeless. By analogy, Jule Eisenbud's brilliant researches (4,5) into the psycho-dynamic complexities of telepathy, thoughtography, and allied psychic phenomena, give reason for optimism in exploring some of these refractory challenges of ufology. Perhaps a careful follow-up of the Port Monmouth case, as in Aime Michel's continuing and provocative studies at Valensole (6) and the South-East of France (7), will eventually lead to a better understanding of what happened and what is happening.

Photograph 5

NOTES

*Billy recalled: "Once in Miami, Florida, in 1961, I saw a shiny, silver-gray, cigar-shaped thing angling out of the clouds. Dave D., his mother and father were with me and saw it too."

†The trouble was later ascribed by Mr. D.J. to a "defective plug."

: At approximately the time of several close sightings and a landing case in Pemberton, N.J., late in the fall of 1959, witnessed by Officer Samuel Cowell, Jr., his two neighbors, Mrs. E. Ahlrichs and Mrs. R. Grover, noticed a foul sulphur odor. From the study of the environment there was no reason to suspect external factors or olfactory hallucination as causes.

§ Mrs. D.J.'s dream is in sharp contrast to UFO Investigator CA's recurrent nightmare of being captured by humanoids near their UFO. "They had large foreheads, big eyes, a slit for a mouth and hair set way back." CA's reaction was precipitated after his investigation of an alleged close sighting of a craft with occupants who reputedly had heads like lobsters with antennae. C.A., a twenty-one-year-old factory worker, was convinced that he was being harassed by MIB: and he claimed many bizarre events, including MIB, visual hallucinations of a menacing alligator head, and the recurrence of unaccountable burning sulphur odors. On one occasion, while disucssing his problems with another UFO investigator (who verified this incident to the author) on long-distance telephone, there occurred an interruption like a rooster crowing, and beeping. Because of many such events C.A. became so panicked that he was unable to work; he sat at home in his living room, and aimed a loaded shotgun at the door for the expected nocturnal visitation of the MIB. C.A.'s past history revealed previous psychiatric treatment in a state hospital and treatment for his current disturbance. He was rejected from military service because of his emotional problems. He had a long-standing fear of being alone, of tall buildings, and of spiders. He had past enuresis, sleep walking, sleep talking, school problems, and two episodes of fainting (possibly due to trichlorethylene which he used in his work). He was deeply enmeshed in UFO literature. From psychiatric examination it appeared that C.A. had chronic paranoid schizophrenia and that his quasi UFO symptoms were chiefly the products of his psychopathology. (For further details about this interesting case see Clark, Ramona A.: "The Ordeal," pp. 27-30 in "The Truth About the Men in Black," Kurt Glemser, 489 Krug St. Kitchener, Ontario, Canada, 1970.)

‡ It should be stressed that Mrs. D.J. had no detailed knowledge of Betty Hill's experience [Fuller, John G.: **Interrupted Journey**, Dell, New York City, 1966] of a painful injection in the navel with a long needle. The only one in the family circle to take a deep interest in UFOs was Mrs. D.J.'s brother-in-law, and this was chiefly **after** the episode. His previous readings about UFOs were limited to occasional newspaper and magazine articles. Unlike the case of C.A., Mrs. D.J. has remained well since her episode.

In a recent interview with Mrs. Betty Hill, the author learned that she has stuck to the account of her experiences, has enjoyed good health, and has an excellent work record. However, unlike Mrs. D.J., who is fearful of further UFO knowledge, Mrs. Hill maintains her interest in UFOs and has collected some instances of presumed close sightings. She has not come across anything like her previous experience.

As an example of speculation versus first-hand study, the eminent psychiatrist and parapsychologist Meerloo, apparently basing his opinion on the

137

account in **Look** magazine of October 18, 1966, wondered if the Boston psychiatrist was totally captivated by the two New Englanders who asserted they had been aboard a flying saucer Dr. Meerloo wondered if his colleague was caught in a temporary psychosis among the three! Cryptomnesia was offered as a possible explanation: i.e., the accounts were unconsciously assimilated, distorted, stored in the memory, and brought out much later under hypnosis (Meerloo, J.A.M.: Le Syndrome des Soucoupes Volantes, **Med. Hyg.** Vol. 25: 992, 1967).

+ The exacerbation of sciatic notch pain and radiation down the sciatic nerve following Mrs. D.J.'s UFO dream brings to mind Mr. O's experience where he had relief of severe sciatic pain following a possible UFO exposure (see FSR for March/April 1971).

¶ Why one family can be affected over a span of time is an intriguing question. A well-documented case involves the Merz family of Oak Ridge, New Jersey, where at different times the grandmother, father, and the son, with additional witnesses, on two occasions all had striking UFO experiences. Possibly, as in the D.J. case, the Merz family had some allied, unusual telekinetic and telepathic aspects. The relationship of the two events — UFO sightings and psychic phenomena — is difficult to pin down.

@ The interview in the D.J. home was recorded on a Sony-Auto-Sensor, thirty-minute casette, using a Sony TC-100 compact-set tape recorder. The beeping of the tape signalled the end of a thirty-minute segment and the need to turn the cassette over to continue. At the point of beeping, which happens only at the end of the recording and when in the "record" position, Dunninger, the children, and Mrs. D.J. remarked on how well this unique patented invention worked. While making the recording, I was careful to aim the microphone at the different speakers and monitor the modulating needle that fluctuated with their speech. A few hours later (in my office) when playing back the recording for analysis, I was shocked to discover that the description of the actual landing, the dream of the little men, the visit to the rooms from where the observations took place, etc., was not recorded. The tape was a complete blank. Although this model recorder and patented auto-sensor tape has been in extended and intensive use, I have never had this happen before or since. When asked for a possible explanation, the tape recorder repairman could not understand how this could happen. The particular tape cassette and machine worked well in my office. Although no explanation is offered, attention is drawn to the peculiar "coincidence" which points out the difficulty in interpreting such data.

‡ While giving a telepathic demonstration at the Huntington Hartford Theatre, in Hollywood, California, on November, 1956, Dunninger was approached by a well-dressed, mannerly group of contactees who told him about their intention of establishing radio communication with "visitors from outside the planet." Dunninger, although he had grave reservations about the group's flying saucer claims, was impressed by their sincerity and behavior.

Dunninger said, "I had them on the show for several evenings where they explained what was going on. I asked them to speak to my audience. One young lady said certain individuals were walking around from another planet and I should tell her which one was which. I said, "None of them." She swore she had seen them float in and out at times, and that a round object would float up to them. She said it with tears in her eyes. She was an extremely attractive young woman, but I didn't believe her. She didn't seem mentally disturbed and she had the audience spellbound. They had nothing to sell — there was no money involved. They published a magazine. They gave me photographs of the so-called (UFO) phenomena which they claimed they had taken of the object in the sky during the time they were on the show (Photograph 5). They left a tape recording with me. They said they were Martians.

The young woman divorced her husband because he failed to believe in what she saw. Their leader was a good-looking fellow who spoke like a reporter. The group acted in unison — what one saw, all the others said they saw. Whether or how they sold themselves the idea of what was going on, I don't know. They didn't appear to be dishonest or ill."

The Los Angeles **Herald and Express,** November 8, 1956, had an article entitled "Men From Mars Fail to Keep Date." The leader of the group later ran for the presidency of the United States.

REFERENCES

1. Duncan, G.M., Frazier, S.H., Litin, E.M., Johnson, A.M., and Barron, A.J.: "Etiological Factors in First Degree Murder," **Journal** of the Am. Med. Assoc. 168 (1958), pp. 1755-58.
2. Robinson, David B. (ed.): **Experience, Affect, and Behavior, Psychoanalytic Explorations of Dr. Adelaide McFadyen Johnson,** The University of Chicago press, Chicago, 1969.
3. Keel, J.A.: **UFOs: Operation Trojan Horse,** G.P. Putnam's Sons, New York, 1970.
4. Eisenbud, Jule, **The World of Ted Serios: "Thoughtographic" Studies of an Extraordinary Mind,** Morrow, New York, 1967.
5. Eisenbud, Jule: **Psi and Psychoanalysis,** Grune and Stratton, New York, 1970.
6. Michel, Aime: The Valensole Affair, **Flying Saucer Review,** Vol. 11, No. 6 (November/December), 1965.
7. Michel, Aime, The Strange Case of Dr. X, **Flying Saucer Review,** Special Issue No. 3, September 1969 ("UFO Percipients"), pp. 3-16.

Chapter 8

Woodstock UFO Festival, 1966 — 1

"The fault, dear Brutus is not in our stars,
But in ourselves, that we are underlings. "
Shakespeare's Julius Caesar, Act I, Sc. 2

"The irrational richness of life has taught me never to
disregard anything, even though it may violate all our
(unfortunately so often short-lived) theories, or what
may at first glance look completely inexplicable. "
C.G. Jung

The understanding of antigravity is central to the supposed method of UFO propulsion and such UFO-related effects as presumed levitation, telekinesis, and poltergeist phenomena. The solution to the *modus operandi* of antigravity could have revolutionary consequences. Although the physics of antigravity and of UFO-related phenomena has been explored with the electromagnetic and electrostatic hypotheses, and so forth, little has appeared on the possible psychiatric aspects of the people who are part of such events.

Background

In psychiatric practice the symptom of a sensation of weightlessness, or antigravity, is not common; yet it is not unknown. It is related to depersonalization, which is seen in a variety of neurotic and psychotic patterns and which can also occur in otherwise healthy people following severe emotional stress. The symptom of weightlessness is also not uncommon in various forms of delirium and drunkenness and in the aftermath of the ingestion of psychedelic drugs, such as mescaline and LSD. Examples of weightlessness, both subjective and objective, are recorded in the parapsychological literature. Also, presumed telekinetic experiences are not unheard of in the histories of patients seen in psychiatry, and such events are actually observed in *statu nascendi* from time to time during psychotherapy (1,2).

With rare exceptions, it is, unfortunately, next to impossible to find someone who can control his telekinetic ability. Psychoanalytic study of telekinetic and poltergeist phenomena reveals that there might be common underlying factors of tremendous splitting anxiety, repressed

The Carriers' house.

hostility, and frustration occurring at crisis moments: i.e., something has to give (3).

Several years ago it was my good fortune to learn of an unusual Woodstock (New York) couple, the Carriers (pseudonym), from a practicing physician and his wife. This report is based on several interviews of the Carriers and others as mentioned in the text, including the referring physician and his wife, the Carriers' relatives, former neighbors, and the police. They all vouchsafed for the Carriers' honesty and absence of past deceptions, hoaxes, hospitalization for mental illness, drug reactions, etc. Four field trips were taken to the scene of the former reputed action for further interviews and photographs. On one occasion the matter was discussed with the eminent telepathist Joseph Dunnin-

141

ger, who was brought close to the locale but who had no specific impressions.

Long before the youth rock festival, Woodstock† had become well known as a beautiful arts and crafts colony in the Catskill Mountains. In her history of Woodstock, Anita M. Smith (4) cites a legend "... that when the Indians were on long marches, they avoided passing through the Wide Clove, because Overlook exerted a drag upon their footsteps. It would be necessary for them to camp for a while before they could muster enough strength to overcome the pulling backward, and could continue their journey." Miss Smith also recorded hearsay evidence from the time of the Revolution, when, "A Tory, named Newkirk, was

†The Woodstock Rock Festival, August 15-17, 1969, was actually held at White Hill Lake, fifty miles south of Woodstock.

about to die, and he was not allowed to go in peace because the Devil threw him from his bed and he had to die alone out in the barnyard (5)!"

This modern UFO account is not a legend. It involves a young couple, the Carriers: the husband was a college graduate and a computer systems analyst, and his wife, who had attended junior college for two years and was her class valedictorian. They rented a small cottage in a relatively isolated area on the outskirts of Woodstock.

After hearing further details of this case from the Carriers' relatives and neighbors in New Jersey, I had a one-hour telephone interview with Mrs. Carrier, aged 25, on July 29, 1969. At that time the Carriers lived in another city far away from Woodstock. The initial contact was followed up by several other phone calls July 30, 1969; September 3, 1969; September 4, 1969; September 14, 1969; and on March 7, 1970, I travelled unannounced to the Carriers' home and interviewed and examined Mr. Carrier psychiatrically.

At that time Mrs. Carrier, who was upstairs ill with the flu, overheard some of the interview; and hardly had I begun with her husband when she shouted down that she would refuse to see me. She was still very upset about the experiences of long ago. However, from these interviews of the Carriers, plus others, it seemed that they were telling the truth as they had experienced it.

They both enjoyed good health and there was no evidence for previous emotional or psychosomatic illness or sociopathic behavior, such as lying, stealing, or dishonesty. The young couple were completely bewildered by the Woodstock events of 1966. The husband independently corroborated most of his wife's account in the presence of a postal clerk (a personal friend), and then privately, in psychiatric interview he expatiated on the more personal aspects of his family's experiences. There were no major discrepancies between his wife's version and his own.

Although it would be desirable if not mandatory to have had many more investigatory sessions and much more information, this was not feasible. However, because of the rarity of such an experience, its similarity to other published UFO reports, and the fact that little field work on this subject has been done by psychiatrists, I felt that even with these shortcomings, these accounts should be presented. All too often the reader is left with such eponymic generalization as "poltergeist phenomena" rather than a genuine spelling out of what was alleged to have happened. Needless to say, the Carriers' experiences are not the type of situation that one sees in the everyday practice of clinical psychiatry.

The following condensation of verbatim statements made by Mrs. Carrier were independently corroborated by her husband. Where indicated his additional comments are appropriately interpolated in the text.

"This happened in 1966, before my son was born. We lived in a remote spot off the road in a house rented from an artist, who had built it as a studio. His niece, who lived next door to us, was a licensed commercial pilot, who flew from New York to Kingston. There were open fields around the house. Approximately fifteen feet from the house was a clump of bushes, then another open field, and bushes beyond that. It is heavily forested around Woodstock. There were high tension wires going across the field.

"In the spring of 1966, we noticed from our living room strange greenish (6) lights in the fields, six feet in diameter. One night, when a friend came to visit from Kingston we all saw something fly close to the car. There was a strange noise that I feared — a high-pitched whine — it was quite annoying. I couldn't blot it out. It was like an enormous vacuum cleaner droning. I could detect where it moved to — the wooded area — then out across the house to Overlook mountain. I heard it many times for months but didn't relate it to the sightings. Whenever a plane came over though, the sound subsided. Then, when the plane went away, it came back to the former level.

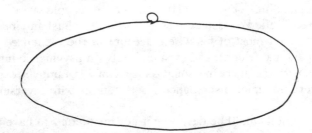

Figure 1. Witness's sketch of Delaware River UFO (see note 7 at end of article).

"One night a strange thing happened. There was a terrifically annoying sound over the driveway. It seemed about six feet above my head. I asked my husband and he didn't hear it, nor did the girl who was staying with us. It was three in the afternoon. Later that afternoon, the girl, another lady, and I were watching TV, when suddenly the sound changed, and the pitch went up and down. I looked at the girl and asked, 'Do you hear that too?' 'Yes,' she said, 'I have been hearing it since three p.m., when I was in Kingston.' No one else heard it. I went all around the house checking electrical outlets, the refrigerator, putting my ears against the furniture and other things, but could find no reason for it. The sound went into a regular pattern of oscillation (7). Then the sound left, and from one corner of the house it went out into the open field. It was so strong that if you stood in the corner you could feel it pass through your ears. It was remarkable; I never experienced anything like it before.

"I put my ear to the wall facing Overlook mountain [and heard] funny garbled sounds like 'Tweety Pie,' then like a lot of sounds in unison, like a voice. I'm positive about this [husband confirmed his wife's and her friends' experiences.] It came three feet above the ground, like mice would talk if they could jabber — but three-foot mice? It went on for more than an hour. We walked around the house and saw nothing (8). Finally we looked out into the field and there was the bright green light. A man that we talked to about it said it was a reflection from window glass, but I went outside and it was still there. My girlfriend and I went out together and watched the light for a while. On one side of the [green] light was a red light, one-eighth the size of the green light and it moved far away from it, becoming a separate light until it disappeared (9). It never stood still but gave us the impression that it was being moved deliberately up and down. I was frightened. Someone can't understand this unless they went through it. The possibility of manufacturing these lights is ridiculous; it was a valid experience.

"(At times) we heard voices, or a voice like a man, thudding clumps, like someone walking. My girlfriend heard it too. Prior to this she ignored it (the other experiences). Once I fell asleep and woke up as my girlfriend screamed. There was a noise on the roof. I told my husband but he dismissed this as too unreal. It was the first time anything like that ever happened to me. We all heard something walking on the roof, one foot after another — not like animals scrambling. It went on for a while, and I became frightened. Before I went to sleep they tried to contact me telepathically — this never happened before! My mind blanked out. (In my mind's eye) there was a stone face (see Figure 2). It was not grotesque, but it was so scary. It was in my mind — inside my head. I said, 'Go away.' I screamed, 'Go away.' It was debilitating. Finally it went away, but the noises from the roof went on. [The husband: "We were frightened. My wife didn't want me to leave for work."]

"The next day, we went out to check. It had rained hailstones (unusual for summer?) all around the house (but that couldn't account for the strange sounds). The grass was flat and scorched. It stayed that way all summer. When I next went into the fields, I thought we might be

145

Fig. 2 Inca head found in Peru similar to hypnogogic visual hallucination reported by Mrs. Carrier. This symbolism is unusual when one considers the fact that Mrs. Carrier was not a devotee of ancient cultures.

overreacting. As the summer went on, many [UFO] reports appeared in the newspapers. The diehard skeptics and nonbelievers came back to the house and changed their attitudes [the husband confirmed this].

"A cousin, who has a cabin high in the mountain, said that he once saw a rocket ship with portholes and that he could see people in it. This was near the Ashokan Reservoir. His uncle had seen things streaking by the mountains that made sharp 90-degree turns — it was amazing. We heard more stories. Then, when my girlfriend and I had our experience people said that strange things were going on in Woodstock and Kingston for years and years."

NOTES AND REFERENCES

1. Schwarz, B.E.: Telepathy and Pseudotelekinesis in Psychotherapy, **Journal** of the American Society of Psychosomatic Dentistry and Medicine, Vol. 15, 4: 144-154, October, 1968.

2. Schwarz, B.E.: Synchronicity and Telepathy, **The Psychoanalytic Review,** Vol. 56, 1: 44-56, 1969.

3. Fodor, N.: **On the Trail of the Poltergeist,** The Citadel Press, New York, 1958.

4. Smith, Anita M.: **Woodstock History and Hearsay,** Catskill Mountain Publishing Corp., Saugerties, N.Y., 1957, pp. 4, 6.

5. Washington Irving described in **The Legend of Sleepy Hollow** (Washington Square Press Books, Simon & Schuster, New York, 1962) an area on the eastern bank of the Hudson, not too far from the Catskills, where as folklore has it, the good people are bewitched and are given "to all kinds of marvellous beliefs: are subject to trances and visions; frequently see strange sights, hear music, and voices in the air. The whole neighborhood abounds with local tales, haunted spots, and twilight superstitions; stars shoot and meteors glare oftener across the valley than in any other part of the country, and the nightmare, with her whole ninefold, seems to make it the favored scene of her gambols" (page 6). And in Irving's **Rip van Winkle** the episode of Rip's time compression should be recalled, "for the whole twenty years had been to him but as one night" (page 55).

6. Schwarz, B.E.: Possible UFO-Induced Temporary Paralysis, **Flying Saucer Review,** Vol. 17, 2: 4-9, March/April, 1971.

7. After preliminary telephone interviews (12/7/68), I made direct studies on March 1, 1969, October 18, 1969, and May 12, 1972, of a family, at their home situated near the Delaware River, who had a series of close sightings and other UFO-related experiences including strange humming oscillations. The couple were artists. The wife was also a registered nurse. Some of their sightings were independently confirmed at different times by the mother-in-law and two English girls (babysitters), who were not told of the previous UFO events. The couple were afraid of alarming them, since they had a problem of getting help for their children, who included newly-born identical triplets.

   Some of the observations of this couple were also confirmed via a letter to me from their neighbor, a prominent psychiatrist, and an exponent of Wilhelm Reich's researches. He wrote me about his own UFO experience:

   "On September 2, 1967, according to notes I made at the time, my wife and I were walking our dogs about midnight, as is often our custom on nice evenings. We had not gone very far when we noticed what looked very much like the moon rising over the ridge about one quarter of a mile behind our house. In color, lumination, and size, it looked very much like the moon as it apparently appears to the naked eye when far enough above the horizon to appear white. This object was, however, football-shaped and had a brilliant, pulsating or turning red beacon on top. There was no undercarriage or other observable protrusions when seen with binoculars through 7X. The illumination of the surface (it seemed to glow from within) was homogeneous to the naked eye, but on close examination with binoculars it appeared to be eight large windows which took up most of the surface of the object. It slowly "drifted" from west to east, but we — and my brother who joined us — were able to follow it for about an hour by going up a nearby hill.

"I later read in the Delaware Valley News that the Goodyear blimp had been sighted in the area that night. When I checked on this with the local Goodyear office, I received a confusing answer. Essentially they weren't sure, and I could only find out for sure by calling Ohio, which I didn't feel like doing. I have since seen a Goodyear blimp and know it is the same size (apparently it has an undercarriage and does not have a beacon on top). Also, it would apparently illuminate in letters or words rather than the way we saw the UFO. Furthermore, what is a blimp doing drifting not more than about one or two thousand feet above ground at midnight over some rural land? Oh, yes, the object made no detectable sound. Since the experience with the [couple], I have seen many peculiar phenomena out here, [and] very often an inexplicable movement of what appeared to be a stationary star. But what I have described above is the most unequivocal."

At the same time that the psychiatrist had his experience, the couple saw "a dirigible-like luminous jelly fish with a red light in the middle (see Figure 1). It must have been at least as big as my studio (size of a small summer cottage)." Late one cold wintry night, when the artist was working in the hilltop studio and his wife was at home in the hollow, the artist had a funny feeling as though someone were looking over his shoulder, and which seemed to tell him that there was something outside.

Finally, he couldn't resist it any longer and he checked. At that point (this was about midnight), his wife telephoned from the hollow and they both observed from their respective vantage points, for a long time, ". . . a Christmas-ornament-like object with revolving brilliant lights about fifty yards away, and about 12 to 15 feet in diameter, sparkling and radiant. There was no noise. My wife said that she had originally gone to bed but then she 'felt' the presence and this compelled her to go to the window [from where she] was watching the object for quite a while before phoning me."

The couple noticed that it dropped a parcel, like a brown paper bag, that floated down very slowly. When they searched for it the next day, however, they found nothing. Additional sightings included a luminous disc that changed shape into something like a perfect chrysanthemum, and then after a "puff" movement a second, similar object was formed next to it. After several sightings, the husband and wife felt they were in telepathic contact with the saucer.

One night the wife had "an awful dream that the UFO landed." There were occupants that were soulless. They treated everyone and everything in a heartless way. "All my wife could remember was that they were in black. Everything was meaningless to them, like we were a tree or something. They had no sensitivity."

About two nights after the wife's dream, the husband was awakened at 3:00 a.m. by a very strong vibration. He related this to a UFO directly over the house. "It was a suction sound. Extreme vibration. A sort of great undulation. It was a hum that could come and go. I thought of my wife's dream. I felt that the UFO occupants wanted me to dress and go outside and meet them. I thought of my family responsibility and I had a healthy fear. I told them in my thoughts why I couldn't join them and that they shouldn't return. After that, I heard it going away and it left. Since that time there have been few sightings.''

The man did not wake his wife during his experience but told her in the morning. And gradually, with the passage of time, they both became deeply involved in religious works — a distinct departure from their past attitude and non-involvement. Although both were accomplished artists, neither of them ever drew (nor would they) what they saw. This was similar to another situation that I studied where I asked an amateur artist to draw what she experienced. Although she diligently tried, she finally destroyed her canvas and phoned me that she couldn't do it (**Journal** of the Medical Society of New Jersey, Vol. 66, No. 8: 460-464 (August), 1969; Case 1).

8. Contactee Stella Lansing, while photographing strange aerial objects, once noted what she interpreted as a chorus of strange, bizarre voices chattering in an unintelligible babble. Her account of this experience was substantiated by an independent interview of several families who lived close to her area and who also reported strange, terrifying auditory effects at different times (see FSR, Vol. 18, 1: 3-12, January/February 1972).

In an unidentified newspaper article of February 28, 1965, mention was made of ''reports of weird music heard floating across Yellowstone Lake, in Yellowstone National Park, Wyoming . . . The sounds resembled the singing of telegraph wires or the hum of bees, beginning softly in the distance, growing rapidly plainer until directly overhead, and fading rapidly in the opposite direction . . . the mysterious music has been likened to the dirge playing on a giant pipe organ, but echoing of distant bells. The sounds have been heard most distinctly in the early mornings on cloudless, breezeless days. The park's naturalist reported that no one 'has the faintest proof of what causes them'.''

Whatever their cause, the great variety of humming sounds are frequently associated with UFOs. A recent article summarizes many similar strange auditory effects experienced by the astronauts (Beckley, T.G., and Salkin, H.: Apollo 12's Mysterious Encounter With Flying Saucers, **Saga** Special UFO Report, Vol. III: 8-11, pp. 58-62 (issued August, 1972).

9. Schwarz, B.E.: Beauty in the Night, **Flying Saucer Review**, Vol. 18, No. 7: 5-9, 17, July/August 1972.

This is the second part of a report of UFO events, in 1966, from the small town of Woodstock — an arts and crafts center which is actually some fifty miles north of the site of the 1969 Rock Festival which bore the same name — in the Catskill Mountain area of the State of New York. The principals, the Carriers (pseudonym), were interviewed in 1969 and 1970 (including a psychiatric interview of Mr. Carrier) and were found to be in good health with no evidence of previous emotional or psychosomatic illness, or of lying, stealing or dishonesty. We saw how the young couple were completely bewildered by the events which began with the observation of greenish lights six feet in diameter in a field near their house, and of "something" that flew close to their car.

Continuing events at Woodstock; Summer 1966

Mrs. Carrier's account continued:

"One afternoon, my girlfriend (age 20) and I heard something like a jet breaking the sound barrier, but it was above our roof. We ran out to look and saw a thick vapor cloud from it: the noise was like a jet — but the vapor trail didn't break up, it lasted a long time — it went straight over the roof to the mountain. Later in the summer a friend (a young man) came out from Boston. We talked about seeing green lights above the fields and other strange things; and later, when this happened to all of us together, my friend went out to check and see if there were lights in the mountain, but there wasn't any. It was in the fields (10). One time there was a power blackout; and the man came to fix it. At that point the light was close in the field and we were so scared that no one went out to see what it was.

"Another time, when my girlfriend and I were looking at TV, we saw and heard the (green) thing; and we got a local Florida station on our TV set (11)! Toward the end of the summer (1966), another friend, who had lived there for several years, told us about Little Buck, a Hopi Indian (12) and his family, who had lived high up in the mountains near the Reservoir. When he heard about my experiences the Indian came to see me. Indians are very reserved people, and Little Buck was reluctant to bring up his own experiences, but after I told him what had happened to us, he said that for years he and his wife wondered if they were insane, because the same thing had happened to them. And that was the reason why they finally left Woodstock. He said, 'They (lights) came close to us and the sound and pull increased so much that we threw ourselves face down on the ground and rocks were strewn about. I yelled at them: "Show yourself!" We ran to a friend's house in fear.'

"One time, when my girlfriend and I were in the house we saw the light and heard the sounds. The vibrations and sensations were so strong that our throats were constricted (globus hystericus?). It was strong — like a magnet above the house — directly above our heads, pulling us up. It increased until the center of gravity was in the center of the stomach. The legs were ordinarily heavy, but this time I felt giddy and was laughing at the novelty of the experience. It was like carrying your body around like a thin handkerchief. We walked around on the tip of our toes. We couldn't force our heels on the floor and I became frightened. We were afraid we would float up toward the ceiling. Then it broke — so quickly that it was like going back into your body. I could feel the heaviness (13, 14).

"Once, [after many of the described events] the niece of the man we rented the house from, the pilot, came to our house to say hello, It was the time of so many reports. She told me about flying back from New York to Kingston, where she saw something so strange that she couldn't

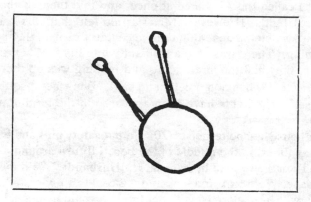

Fig. 3. UFO, as seen by the 12-year-old. The Tappan Zee bridge crosses the Hudson River just south of Nyack (see sketch map)

describe it (15). She had a young boy with her, and she told me about a friend of hers who works for the Kingston paper. She also told me how her niece (16), who was sixteen years at the time, said that several years ago she had been in the middle of Woodstock on the green, and saw a thing like a ship with portholes. It stopped and landed on the green. The door opened and then closed. The girl said she was so terrified that she didn't tell anyone outside her family for two to three years. Last summer I heard, from a friend, of another sighting where there were thousands of people at the fair, close by, and they saw an object hovering above them (17).

"The other mountain, in back of our house, has Clarence Schmidt (18), the artist, living there. He is an old man with white hair and beard. He has a lot of mirrors around his house that reflect on the water and he can look out on the reservoir. There is something funny about this. We'd seen bright lights around his house all summer. There might be a clue there. Once we stayed up late one night to talk about him. Then we decided to go and see him. We stopped in town to buy some cookies, and as we were about to take a turn — our intention was to go straight up the road — in a split second my husband impulsively wheeled the car to the left. He just cleared a truck ahead of us with a huge blade on its back, which fell off and hit the pavement. It was a close call.

"Once, toward the end of summer, in the middle of the night, my husband and I were in the house and we heard a voice over a loudspeaker, like a megaphone, saying 'No. A little to the right. Over there.' It was very strange, for there was nothing there. I was so frightened that I called the Air Force at once, and told them of this and the (associated) lights. [However, Mr. Carrier felt that this was due to people with walkie-talkies, although he couldn't explain the incongruity of the timing.] There was also a brilliant white light. When the policemen came, they had the siren going and nothing was up there. One of the policemen (19) listened quietly and said, 'Don't be upset. I've seen them myself.' The lights have even appeared in the form of a cross in Kingston.

"Our house had poltergeists (20). I'd put safety pins and baby lotion down many times, in the middle of the bed. I'd turn around and they'd be gone. Then they would be back later. [Husband: "We'd miss things. It was insane. We'd look and look and we couldn't understand it."] My girlfriend, who lived close by with her family, would hear a car drive up. They would look out, and see nothing. They would hear the crunch on the gravel, doors slamming, footsteps, a knock, and then nothing. She said this happened several times.

"The night that May came to the house we aimed an old movie camera at the (green) light and tried to get some footage. After that a few people came to the house and a lot of negative things happened to us. Things were being lost that never happened before. My husband didn't believe me. The light and steady noise you could take in your stride, but we heard funny noises from the house — high-pitched. [Husband: 'High-pitched screams.'] Once the two poodles came back very frightened. There was a funny crackling sound, like the kind that comes out of a hi-fi set. My husband heard it too. [Confirmed.]

"One night we heard a noise like someone yelling, "Help." But it was a crackly, taut voice, the stereotyped spooky voice. Then our house was robbed and the movie camera taken. The film had not been

152

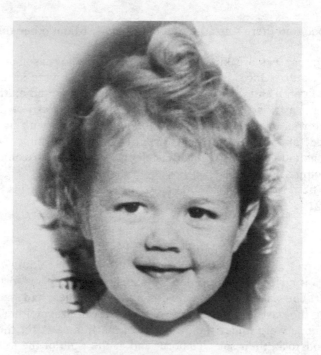

Fig. 4a: Merz grandchild

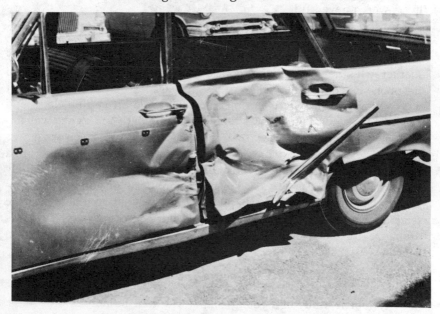

Fig. 4b. Similar image on damaged car

developed and there was a lot of footage on it. Many other things were stolen.

"Our car was breaking down all the time for no reason at all, and it wouldn't start. Once, my husband's friends and I were sitting on the screened porch and we heard some funny crackling sound on the gravel. 'That's it,' a friend said, and there was a brilliant flash of light, as if someone was taking his picture. The fellow who was with us later disappeared, and we haven't heard from him in a long time. We would have constant harassment on the telephone: clicks, disconnects, and funny sounds.

"When we moved to the city we dismissed all this from our minds (21)."

★ ★ ★

We emphasize that neither Mr. or Mrs. Carrier nor their immediate families had a past history for various diseases, including brain syndromes, injuries, temporal lobe epilepsy, delirium or drug ingestion (22). The Carriers, like many other young couples, had smoked marijuana in the past, but at the time of their experiences neither they, nor their friends were under the influence of marijuana. After the Carriers left Woodstock, their son was born, and at the time of the study (1969-1970), both mother and child remained healthy. Her pregnancy and delivery were uneventful.

At the conclusion of my (BES) original telephone interview of Mrs. Carrier (7/29/69) at 9:30 p.m., the electric lamps of my recently deceased father's office, where I was working, suddenly went out. My mother, who then entered the room and who did not know the content of my phone talk or anything else of these researches, remarked how odd it was, since the lights were on timers and set to go off at 10 o'clock, and should not go off at 9:30. I was unaware of this data and as she was unaware of my odd interview; so I checked the clocks to see what was wrong. There was no explanation why the two lamps went out within a half minute of each other at this earlier time and almost immediately following this call. There was no evidence for a local or general interruption of the house current. Perhaps this episode illustrates how possible telekinesis might occur under emotionally charged conditions. If records are kept for such minutiae over the years, a pattern of built-in controls (23), as also happens in telepathy, can frequently be observed.

Summary
Psychiatric study of a young couple who had numerous presumed UFO-related experiences over a period of months, tends to support the

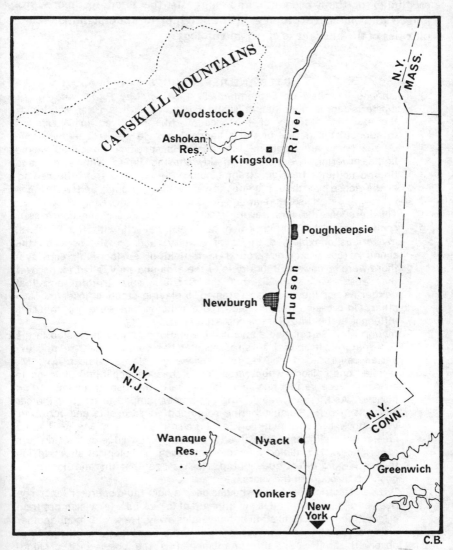

Part of the State of New York, showing the location (within the dotted boundary line) of the Catskill Forest Reserve, and the position of the country town of Woodstock. Abbreviations employed at the inter-state boundary lines: N.Y., New York State; N.J., New Jersey; CONN., Connecticut; MASS., Massachusetts. The Tappan Zee bridge referred to in reference 15 crosses the Hudson River close to Nyack, N.Y.

credibility of their accounts and suggests the need for more prolonged and intensive probing in the attempt to understand the complexities of the interphase of psi and ufology.

NOTES AND REFERENCES

10. Telephone interview on September 25, 1969, of Mr. P.M., who had a master's degree in mathematics and worked with Mr. Carrier, confirmed the essential features of the account. Mr. M. lived in Woodstock throughout the period of these happenings. He was frequently at the Carrier home and spent nights there. He specifically recalled seeing lights hovering over the cornfield, chasing lights with a car and finding nothing, hearing strange noises outside and from the ceiling of the house ''as though someone was walking around and yet no one was — it is an isolated area —'' sound of cars driving in and out yet there were no cars, sewing-machine-like sounds in the house as if coming from the ceiling which he heard himself with the Carriers, mysterious unexplained thefts of jewelry, and on one occasion the sound of cows moving around in a field of six-foot-high corn, yet there were no cows within a mile of the area and they failed to discover the cause. Mr. M. said that the Carriers were truthful and that neither he nor they were accustomed to playing practical jokes on each other. On occasion they all had used marijuana, but were not under its influence at the time of these odd experiences.

Although Mrs. Carrier had a mystical inclination and was interested in the supernatural, it should be stressed that her possibly UFO-related experiences preceded her reading knowledge of the subject. Mr. M. recalled one episode when Mrs. Carrier had begged him not to go to an Army Reserve meeting in Massachusetts because of an impending disaster. As Mr. M. was driving up, a deer jumped in front of the car and smashed it. Because of the continued weird events and terror in Woodstock, Mr. M. finally left, as did also the Carriers. Mr. M. had no idea of my preliminary investigations nor my knowledge of the Carrier's experiences. He denied any relevant psychopathological stigmata, on tangential and direct questioning. He has been healthy and has had a good job throughout the years.

11. C.D.B., an electrical engineer who has been a ham radio operator for thirty-five years, told me that it is not unheard of to pick up a television program originating from a local station many miles away. He wrote about another unexplained phenomenon occurring in radio transmission. ''It has been observed rarely . . . this phenomenon is the observance of long-delayed echoes by both the originators of transmissions and by others. Since radio waves travel with the speed of light, you wonder where they've been all that time.'' Two relevant references originating from the Radioscience Laboratory, Stanford University, and supported in part by the Office of Naval Research, are: Villard, Jr., O.G., Graf, C.R., and Lomasney, J.M.: Long-Delayed Echoes . . . Radio's ''Flying Saucer'' Effect, **QST** [Radio Amateur's Journal] 38-43, May 1969; **ibid.**: There Is No Such Thing As a Long-Delayed Echo AR . . . or, The LDE Mystery Deepens; **Quest**: 30-36

(February) 1970. A spectacular example of a possible LDE if verifiable is presented in Edwards, Frank: **Strangest of All,** chapter headed "Signals From Space," pp. 165-166, Ace Books Inc., New York, 1956.

12. In **The Sky People** (Award Books, pp. 104-106, N.Y., 1970), Le Poer [Trench — ED.] writes about some of the UFO-related myths in the legends of the Hopi and their supernatural friends, the Kachina, who believed they originated from the skies. "If the Hopi and Kachina had a link long ago with Mars, could the Kachina today, in their ritual dancing still wear the symbols of two Martian satellites?"

13. From the **World** of Coos Bay, Oregon (September 28, 29, and October 10, 1959) and personal letters to me, Leo Bartsch, a real estate agent, described an early morning episode: "I was lifted right out of bed. I was weightless for [about] a minute." At the same time as his experience, he subsequently learned that a Mrs. Carlson and her two sons had seen (and reported to the police and the Air Force) a brightly colored, mysterious, low-flying object. In an article entitled, "The UFO, a change in my life," Mr. Bartsch described his experience (as told to his wife at the time): ". . . something out of the universe just went low over this roof. Although I saw and heard nothing, I knew it. How or why, I do not know . . . my arm became normal instantly. Then I realized she [the wife] must be thinking I had a nightmare. So I told her to look at the clock and be sure to remember the time, as I said, 'someone saw it and it will be in the newspapers.' I even wondered why I was saying this when I had not heard or seen a thing. And when the next issue came off the press, there it was, September 28 (my birthday), the 1959 issue of the **World,** Coos Bay, Oregon . . . This woman and her sons lived only three miles from me. From where she lived, the direction of her sighting was directly over my house, and she stated it was low."

He attributed the immediate healing of his left arm, which at the time of the experience felt "like a sparking, electric contact," to the UFO, and soon afterward started attending flying saucer meetings. He became a knowledgeable fundamentalist in his interpretation of the Bible. It is regrettable that there was insufficient medical evidence or observation to document and speculate upon this alleged effect.

14. In a bizarre experience H.D. Stocks reported (Red Sun That Rises Straight Up, **Air Facts, The Magazine for Pilots**, Vol. 33, No. 10, 50-55 (Oct.) 1970, also see FSR, Vol. 15, No. 3, May/June, 1969) how, in association with an eerie glow and a feeling of detached unreality, he noticed,"with amazement that they (a flock of sheep) all appeared to be standing on tiptoe, like ballet dancers, with their heads held unusually high, just as if they were suspended in space with their hoofs barely touching the grass." Mr. Stocks and the farm manager, Jock Marais, then experienced "a peculiar feeling, almost of weightlessness." This experience was related to an ancient Zulu legend of the sun "that raises straight up into the sky after devouring some of the tribe's cattle." After the sensations of weightlessness appeared, Stocks had a most peculiar, near-immediate experience in his airplane, which had "an incredibly rapid accelerating ascent," associated with instrumental changes and

"strangely no feeling of the G force." (For a well-documented similar experience see Sanderson, I.T.: **Invisible Residents,** Chapter 9, "Supramarine Time Anomalies," pp. 143-156, World Publishing Co., New York, 1971.)

This episode, which occurred in Natal, was "forgotten" until a very peculiar related experience, "halfway across the world, almost exactly a year later, the 15th of June." While flying with a man who was one-quarter Cherokee Indian, they were amazed to suddenly see an "eerie pinkish glow, more intense in the center of the circular object as it shot straight up into the sky." With appropriate details Stocks describes how they had a sensation of "no G force, and my camera, which had been lying in my lap, now felt light as a feather to my touch."

After Stocks and his passenger had landed they compared notes on their experience, and by a peculiar coincidence, a farmer then telephoned them to describe his strange related phenomena. They flew over to the farmer's ranch and were amazed to hear how a herd of white-faced Herford steers had stood in a semicircle in association with a pinkish glow, an absence of sound, a peculiar weightless feeling — and "one of the oldest steers was missing." One of the ranch hands, an American Indian, recalled a legend of "the sun that rises straight up." This account was confirmed by Stocks' friend who had heard the same story from his Cherokee grandmother. Stocks' experiences were reported to **Project Blue Book.**

15. After a preliminary telephone interview on October 29, 1970, Mrs. Gale Brownlee, a licensed commercial pilot, with a flight instructress rating, was interviewed in her home on February 14, 1971. Present at that time was William Salvucci, a prominent local restaurateur. Both of these people recalled hearing the Carriers describe "what she saw and felt — told goofy things. I didn't get the impression that she was imaginative. She genuinely believed, and, whatever it was, she was terrorized." Mrs. Brownlee was free of any relevant psychopathology. She described her own sighting, which was reported in **The Daily Freeman** (Kingston, New York, Saturday evening, April 23, 1966). A twelve-year-old passenger and she were returning by aircraft: "We were at an altitude of about fifteen hundred feet. When flying over the Tappan Zee bridge we looked out and saw the object. It was high above us and appeared as a bright green and yellow flare, travelling in a north-north-west direction. A green and yellow flame appeared to be shooting from the UFO, which was travelling at a high speed like a satellite."

As reported, the object was witnessed from other vantage points by many people. On telephone interview (10-29-70) of the young man who was the original passenger, his account was as reported, except that he recalled that the object was noiseless and there were no physiological effects.

16. Mrs. Brownlee's sister, Mrs. E.K., and her friend, Miss E.H., when interviewed on the telephone (10-29-70) recalled the golf course UFO episode of 1958: "It was approximately 11:00 p.m. There was moonlight, and no clouds. There were three oval-shaped [craft], with domes on top, hovering about one telephone length over the airport.

They had windows with slots all around. There were no lights. They were gunmetal grey and there was no noise. We had a weird feeling before we saw them. Our observation lasted 5 to 10 minutes. We were scared and stayed in the car. It had no affect on the motor or lights. One UFO came back and it was just sitting there; then two went back and forth. We told our parents and many people. They didn't believe us.''

The friend, Miss E.H., said: ''Spooky effect. Strange-appearing — out of the ordinary. Not like a plane or a helicopter — no noise. One object was elliptical.'' Both ladies were of good health and had no previous or subsequent experiences similar to this. This was one of the most moving experiences of their lifetime. This event took place a very short distance from the Carriers' home.

17. On direct interview of the then current occupant of the Carriers' home (2/2/71), he reported no strange events in his home since he lived there, but he recalled a Woodstock rock concert in August, 1969, which was tape-recored by N.Y. radio station WBAI (Pacifica Foundation). At that time everyone was amazed, because a UFO hovered above the audience. This event took place about one mile from his home. It was impossible to check out this story further, and the gentleman could not locate the tape. See Figure 3 for his drawing of what he saw.

18. Rehberg, W.: Clarence Schmidt of Woodstock, **The Newark News** Sunday Magazine (cover story), Nov. 29, 1970. In my interview of Mr. Schmidt on Sept. 13, 1969, he denied any knowledge of UFOs. However, it appeared that he was an observant old man, and with more time the results might have been different.

19. When contacted on the telephone, the chief of police of Woodstock vaguely recalled the Carrier incident. However, the officer who made the house call during a particularly trying time remembered entering the complaint on the blotter but with no details. He chiefly recalled the Carriers' terror. Both the officers remembered Mrs. Brownlee's personal experience. When State Tropper CVW was phoned, he was initially reluctant to discuss his own Woodstock observations of a ''red-green-blue standing-still object that also went like hell. It appeared to be a mile away, then over the street and I observed it for four hours. I counted seven or eight of them. There was no influence on the car, lights, compass, or wristwatch. The other officers saw it too. I contacted Stewart Air Force Base but took a hell of a beating and harassment because of this. They convinced me it was ice crystals. But it was quite a thing to see. This was in 1967'' (near the area of the Carriers' sighting).

20. The relationship between parapsychology and ufology is difficult to define. If levitation, teleportation, materialization, and dematerialization were easily demonstrated facts, which they are not, these would be the most reasonable explanations for much UFO phenomena. Many of the presumed associated telepathic aspects of ufology are assumed to come directly from the UFOs of the entities. However, this might be too superficial a view of a much more complex problem. For example, from my experience in psychotherapy, it is not unusual to have highly polarized, poorly repressed ideas telepathically sent or received. Of course when

159

one is worked up and excited about a subject as fascinating as UFOs, this can be an excellent **modus operandi** for telepathic leakage from the physician investigator to the witness, and totally without the witness's awareness of what is going on — an unconscious process. Thus, this greatly simplified process alone could be a suitable explanation for much of the supposed UFO-associated telepathy and other paranormal phenomena, without any need to invoke its origin in the UFOs themselves.

As an illustration, there is the Merz case (note p. 26, FSR, Vol 17, No. 2:4-9, March/April, 1971 where three generations of a family saw UFOs at different times, and in some instances under well-controlled conditions with countless other observers. The grandmother, who never took herself seriously, also has had many lifelong non-UFO related psychic experiences. For instance, when her grandson was injured, a picture of her sister (who was psychically talented) fell off the wall. At another time, when Mrs. Merz's husband and son were involved in an auto accident many miles away, Mrs. Merz, in the presence of her granddaughter (whom she had raised since age five), had a premonition that something horrible had happened. She was very attached to this granddaughter who was the only one of the five grandchildren who resembled herself. When Mrs. Merz later found out what had happened — her husband and son knew better than to try to conceal such news — they were more surprised than anyone else to see that the polaroid picture (of their damaged car door), taken by the mechanic for insurance purposes, showed a resemblance to the favored granddaughter through a coincidental deformity (see Figure 4a and b). Unfortunately, I could not borrow the best picture of the granddaughter, which showed her bangs and which was a better resemblance to the image on the damaged car door.

These accounts become so complex that it is almost impossible to find a cutoff point for the psi material **per se,** let alone relating it to the UFOs. The Merz case involved the later haunting by the same favorite aunt and psychic who "came back" on many occasions with warnings which checked out. In her lifetime the aunt was a snake charmer with a circus for many years, had many unusual psychic experiences as did her sister, the grandmother. Thus, do UFO experiences happen to odd people? Or, are people who are accustomed to out-of-the-run-of-the-mill experiences — like psi stuff — more likely to become aware of other strange events such as UFOs? Or do UFOs (or what is behind thim) take advantage of such biologically and psychopathologically vulnerable individuals?

In many cases, why should one have to resort to the hypothesis of implanted lies, false prophesies, etc., when observation of non-UFO-related psychic matters in paragnosts reveals the same pattern: i.e., an inexactitude and a groping for correctness. For example, anyone who has followed the careers of some of the publicized prophets will note the infrequency and vagueness of their hits, and their many outlandish errors. Although such "errors" are at times parapsychologically correct — they are more often, perhaps, examples of the paragnosts' own projected psychopathology and fumbling attempts at synthesizing their impressions (see Tenhaeff, W.H.C.: Proceedings of the Parapsychological Institute of the State University of Utrecht, Nos. 1-3,

1960, '62 and '65).

Thus, much more spade work would be indicated in cases like the Merz or Carrier families and in other published reports, before jumping to an unjustifiable **pars pro toto** conclusion. The UFO and psychic phenomena might be related; yet there are also differences that must be taken into account. It can be erroneous to try and place them all under one umbrella.

21. When scouting the area for additional opinions, I noticed the name of a psychiatrist who was formerly affiliated with our local hospital in Montclair, New Jersey, and with whom I was acquainted from departmental meetings. When I telephoned him (11/2/70), he claimed no knowledge of UFOs and was most reluctant to discuss the subject. It is of interest that at the time this man practiced in my town, he had much pressure on him because he was allegedly a follower of Wilhelm Reich, and such practices as espoused by Reich were far from the mainstream of practice.

It is of interest that in his writings Wilhelm Reich called attention to the possible connection between his Orgone energy and flying saucers. This would be an interesting subject for someone to undertake who is thoroughly familiar with the controversial researches and personality of Wilhelm Reich. Either Reich was a genius years ahead of his time, or a once brilliant man who succumbed to the insidious effects of psychosis. Some interesting and conflicting references about Reich and UFOs are:

Steiger, Brad, and Whritenour, Joan: **New UFO Breakthrough,** Award Books, New York, 1968: Ch. III: "The Silencing of Wilhelm Reich," pp. 29-37.

Hoppe, Walter: Autobiography, **The Journal of Orgonomy,** Vol. 3 (No. 2): 155-165, Nov. 1969.

Reich, Ilse O.: **Wilhelm Reich, A Personal Biography,** St. Martin's Press, Inc., New York, 1969, pp. 110, 115, 119, 122, 129 146, 150-151.

Eden, Jerome: **Orgone Energy,** Exposition Press, New York, 1972, pp. 69-74; 149-153.

Schatzberg, A.F.: Wilhelm Reich: Self-Destined Victim and Social Casualty, **Archives of General Psychiatry,** Vol. 27 (No. 1: 67-72, July, 1972).

Mention was made elsewhere (**Proceedings of the Eastern UFO Symposium,** January 23, 1971, Baltimore, Maryland, published in 1971 by Aerial Phenomena Research Organization, Tucson, Arizona: page 12) of a world-renowned physiologist who had a close UFO experience that was initiated by telepathy. This researcher, famed for his many contributions, was a former student of Reich and performed numerous successful but unpublished experiments. Although many years later he privately upheld to me the validity of the earlier researches and his UFO experience, few knew of his interesting and significant association with Reich earlier in his career. He was still intrigued with the possibilities of UFOs and orgone energy.

22. Although the study of the Woodstock events is, unfortunately, incomplete from the psychiatric viewpoint, attention might be directed to the experiences of the astronauts and cosmonauts, some

of whom reputedly had UFO or UFO-related experiences. While voluminous data has been published on the telemetric monitoring of their various physiological functions and other data, as far as I am aware, there have been no psychiatric reports of these brave men. If the matter is as it seems, then it might be asked why has exclusive attention been given to the "objective" aspects of the astronauts' experiences, while neglecting the correlative subjective, or human aspects. Unless such anamnestic anecdotal data about the astronauts' UFO experiences (see **Condon Report,** pp. 204-208, New York Times Books, 1969) exists in presumably classified files, this omission could be reprehensible from the broad scientific and ufological viewpoint; e.g., clues concerning the extraterrestrial vs. ultraterrestrial hypothesis. Furthermore, if the popular accounts of some of the astronauts developing various presumed emotional problems are creditable, then the lack of intensive pre- and post-flight psychiatric (and parapsychological?) study of these highly trained and programmed astronauts might have left them unduly vulnerable to their emotionally charged explorations.

Unlike the largely anecdotal data obtained from the young Woodstock couple, the accounts of the highly trained and technically sophisticated astronauts might have given clues for such questions as: (1) Are the UFO and UFO-related events "real"? (2) Might such events be related to possible psychodynamic factors, and if so, in what way? (3) In what ways might these almost experimentally observed factors have influenced, if at all, the astronauts (and vice versa)?

If such psychiatric investigations have not been undertaken previously it is hoped that NASA, which has not overlooked myriad other aspects, will consider future flights as an ideal opportunity for such studies. It is regrettable that the Condon Report was inexplicably remiss in such an opportunity by not tackling close UFO landing or occupant cases from the psychiatric viewpoint.

23. Schwarz, B.E.: Built-in Controls and Postulates for the Telepathic Event, **Corrective Psychiatry and the Journal of Social Therapy,** Vol. 121: 64-82 (March) 1966. Some key articles on psi and ufology which have appeared in FSR are those by Charles Bowen, Gordon Creighton, P.M.H. Edwards, Janet Gregory, John A. Keel, Ivar Mackay and Aime Michel.

Chapter 9

UFO Landing and Repair by Crew

PART I — THE REPORT

By TED BLOECHER

Investigation of a report of an incident at
New Berlin, N.Y., U.S.A., on November 25, 1964

Information about this previously unreported UFO landing and occupant case came from Alexander D. Mebane of New York City, long-time friend and colleague. Lex Mebane had learned of the incident through a mutual friend of his and the primary witness, Mrs. Mary Merryweather.* The intermediary, Miss Charlotte Ronald, had spent a weekend with Mary at the latter's family home near New Berlin, New York, in the early fall of 1970 or 1971. At that time, the two women observed several unidentified lights along the crest of a nearby hill. This incident prompted Mary to disclose her observation of some five or six years earlier, at which time she observed two landed objects and the repair of one by the apparent "crews." Miss Ronald, knowing of Lex's interest in the subject, told him about her sighting as well as the earlier observation by Mary Merryweather on December 12, 1972, requesting additional details on the occupant case, but received no reply.

On June 2, 1973, I called Mary long distance, introduced myself, and explained my interest in obtaining a first-hand account of her earlier sighting. Apparently satisfied that my inquiry was genuine and that I was not just some curious "nut," she willingly provided additional details about the incident. During the course of our half-hour phone conversation, it became evident that the witness was providing a coherent and straight-forward account of a most unusual and possibly important UFO event, and that adequate details could not be gathered in a single telephone conversation. She therefore agreed to a personal interview at her present home in northeastern Pennsylvania and the date was set for Sunday afternoon, June 10, 1973.

Interviews

This report is based upon notes taken and a lengthy taped statement made during that three-hour interview, in which Mary described the landing of two objects on a nearby hillside and her subsequent four-hour observation of the repair of one object by the two crews — a group

*This is a pseudomym.

of perhaps as many as a dozen "men." In addition, further information was obtained in a number of subsequent telephone calls, as well as by answers provided to a series of specific written questions that were submitted to the witness following our June 10 interview. These questions and answers are included in an addendum to this report.

Because of his experience in interviewing many UFO witnesses involved in similar incidents, I advised another colleague, Dr. Berthold Schwarz, psychiatric specialist of Montclair, N.J., who is well-known to readers of FSR as consultant and contributor, of the New Berlin case. Dr. Schwarz contacted Mary and, with her consent, met with her for four hours on August 14, 1973, at which time valuable additional information about the witness, including hypnotic-regressive data, was obtained. It is hoped that the results of this independent interview will be made available to Dr. Schwarz at some future date.

In addition, it is anticipated that an artifact, found by the witness at the landing site a day or so after the incident, will be provided and subjected to appropriate laboratory tests to determine if analysis can comfirm its uniqueness. If this is the case, an addendum report will be prepared regarding the results of such tests.

Mary Merryweather has at no time sought publicity as a result of her unusual observation; to the contrary, she has gone out of her way to avoid it and has discussed the incident with no more than a dozen people, most of whom were family members or close friends.

Location

The location of the site of the incident is about one mile north of the center of New Berlin, N.Y., on old route 80, just northwest of an area known as Five Corners (Latitude 42 degrees 39'; Longitude 75 degrees 20'). The UFO landings were made on a hilltop about 1300 yards northwest of the observers' locale. The date was Wednesday, November 25, 1964; Mary is quite certain about the year, as 1964 was the first year of her marriage. Likewise, she is definite about the date, as November 24 is her parents' wedding anniversary; the incident occurred during the early morning hours of the following day, from about 0045 to 0455 EST.

Besides Mary, who was about 20 at the time of the sighting, a second witness was her mother-in-law, at whose home she was staying. Mary grew up in the vicinity of New Berlin. From 1962 through 1964, she attended Ithaca College, where she majored in Music. She married her husband, Richard, a chemical engineer, in 1964 and, at the time of the sighting, they resided in the Syracuse. N.Y., area. During Thanksgiving week, 1964, Mary and Dick were visiting their parents in

New Berlin. On November 25, Mary was staying with her mother-in-law to keep her company, while Dick and his father, with several other local men, were off on a hunting trip.

At the time of our interview in June, 1973, the Merryweathers had two children: a son, about six-years-old, and a daughter, about four; in July, 1973, a second daughter was born.

Since our initial telephone conversation in early June, Mary has been most cordial and helpful in providing details about the events of November 25, 1964. As far as this reporter is concerned, the primary witness in the case is entirely credible. Her account must be considered an accurate and true report, to the best of her ability, of what she perceived to be a real, and unique event.

The following Narrative is derived from Mary's own first-hand testimony; apart from minor editing to remove non-essential material, and revision to maintain proper sequence, the words used to describe what took place in 1964 are entirely those of the witness. Transitional sections (in brackets) have been derived from notes obtained during our interview and from our several phone conversations. A list of specific questions and answers is included in an addendum.

Narrative account by the witness

"Dick had gone hunting with his father and I was staying with his mother so that she wouldn't be alone, in New Berlin, north on Route 80, at Five Corners. It was about 12:30 at night and I decided I couldn't sleep very well . . . so I turned on the television. There was an old movie I had seen several times; it wasn't very interesting to me and I got up and got a ginger ale, and decided I'd look outside and see what it was like.

"It was unusually clear for a November night . . . it had been snowing that year, often in the evening, and (had been) cloudy, over-cast and miserable. But this night was light and very, very clear. An unusual number of stars were visible; the moon was out, very bright.

"I stepped out on the porch and it was cold, so I . . . got my coat and went out again. I was looking at the stars and trying to figure out where the constellations were and I noticed a falling star. I was looking north northeast and it fell in an arc, as it usually does, in an easterly direction, toward the horizon.

UFO observed

"Then I saw another one, only instead of arcing along the horizon, it came straight down. I saw it in about the same spot as I saw the other one. It appeared to come down directly over the highway (Route 8, which runs north out of New Berlin TB), or a little bit east of the highway,

165

down by the Five Corners. Then it followed along the brook . . . more or less parallel to Route 80, which comes directly across in front of the house. I realized how strange it was, because . . . it was clearly visible and the hillside above the creek and on the north side of the road was visible above the object. It occurred to me that this was an unusually bright light, a brightness and intensity that I had never seen before. Mercury vapour lamps are extremely bright, but this particular (light) was even brighter than that.

"Not only was the visible part (of the sighting) strange, but there was a kind of low hum, like a drone-hum combination, like a . . . water pump running kind of laboriously, and it never changed pitch, it was about the same.

"I think that my mother-in-law got up to come to the bathroom and I spoke to her as she came through the living room. I opened the door and said, 'When you get through, I want you to step out here and take a look at something.' At this time she usually would let the dog out. They have an English Springer Spaniel, very devoted to Dick's mom, and she always went out at this time of night.

UFO approaches

"The next thing that happened was a car, probably some young people coming home from a movie, came north from New Berlin and turned left at Five Corners and was coming along the highway between me and the creek bed, along where the vehicle was travelling. It was travelling rather slowly, and this car kept on going . . . Then another car came by, probably a minute and a half later, and they slowed down and pulled over a little northwest of the house, kind of on the shoulder of the road, and this flying object slowed way down, practically to a stop. Then it did stop and hovered for a moment, and then it came back towards me, back past where this car was, and they started right off (the car — TB) and were on their way!

(At this point several things happened almost simultaneously: Mary's mother-in-law had come to the door, opened it, and was about to step out as the object began moving rapidly back toward her daughter-in-law, who at the time was standing on a slight rise in the middle of the driveway; Mary, alarmed at the sudden motion of the object towards her, made a hasty retreat to the porch; the car, of course, 'burnt rubber' as it took off up the road — TB.)

"When the thing had started to back up, I decided that maybe I was a little too close, and I backed up too! I was within a good sprinting distance to the front door. My mother-in-law started to step out on the porch and she saw this thing, and she swung the door right around again

166

... She kind of left it open a little bit, as if she didn't want me to be alone, but she wasn't going to come out there, either! She said she definitely thought 'that was very strange,' and wished that I'd come back into the house. I turned around and said no, I didn't think I would. The object came to a stop at a point several hundred feet directly across the road from the house and hovered there ... I felt like I was being observed, as much as I was observing.

Animal effect

"And then she tried to persuade the English Springer to come out, so that I'd at least have some company, and the dog would not come out of the door. She wouldn't even come past my mother-in-law's legs — she just lay there and I could see her shaking, she was just quivering.

Landing observed

"Then another car came by and slowed down. This was the third car. They slowed down and the vehicle started to go along at the same speed as the car was travelling; they (the people in the car — TB) appeared to become frightened, and they floored it and got out of there. It kept on going slowly, when this other car decided to leave ... very, very slowly along the valley; it followed along the creek bed, followed that up the hillside ... It kept going north northwest and went up the side of this mountain about 3800 feet away, according to the scale on this topographical map. Then it settled down just below the ridge of the hill, and I couldn't hear the humming sound, the drone, but I could see the light, it was still there. My mother-in-law said, 'Now will you come back into the house?' And I said no, get me the binoculars, which she did.

"My mother-in-law called to me from the front door and said that I could see a little better out of their corner dining room window, which faced north northwest, and would I come and try, because she didn't want me to get cold. I'd been out there quite a while and I was getting cold, so I did. She'd been watching from the dining room window and I found that I could see better ... Anyway, sometime after it landed, probably two or three minutes, I went into the house. My mother-in-law felt considerably better, and I was more comfortable and warmer. And the dog still hovered at her feet. She followed her everywhere. She was just petrified, she literally shook.

(According to Mary's time-table, she went indoors a little after 1:00 a.m. — TB.)

Occupants observed

"As I watched out of the dining room window, I tried to look through the binoculars and I couldn't see because of the glare on the lenses. She said, 'Tip them up and down,' and I did, and it cut the glare off so that I

167

could see what was going on. There seemed to be movement around this vehicle. My mother-in-law said to me, 'What do you see?' and I said, 'Well, I can see light, and there seems to be movement around there . . . You know? It looks like men to me.'

"I couldn't tell the shape of the object, except that the light seemed to be underneath it and it apparently was setting on legs, because the bottom of the object was up from the ground, far enough so that these — I'll call them 'men' for lack of knowing who they were or what they were, because they were built like men — could get under this thing, if they got down on their hands and knees, or sitting down; they lay down under it like a man does working under a truck or a car. But they had more room than they would have if they had been under a car or a truck.

"I could see them coming around this vehicle and they brought with them their boxes of tools, like tool chests or something, and one of these chests took two men to carry it. I don't know if there were two (chests) or three, but I know there were more than one. They appeared to be coming around something in a semi-circular movement, as if they were walking around a round vehicle, or something that had a round shape to it. I couldn't see the shape of it because of the bright light. It appeared to be light on the bottom of the object . . . that was so intensely bright I couldn't make out the form of the objects.

"I asked her (mother-in-law) to take the glasses and tip them up and down to see if she could see movement, and she did; and she said, 'Oh, definitely, I can see them.' And you could tell when she saw (the figures), because she stiffened, you know. It alarmed her, and she said to me, 'Definitely, I see them.' She said, 'Now you watch them and you tell me, because I don't want to watch them any more.'

Humanoids described

"Now, to describe the 'people' that I was seeing: there were about five or six . . . They seemed to be dressed in something like a skin diver's wetsuit. It was a dark color, and their hands were visible apart or out from the wrist of the suit; their skin was lighter than the suit they were wearing. They were built like men: their heads were on necks, which were on shoulders, etc. I could see the muscular build of them, their spinal column; they were standing on two legs like we do, and they worked with arms and hands that were like ours. The only difference was that they were slightly taller than we're accustomed to seeing people — between six and a half to eight feet tall.

(Mary based her estimate of height on the size of the bushes she could see in the lower portion of the field on the hillside — TB.)

"The only ones I could see well were the ones up close to the vehicle

168

where the light was shining on them, and most had their backs to me, or their sides. They did have lighter skin on their faces and necks, like their hands, because I could see the sides of their faces and necks, some of them ... I don't think they had anything on their heads. They seemed to have hair like we do, although their hair wasn't long, as is the custom today for men to wear their hair long, as they do. It seemed well-barbered, fairly close to their heads. The profile of their faces on the men that were on the ground, underneath the vehicle, was like the profile of a man's face.

Occupant activity

"They were working on this vehicle like I've seen my father work on farm machinery; they seemed to have wrenches and screw drivers, and tools like a man would use to work on a piece of machinery that had gone bad, or (on) a motor. They took something out from underneath the center of their vehicle and let it down, gently, with their hands. I don't remember if they wore gloves or not to do this. There were a team of about five 'men'.

"Sometime before this, about five to seven minutes after I had gone into the house and found that I could see better out the dining room window, my mother-in-law got up and when she started to turn around she said, 'Oh, there's another one!'

Second UFO Lands

"I took the glasses down and I could see another vehicle coming from the west southwest, going east northeast, and it settled down on the crest of the ridge, just above where this other vehicle had settled. Four or five more 'men' joined the ones who were working on the ground. It was just after they (the first crew — TB) had removed whatever they took out of the center of it, which seemed to be like a motor or a power supply, or something ... The four or five other 'men' joined them ... and they also began to work. I could see 'men' standing in the foreground, down the hill a little way. I could see them cutting long — what looked like — heavy cable, because it arced, or fell in a loop as they were holding it between them. They were cutting it in exact lengths and they worked quite hard at doing this. I don't know whether it was because it was so heavy or cumbersome, or large, or what the reason was, but the cable appeared to be dark, and they used it in fixing this piece of machinery.

"Repair" work continues

"They left this — what appeared to be a motor or a power source — directly underneath where they took it from and didn't take it way from

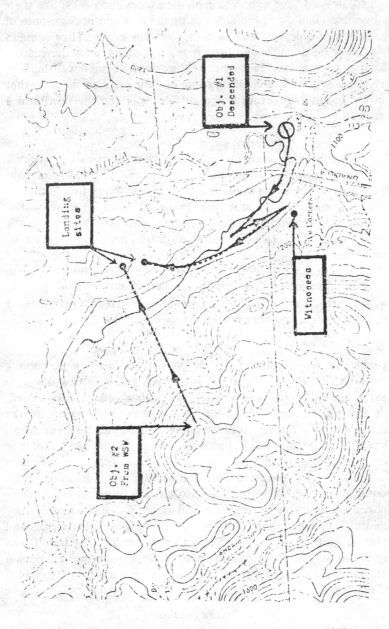

Map of the hilly area just to the north of New Berlin showing locality of the witnesses and the UFO landings.

there, they left it there and worked on it. When I saw that, when they sat down to work, my mother-in-law told me that it was quarter after one. And while I watched them work, and cut and struggle, they were walking around, were sitting or half-lying down, leaning on an elbow and kneeling. There were about ten or twelve 'men' in total — I couldn't be absolutely sure, because they were coming and going, and bringing things and taking things back to the vehicles.

"I couldn't see the figures without the binoculars. The only thing I could see without the binoculars was the light — well, the two lights. I could see the light below the crest of the hill, and the one above it, and the one above it was not as bright. It was as intense, but it wasn't as large . . . The one at the top of the hill would have been smaller than the full moon, and the one below would have been three times larger. Whatever was wrong with the vehicle seemed to be connected with the size of the light.

"Periodically, my mother-in-law would tell me what time it was, and she decided to stay up with me, she said, mostly because, 'Number one, I can't sleep till they leave or something else happens, and, number two, I wouldn't leave you here alone for anything in the world.' And, she said, 'The dog is scared to death; she's almost as frightened as I am.' I wasn't particularly afraid, I didn't feel any fear. She said she was frightened because she had never seen a light like that before. She wanted to know if we should call the police, or some authority, or maybe the government, a U.S. government agency of some kind; I looked at her and she looked at me and I said, 'Well, I hate to,' and she said. 'So do I.' And I said, 'You know, if we call someone, they're going to come here with guns and firearms and bother them, and they just want to get that thing fixed and get away.' And I just didn't want to be bothered with whatever trouble might occur from it, and she felt the same way. At that time we didn't think of the trouble that might happen to us because of it, but we were thinking that they just want to get this thing fixed and get away, and we didn't want them bothered by some stupid persons.

"I'm convinced they knew I purposefully didn't call the authorities . . . I'm sure they saw me after that car decided it would go away — I felt I was being looked at by numerous eyes. I don't know if you can tell; I can tell if somebody's watching me. I felt like I was being watched, intensely. My mother-in-law remarked on that, that she also felt that we were watched. She said, 'I can't explain it, but between you and me and the wooden fence, I am sure that they realized that we did not call the authorities, that we weren't going to, and wouldn't.'

"Difficulties" observed

"At exactly four-thirty by our kitchen clock, the 'men' got down in a

171

team and there were nine of them — there were some behind, a group of three, that were evenly spaced around this piece of machinery; and then there was a line of 'men,' six 'men' behind them; they seemed to be holding something, or seemed to be ready with something. Maybe each one of them had tools, I couldn't see that, but they all seemed to be working together. They got this thing ready, and there seemed to be a man underneath who was the leader, and he would gesture to them as if to say, 'Now take it easy,' and he used both his hands to gesture with ... They got a hold of the thing and they seemed (to be) working together, and he seemed to be saying, 'Now, we'll move it.' Then, all together, they picked this thing up and moved it directly upwards and tried to fit it into the bottom of this vehicle. It went right up, maybe eight inches ... and then it seemed to go off at an angle. You could see the bottom, like a plate, or like the bottom of a motor; you could see that, because the light very abruptly ended there and it was circular, like a dinner plate. As this thing went up in and then went off, at an angle, the bottom of the thing you could see was tilted, instead of being level. As they tried to get it in, they were turning it, too, like screwing a screw in; they turned it a little, and it went back a little bit, but it wouldn't go up in there the way it should.

"They got it up into the vehicle, I think except for the last three, maybe four, inches of it, and it was just off, it wouldn't fit, it wouldn't go. They couldn't get it to go any further, so then they carefully retraced everything they had done and set the thing back down on the ground again. They worked on it another ten minutes, and then they tried it again, the same method, and it wouldn't go ... They retraced their steps again and put it back down on the ground and worked on it another ten minutes. These 'men' that had been cutting cable, cut something else that was like cable, only it seemed to be a little lighter ... and they cut shorter pieces. They worked, and they were hurrying — you could see how they were rushing with this.

"They tried it again a third time. They lifted the thing up in there and they got it closer to going the way it should have, then it was the other two times, but it just wouldn't go. It lacked about an inch and a half of being right and it was off at an angle; they couldn't get it in there the way it should have. One of the 'men' who was with the three who had a hold of it, and then two or three 'men' back down the line, made a gesture like, 'It's not going to work!' They were exasperated, anxious for it to go in right, and it just wasn't working.

"Then they took this thing out again and set it on the ground and worked on it for ... maybe three minutes, and the man who seemed to be the leader gestured to them as if he was saying, 'Well, now take it easy, we'll try it once more, and try to get it to do what it ought to.' He was on the left side of this motor. I couldn't hear them, of course, but that seemed to be about what he was saying. And they very carefully picked the thing up and it went back in.

Success, and departure

"There was just enough of the extra light that I could see the front part of the vehicle (the part toward the witness — TB) was round, and the bottom tapered up. Now, whether it tapered up to a cone-shape or was rounded on top, I don't know ... Just before they got this thing into the center — and it seemed to be cylindrical, I don't know what the top was like — this intense light came out from underneath the vehicle. Anyway, they got it to fit in there and they seemed to be very pleased. It was a minute before five minutes of five. I could see them quickly pick up everything they could pick up and the 'men' from the vehicle above them on the hill ran with their material up there; these 'men' were running like a man running with something extremely heavy, two 'men' with the tool boxes — the one that required two to carry. There were at least two more tool boxes, other than the one that took two 'men' to carry, because there were two other 'men' who were laboriously running. They ran around the side and I didn't see them after that. It looked like they were picking up cable pieces these other men had left just before that; they ran up the hill with them, and I didn't see them any more, either.

"At five minutes of five, the vehicle on top of the hill left — and it shot off, almost like an instantaneous disappearance, in the direction that it had come from, west southwest. A minute later the other vehicle rose straight up, went to the crest of the hill, rose a little further again, and shot off in the same direction that the other one had left in, at the same speed. And that was it. It had been a long night.

"The next afternoon I got up and I said to my mother-in-law, 'I want to go up there.' She said she thought I should. Now my mother-in-law is quite heavy, and she's a tall woman, nearly as tall as I am, but she has arthritis and bursitis, and it's hard for her to get around. In order to get to the top of this hillside — they use it for a hay field and they cut alfalfa and timothy from there for feed — it's expansive, but there's quite an incline to get up to where the field is, where those vehicles were. I had to cross through two barbed wire fences and I had to go through low berry bushes and on the steeper part of the hillside. And she couldn't get through there.

"But I went to the farm house, which is fairly close to the road — this property belongs to them — and I asked them if I could go up there, and they said yes, that I could, and they kind of looked at me strangely and I didn't offer an explanation; fortunately, they didn't ask, so apparently they hadn't seen anything, or hadn't been aware of anything having happened. I said thank you and I went up there; Mom sat in the car, 'I can't walk up there but I can sit in the car and watch!'

Marks found

"I searched around up there and I found, at the top of the hill and down from the crest at the same angle I had been observing the night before, three places where something cone-shaped and round at the bottom, very heavy and spaced in a triangle about 15 to 20 feet to a side, had set into the ground. They were at an angle like they were the legs of a tripod, (with) something on it that was very, very heavy, because one of them had set on a rock and had broken it, and gone down a little ways into the ground where it was bedrock, or maybe shale. The impressions on the bare ground that didn't have any rock underneath were about 14 inches wide and up to 18 inches deep. The shallowest hole was about four inches deep.

"There were two sets of these, one at the top of the hill and one down the slope. They were set like an equilateral triangle — one hole wasn't any further from the other two.

Artifact found

"I searched around and then remembered the 'men' cutting cable, and I went on down the hill where there was a lot of tall grass and so on, and began to look around. I don't remember whether I found it that day, or when Dick and I both went up there after he came back from hunting, but it seems to me it was that day. On the ground, about 50 or 60 feet below the lower set of holes, I found a three-inch piece of what looks like cable. It looked like a strip of something they had missed. The outer part of it looked like the wrapping, something like a brown paper towel, only it wasn't like our paper towel. It felt rather like that and was dark brown in color. It seemed to be a wrapping for a cable, tubular. And in the center of it — it had been cut out laterally — you could see the strip, maybe an inch wide more or less, something that looked like very finely shredded aluminum strips laid in there, and it was as long as the piece of paper and had been cut, and had the color and feel of aluminum, although it wasn't aluminum. It didn't behave like aluminum. Aluminum will crumple and this wouldn't crumple. You couldn't crease it. It was inside, strips of this, laying inside the paper. You could remove the inside, for the outside paper had been cut along the length of the piece, but it was all together.

"That's what I've got. It's at my mother-in-law's, unless it got thrown away. She wanted to put it up, and I wanted to put it up — you know, keep it, put it away, not let anybody get their hot little hands on it. It was very light. It had practically no weight to it at all, including the paper."

(The artifact has not been located as of this writing, December 15, 1973 — TB.)

Part 2
Further details of the New Berlin landing report of 1964
Ted Bloecher

The first part of this report of the investigation into the events stated to have been observed at New Berlin, New York, on November 25, 1964, dealt with the remarkable account given by the witness (known by the pseudonym "Mrs. M. Merryweather") of the landing of two UFOs, and of ground activities by the occupants which could well answer the description "repair work."

After my first hearing of the account I posed a number of questions in questionnaires that I sent to Mrs. Merryweather, which she kindly filled out.

General questions, with witness's answers

Question 1: When was the house built where the sighting took place?

Answer: About 1945.

Q 2: Was the noise of the object different from that of a helicopter? Louder, softer?

A: Yes, softer, no whap-whap! Just a low hum.

Q3: Did you observe the object through binoculars while it was still airborne, before it landed on the hilltop?

A: No.

Q 4: On tape, you describe the men as having five fingers. Could you see five fingers?

A: I'm not positive. They did not have a peculiar way of handling tools or gesturing — nearly sure they did have five fingers (hands didn't look odd to me).

Q 5: Where and with whom did you have Thanksgiving dinner that year? Was Dick there?

A: Both families. Yes — held after Thanksgiving was past!

Q 6: Where and when did you go to college? What was your major?

A: Ithaca College, Fall 1962 — Spring, 1964. Music.

175

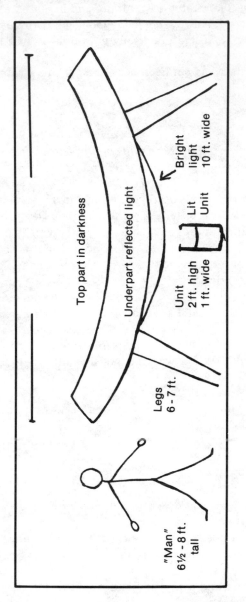

Top part in darkness

Underpart reflected light

Bright light
10 ft. wide

Lit
Unit

Unit
2 ft. high
1 ft. wide

Legs
6 - 7 ft.

"Man"
6½ - 8 ft.
tall

Above and below right: Copies of Mrs. Merryweather's sketches which accompanied her answers to the questionnaire.

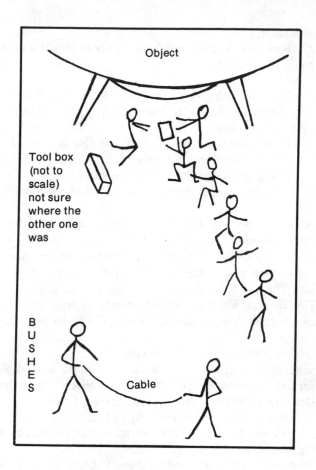

Object

Tool box
(not to
scale)
not sure
where the
other one
was

B
U
S
H
E
S

Cable

Q 7: How many pairs of binoculars were at the house at this time?
Could you have used a pair stronger than five power?

A: Only (1 pair). No.

Q 8: How did you know the figures were larger than normal? Were
there any reference points (bushes, fence posts, etc.) that could be used
for reference?

A: The bushes down the hill were about 5 feet tall and "men" were
1½—2' taller. The men "cutting cable" were close to these.

Q 9: How wide were the holes in the ground? Did they taper?

A: About 14" across, and 18" deep. Yes (they did taper).

Q 10: You said several were as deep as 13 inches. What were the
shallowest?

A: And deeper. About 4" (the shallowest).

Q 11: About how far apart were the two sets of landing marks?

A: 40-50 feet.

Q 12: About how far downhill from the lower object's landing marks was the cable you found?

A: 50-60 ft.

Q 13: When did Dick go up on the hill with you? Did anyone else go?

A: The day after returning from hunting, the Monday after the sighting. No (no-one else).

Q 14: Did Dick see the holes? Did anyone else see them?

A: Yes, but no-one else that I know of.

Q 15: To approximately how many people have you described this incident over the nine-year interval? Any peculiar reactions? Repercussions?

A: About 10 people. Peculiar reactions? Yes, but that's another story! Repercussions? Yes, you and Dr. Schwarz!! Ha Ha!

Q 16: Have I overlooked any important questions that may have occurred to you since our interview? If so, please itemize.

A: Yes. These are as follows:

a. The English Springer did go outside shortly after the sighting and seemed herself. She seemed to have no ill effects from her apparent fright.

b. Drawing for sketch has hilltop too close.

c. Several times (I) observed something being passed along to the men under the object working on the "power source" (?), or "motor."

d. Drawing of arrangement (approximate) of men.

e. Tool boxes about 3 or 4 feet long by 1 ft. or so.

f. (There) was a circular path "worn" — hay stubble mashed down by walking around an object.

g. I did see "men" come and go around object, while working.

Signed: "M. Merryweather"
Date: August 17, 1973

Secondary list of questions regarding
object and its size

1. At "A" please sketch in figure, comparing with height of object. *Stick figure!* (This was done and included in drawing — TB.)

2. Can you estimate the width of the object? 25 to 30 ft.

3. Can you estimate the length of the "legs?" 6 to 7 feet.

4. Were the legs light or dark? Did they taper, as in sketch? Light, and tapered.

5. Can you estimate the size of the light underneath? About 10 ft. wide.

6. Was the light comparable in size to "3 full moons" (as on tape) or

was the entire lighted underside that size? The light directly under the object was that size — between the legs.

7. Can you sketch a line across the object indicating where light and shadow met? Did line arc upward or downward in center? (See drawing, separate page — TB.) Downward.

8. Can you estimate the size of the unit that was removed? 2' high and 1' wide.

9. Was this unit luminous, or lit by the reflected illumination of the light? Luminous on top — not on bottom. (See drawing.) Very intense light from object.

10. Can you estimate the distance from the ground to the underpart of the object (or light)? 4-5 ft.

11. What positions did the "men" assume under the object as they worked on the unit? Sitting to replace and half lying down to remove, leaning on an elbow and kneeling.

12. Was the ground around the area illuminated by the light? How far? Some —perhaps 40 ft.

Signed: "M. Merryweather"
Date: August 17, 1973

Comparative Commentary

Among the ambiguities of the UFO-occupant related reports are the widely varying and often contradictory descriptions of the appearance and behavior of the reported entities. But along with these often conflicting details there may also be found certain features of similarity that are worth noting. It might be helpful, therefore, to cite several examples of UFO occupant reports that contain details similar to those reported in the New Berlin case.

Human UFOnauts, as unlikely as the idea may seem, are not novelties with the New Berlin report: quite apart from the contactee literature, many cases of human-appearing entities have been recorded in association with close encounters with UFOs. For example, among the Air Force's "unexplained" UFO cases is the reported encounter by Eddie Laxton at Temple, Oklahoma, on March 23, 1966; while driving to work early in the morning, Laxton came upon an object in the road, blocking his passage. "Standing beside the object was a man dressed in a suit similar to clothes worn by members of the Air Force, Laxton said. The man wore a cap with the bill turned up (1)." As Laxton got out of his car to check, the "pilot" climbed aboard the vehicle which ascended straight up for about 50 feet and, without stopping or turning, swiftly shot off towards the south — a departure very similar to that reported in New Berlin.

Laxton's UFOnaut was as human-appearing as one could find: having had a good close look, he said he could recognize him immediately if he ran into a crowded bar. There are, however, a number of larger-than-life human-type UFOnauts more closely related to the crew seen in New Berlin; in one particular case, even the dress of the reported UFOnaut is identical to the uniforms worn by the "men" seen by Mrs. Merryweather and her mother-in-law.

On the evening of August 7, 1954, according to a local press account (2). Gabriel and Henri Coupal, 13- and 11-year-old sons of Mr. and Mrs. Phillip Coupal, who lived near Hemmingford, Quebec (just north of the New York state line above Plattsburgh), reported having seen an object land in a field on their farm, and its "pilot" get out. In a taped interview, a few weeks after the event (3), the boys and their mother described in more detail the circumstances of the encounter.

The two boys had gone off to one of the fields to pick peas following supper. Hearing a buzzing sound "like bees," Gabriel looked up to see a luminous and multi-colored object descending near a barn; hovering some feet above the earth, the spherical, 9-foot object turned black and a shaft appeared at the bottom, extending downward into the ground and, according to the older boy, "making like a ladder." An opening appeared and a very tall man emerged. Badly frightened, Gabriel grabbed his younger brother and the two fled to their house. As they raced home on the back of their single horse, Henri looked back and said, "I see a big man coming after us."

According to notes made from the taped interview, the boys described the "man" as being seven or eight feet tall and dressed in a skin-tight, black rubber suit, except for his head. He was well-built and carried in his hand what the boys described as a "machine gun." Apart from their description of the man's "great big round eyes," he was entirely human in appearance, although his black hair "was not combed like the men around here," being cut "differently" and "not very long." These details correspond neatly with the New Berlin UFOnauts.

The interesting thing about the Hemmingford sighting is that while no further observations of the "tall man" were made, Mrs. Coupal reported that the object remained in the vicinity for more than an hour following the boys' initial encounter, apparently touched down briefly several times in the neighborhood. It was observed by a large number of people, including Mr. C.E. Petch, a Hemmingford agronomist, and Mr. and Mrs. Douglas Laurie, over whose home the object briefly hovered. Further, Mr. Petch, examining one of the reported landing sites, told of finding traces in the ground and skid marks in the grass.

Regarding the specific activity of the New Berlin Ufonauts — that is, the lengthy repair of a particular unit believed by the witness to be some kind of "power source" — an examination of the UFO occupant literature so far fails to disclose a reference in which similar activities have been reported in such detail. (Perhaps a reader of this report can provide an appropriate example.) There are numerous reports of observations, however, in which the reported Ufonauts appeared to be engaged in some general or unspecified kind of "work" on or near an unidentified object.

Near Joyceville, Ontario, for example, a Toronto resident named Stanley Moxon was reported to have observed two small, white-clad "men" near a landed object while he was driving in the area on the night of August 23, 1967. The Ufonauts "seemed to be at work around their machine," press accounts relate (4). While Moxon was maneuvering his car so that he could throw the headlights on the scene, the little men, ceased their "work" and quickly entered the object, which then ascended at high velocity. If their "work" was mechanical repair of the type reported at New Berlin, the press accounts fail to specify it.

It might be fairly asked if the details mentioned in the above cases that correspond to those in the New Berlin report could have been "borrowed" in order to enhance the credibility of the latter case, or for some other reason. This is not at all likely, as far as this reporter is concerned. The Hemmingford case has not been reported in any detail in any of the available UFO literature in this country. It is improbable that Mrs. Merryweather would have had access to these particular details, even if she was familiar with the UFO literature. (She is not.) Furthermore, it makes little sense to select only isolated details from certain cases as supportive data for an allegedly fabricated report: each case is quite distinctly different in its overall circumstances and the variations are actually more notable than comparisons. Most important, however, based upon my own familiarity with the primary witness in the New Berlin case, it is simply not within her character or dispostion to have "borrowed" isolated details from other reports to use as a basis for creating a false story of her own.

The significance (if any) of comparing certain details from the above references to similar features in the New Berlin case remains uncertain. No clear-cut patterns can be derived from such tenuous and isolated comparisons. On the other hand, how will we ever begin to understand what potential significance is contained in these data if they are ignored or overlooked?

NOTES

1. Lawton (Okla.) **Morning Press,** Thursday, March 24, 1966.
2. Huntington (P.Q.— **The Gleaner,** Wednesday, August 18, 1954.

3. Interview with witnesses by Dr. Adolph Ditmar, August 28, 1954.
4. Kingston (Ont.) Whig-Standard, Thursday, August 24, 1967.

PART III
NEW BERLIN UFO LANDING AND REPAIR BY CREW

A Psychiatric-Paranormal Survey of the Principal Witness

Ted Bloecher, pioneer UFO investigator, recently reported a spectacular UFO landing and repair by its crew in New Berlin, New York, on November 25, 1964 (1). In 1973, Bloecher conducted several interviews of the people involved, including a face-to-face meeting with the chief witness, a 29-year-old housewife, Mrs. M.† These data were supplemented by telephone interviews and letters. The UFO experience, which also partially involved Mrs. M's mother-in-law, was observed over four hours while two crews from the grounded UFOs — "a group of perhaps as many as a dozen men" — "repaired" one of the craft.

Bloecher's investigation consists chiefly of Mrs. M's narrative, a map, drawings, and an addendum of questions and commentary. Among much interesting information, Bloecher mentioned an artifact found by the witness at the landing site, shortly after the incident. It was Bloecher's impression that the witness and her family were credible. However, because of the uniqueness of the experience, the M family avoided all publicity and discussed the incident with no more than a dozen people, most of whom were family or close friends.

Because Bloecher appreciated the possible value of collateral psychiatric study in cases such as this, arrangements were made for interviews of Mrs. M. who was seen on August 16, 1973 in her home in rural Pennsylvania. At that time all the facts of the landing and repair were confirmed during both direct interviews and hypnotic regression. The visit lasted four hours and most of the material was tape-recorded. The data that follow were also expanded by written material and during an extended phone call on June 19, 1974.

Mrs. M's description of the two landed UFOs, the entities, and the strange goings-on is similar to many reported worldwide observations (2). Psychiatric examinations were conducted in the patient's rural home and showed her to be a healthy, open, straightforward young woman. She stuck to her story and presented a well-organized account.

† (The pseudonym "Merryweather" was used by Ted Bloecher in his report to FSR — EDITOR).

182

When her data from disparate sources and times were reviewed there were no inconsistencies (3). She frequently laughed when elaborating on some of the details, such as the ufonauts attempting to repair the craft, handling the tool boxes, cables, etc. She said she was more curious than frightened.

Aside from Mrs. M's recalling previous (and one more recent) UFO experiences (4) there were few other clues to this study; and if the interview had been terminated at this point, one would have concluded that there was nothing more to be gained by further questioning. However, a combined psychiatric-paranormal survey quickly uprooted data, which had been shut off initially, and which yielded a picture that led to surprises and that had possible relevance to the UFO experiences.

First, the UFO sighting happened on the wedding anniversary of Mrs. M's father and mother, and at the Thanksgiving holiday. Mrs. M made little of these connections, and aside from this, it appeared that there was nothing of deep personal significance, actual or symbolic, that immediately preceded or which led up to the sighting.

At the time of the landing her husband and father-in-law were away hunting and she and her mother-in-law were staying up to watch a late TV show — a musical. According to Mrs. M, an unidentified auto and passengers, at an early stage of the sighting also witnessed some of the strange goings-on. Her dog "Lady" was frightened. Also, Mrs. M. felt that the entities had seen her because an outside light that was on the house was red, she had a red bathrobe on, and it was very clear that night. Most of her observation was done with field glasses. Mrs. M. is near-sighted, but at the time of her experience she had fully corrected spectacles. She and her mother-in-law decided not to call the authorities and possibly cause a row and obtain unwanted notoriety.

The next day Mrs. M was joshed by her husband and father-in-law, but she and her husband walked up to the alleged landing site and found equilateral-triangle impressions in the ground. They searched for the cable artifact, which George (pseudonym for her husband) found and placed in his mother's house for safekeeping. Although George is a chemical engineer, he did not press for analysis of the "cable"; "It looked like thin aluminum strips that were small, maybe a 1/16th of an inch, flat, and there seemed to be an insulation, like strips of paper. The strips were parallel to the cable. They didn't feel like aluminum. It was light." Although the family searched for the artifact, they have yet to find it (June 19, 1974).

Family History

Both Mrs. M's parents were of old American stock. Her father, an only child, high school graduate, and successful farmer, could not attend college because he had to care for his father who was ill. He was described as a widely read man. Mrs. M. recalled many episodes of everyday telepathy between her father and mother. Her father's temper was recalled as "even." He attended a nondenominational Christian church. Her paternal grandfather had died when Mrs. M. was eleven. She was very much attached to him, and more will be said about him later. The paternal grandmother had died of breast cancer in 1971. Mrs. M felt that she was never particularly close to her: "She wanted me to be perfect." Since the death of the grandmother, Mrs. M. has felt some kind of forgiveness from her grandmother; e.g., "She wasn't given time to let us know how she loved us — she wanted to talk to us."

Mrs. M considered her mother, a college graduate who majored in history and once taught high school, a very intelligent woman. The mother was the second oldest of eleven children, and her family was poor. Mrs. M recalled many episodes of telepathy between her mother and herself. For example, when Mrs. M was washing dishes in the kitchen and the mother was sitting in the living room wanting a pair of sewing scissors, Mrs. M got them for her. The mother was described as "terrific at finding lost things for her husband." The mother is an Episcopalian.

Interestingly, Mrs. M's mother and father had a common seventh-or-eighth generation ancestor who was a citizen of colonial Massachusetts and who had been tried and acquitted of being a witch. In her associations Mrs. M. compared her personality to her parents' personalities and presumably to "the witch ancestor" when she said that: "she knew what she liked and didn't like a strong personality."

Mrs. M has a fraternal twin who is five minutes younger. She is closely attached to him. He is a farmer and, with his family, lives near his parents. She recalled her father's oft-repeated comments: "One of us would answer a question that the other twin had not asked verbally. This happened many times — we also seemed to know when one of us was hurt or in danger." She also has a brother two years older who had been married, divorced, and remarried. This brother, a music teacher, has perfect pitch and is left-handed.

Mrs. M left college after the third semester to marry her husband, an agnostic, who was then a student at a technical institute. He is old Colonial stock on his mother's side and of German-French extraction on his father's side. At the time of deciding whether to marry her husband she was going with another man of whom her parents disapproved. One day when Mrs. M and George (her future husband) were talking about getting married: "Grandpa [paternal] appeared in an unusual light in the dining room. It was a white light that spread out, and as it spread out

I could see him standing there in white robes. I was surprised. He was smiling at me. I interpreted it as being that he approved of George and it was a comfort to me." Mrs. M had not had any psi experiences with her husband unless one includes the alleged haunting, which is described below.

At the time of the UFO landing/entities experience, Mrs. M, age 20, had been married for one year. She was not pregnant (5). In the subsequent years and at the time of the psychiatric study (1973), she had a son, age 6, a daughter, age 5, and infant daughter whom she described as "exactly like me". The pregnancies and deliveries were uncomplicated. The children were born through natural childbirth. Mrs. M noted many family instances of possible parent-child telepathy (6).

Some psychodynamically significant facts of Mrs. M's life included dissociative traits like sleepwalking and sleeptalking. She denied automatisms; e.g., "I hate the ouija board, and it won't work for me." Prior to the interview, she had never been hypnotized.

She had attended several schools and was a good student. Both parents handled the discipline: "The worst thing a child could do was lie. There was never any deception. But we were punished for being inventive. If there was a lie, we'd sit down together and talk about it. Mother and Father's kindness was the discipline." She enjoys singing and can play the piano and the guitar by ear. She had been molested twice as a youngster: "It crops up as a ghost, every now and then."

Significant Past Experiences

1. In her childhood Mrs. M had a tonsillectomy under ether anaesthesia: "It was a black void and I could see sheets of metal all crumpled — awful scared — it accelerated — changed directions, but was nothing like the drone, or in other ways like the [UFO] experience."

2. *Out of Body* (7): Once, on a Christmas day, at age 15, Mrs. M had a severe asthmatic attack and bronchial pneumonia. Her parents were very concerned. She recalled how she was propped up in bed, with a vaporizer on. Suddenly: "I couldn't breathe and nothing seemed to matter. I didn't pass out, but — I came out of body. I stood on the floor by the bed and looked at myself. I gazed around the room, walls, and ceiling which then seemed to disappear as I began to travel. I went to the right and I was up higher than the house. I wasn't travelling distance as much as I was travelling space and time, and I could see both where I had come from and where I was going.

Then there was a light, off in the distance. It was growing larger, and in that light I could see people working. They were dressed in white robes. My grandfather was there and he was also dressed in a white

185

robe. He seemed to be in the forefront, closer to me than the people who were working in the background. He seemed to be waiting for me, but he was not smiling. I stopped halfway between where I was going and where I had come from. There was music, such as I had never heard before in all my life. I looked back and thought 'Dead, you know.' I turned around and looked back again at Grandpa and where I was going. Then a man stepped up behind me and took hold of my right shoulder with his right hand and wouldn't let me turn around. I started to turn to look at him, and I could feel the light from behind me as if it were emanating from the person, as he said to me, 'You may go there [death], or you may go back [life], but if you go back I have work for you to do, and your life won't be easy for you.' I made up my mind to come back, and Grandpa seemed to turn around and go off.

I came directly back — at once. Next, I was standing beside the bed and I was getting into myself. It hurt to get back in my body. I did not seem to be asleep any of this time. I don't remember not being conscious of where I was or what I was doing. When I got back into my body, there was a little struggle to start breathing again, but I began. I've never forgotten that experience. I told my mother and father and later my husband about it. I think I died. Years later, when I got my (Mormon) blessing from the Patriarch, he said almost the same words to me that happened in this experience."

3. *Mormon Church*: One year after the UFO landing, Mrs. M joined the Mormon Church. "When I was investigating the Church, I spoke to the elders about it [UFO experience]. I became a Mormon because the church is true." She did not elaborate on this but felt that her conversion was unrelated to her UFO experience. Interestingly, Joseph Smith, the founder of Mormonism came from Elmira, which is close to Mrs. M's childhood home. Her statement was in contrast to some reported analogies between reputed contactee experiences and Mormonism (8). Much of her interest in genealogy was compatible with the tenets of the church in this regard. She said that since joining the Mormons: "People who are close to me never have anything bad happen to them. For example, I have been involved in many situations where a horrible auto accident should have happened, but it didn't. I don't consider myself superstitious. I believe we're in the millennium and Armageddon is approaching."

4. *The Good Samaritan*: "My Patriarchal blessing tells me that people will come to me for advice and I will be able to give them wise and sound counsel. Many times I've had total strangers come up to me and ask things that are very personal, and I've been able to help them. I feel I've been chosen for this.

"I particularly remember one incident. A woman came up to me in a motel lobby in Maryland and asked, 'Are you staying here at the motel?' I said, 'Yes, I am.' She said, 'Well, my husband works for the chemical plant and we're staying here.' She then remarked on what a beautiful day it was, and then said to me, 'I have a problem. And I'd like to have your help.' You could have pushed me over with a feather when she asked me this.

"So she came to my room, and we sat down and had lunch while she told me about her problem. It was very personal. 'Could you give me sound advice?' she asked. I thought about it for a few minutes, and although I can't remember what I told her or what her problem was, she looked at me in tears and said, 'Thank you. Now I know that's what I should do.'"

5. *Haunted Apartment:* Two years after her UFO experience, when the husband was attending college, they lived in a five-apartment building and she recalled a possible haunting there. On occasions, when Mrs. M was home alone, she would hear sounds like marbles being rolled across the kitchen floor. Although she checked everything out, she could not find an explanation. Her husband scoffed at this until one day when he also heard the sound. He grinned and said, "Your friend is back!" He listened, went into the kitchen, turned on the lights, and it stopped!

On numerous occasions she also heard something like a broom handle being bumped against the ceiling (or her floor) downstairs. This annoyed her because she was the only one in the apartment at the time, and she could never find an explanation. She complained about this to her husband who also subsequently heard it. Finally, the sounds went away.

6. *Missing Objects:* Like her mother, Mrs. M was also gifted in finding missing objects. "Once, Dad lost the string and shock assembly from the hay mower. This is an essential part that is needed for loading and baling. Dad and my brothers searched for it and couldn't find it. Mother, who was good at finding missing objects in her own right, couldn't go, so she told Dad to ask me to see if I could help. So he told me where he had worked last, and I began to walk around. I then asked my twin to get in the truck with me and drive around the field. Suddenly I said, 'Stop.' And there it was, down in the field."

She also recalled: "Material for genealogical research has appeared out of thin air. Once, in Baton Rouge, I was grabbing a heavy county record book when it fell off the shelf and opened to the page that I had been searching for, for over two years — it had all the information I needed about my mother's grandparents."

7. *Haunted House:* A later haunting, in her current country home

and years after the sighting, concerned the alleged ghost of the former owner who in life was supposedly very fond of the house, to which he had built an extension. She recalled these episodes:

"I'd bolt the cellar door so that my son wouldn't fall down the stairs, and yet I'd find the door open. This happened repeatedly and would make me very mad. Also the other doors would be open and the cellar lights would be on. And the radio went on once. Also, once when George went to work and left the radio on, I heard a man's voice say: 'Helen (pseudonym).' It sounded as though it came out of the hi-fi set, yet that wasn't on! At that time the kids were looking up and smiling as if they saw something. On another occasion, the children were looking at a picture of my paternal grandfather which was given to me by my mother. David, who had just learned to talk, said: 'That's Grandpa Stark (pseudonym).' I asked, 'How do you know?' He replied, 'Oh, we saw him (phantom?).'"

Mrs. M. continued: "Mr. Campbell (ghost) bothered me. He hounded me if I didn't open the draperies. Every time I went into the room, he'd do this to me — as if somebody was taking hold of me. If I opened up the draperies, I had a feeling he would leave. One day I played a game with the draperies. I made the bed and closed them, but after one or two minutes I felt as if someone were standing in the room and wanted me to open the drapes. I did so and the feeling left.

"I'd also find the lights on in the middle of the night both outside and inside the house. The neighbors would report this when we came back from a trip to town. One day I went to the store while a neighboring girl came to sew. She saw a man disappearing into the guest room. He was dressed in gray pants, brown shoes and a plaid shirt. It scared her to death. I came home, she was not there, and the back door, which was previously locked was open."

Nearly one year later (June 19, 1974), Mrs. M. reported further evidence for the haunting: "Our 'friend' turned all the lights out and left the doors open."

8. Strange Phone Calls: Mrs. M recalled receiving strange phone calls prior to the UFO-landing experience. Once, before her marriage, a man's voice asked her name, age, and whether or not she was married and had children: "Like statistical data — there was no reason for it. I don't know why I even answered him. Usually I just say 'you have the wrong number' and hang up. He was polite. The last time this happened the man had a Scottish accent. I did not have any idea who he was. He asked me questions: I can't remember it all, but it seemed to be connected and have some purpose."

9. Phantom Driver: "While driving on the highway to Kingston,

New York, I saw a car behind me in my rear-view mirror — I could see her — a middle aged woman, and her face was blanked out. I felt awful and thought she was going to die. It was horrible (9)."

10. *Premonitions:* "I get odd feelings about people — even premonitions about myself. For example, one summer, when we were in high school, my twin brother and I decided to go to the Vermont State Fair. I looked forward to this, and we made plans to go with our older brother and his wife. The night before I couldn't go to sleep — I felt funny — and began to cry for no reason. I cried and cried. I woke up two or three times and decided that Bill and I couldn't go because we would be killed. I was sure of it. I went downstairs and told Mother. Bill came in and asked, 'Why not?' I said, 'Something is going to happen today and we'll be killed.' He asked if it was all right for our older brother Johnny and his wife Susie to go. I said sure, but we couldn't. Bill accepted it, 'OK, we're not going, and don't feel bad.' Of course I was in tears and disappointed. It was awful. My father said, 'Now, daughter, don't feel bad. When you have a premonition like that, obey it.'"

Mrs. M recalled hearing how, once during her father's courtship of her mother, a premonition he had was verified by a near-fatal auto accident.

11. *Animals:* "When I was a girl, wild cats would come to me that never went to anyone else. Also, when I'd walk through the woods, I could approach the deer, and they would just stand there and look at me. It's strange. I don't know why. Dogs would like me too. They don't continuously bark at me (when they do at other people). Never did a dog bite me. There is a dog down here who won't even go to the people who own her, but I'll call her and she'll come right to me."

12. *Confirmation through Hypnosis:* A deep hypnotic trance was quickly obtained (10). Mrs. M relived the UFO — landing experience and invoked the essential details. While entranced, Mrs. M noted that the entities were Caucasian, they wore dark suits, and one of them had blonde hair.

13. *Motion Pictures and Thoughtography:* Although Mrs. M was unfamiliar with thoughtography (11) and had no memory of possible "spirit" pictures in the old family album, among snapshots, and the like, she recalled some recent developments (telephone conversation June 19, 1974) where two different friends of hers "accidentally took clear pictures of an airplane in the clouds and got back (1) a picture of a white-robed man and (2) on a separate occasion when a camera was aimed at and snapped a clear sky, and a different person developed the film, the print was of Christ in white robes."

She promised to try to locate the material and sent it for study. Her

189

results are not unlike the description of Jesus appearing on a turned-off television set, and some of Mrs. Lansing's work (12).

In conjunction with techniques used by contactee Mrs. Stella Lansing, motion pictures were made of Mrs. M, her children, pets, and the inside and outside of the house. A frame-by-frame analysis of the films revealed nothing unusual. It can be speculated that the results might have been different had the pictures been taken by Mrs. Lansing, in view of her past results when others who were simultaneous filming usually failed.

14. Parting Shot: When I was leaving Mrs. M, she pointed out a house some distance down the road and told me how she always detested that house and always associated it with bad news, until one day she told her girlfriend about her feeling. The girlfriend, who knew something of Mrs. M's paranormal experiences, howled with laughter. Finally, she blushingly informed Mrs. M that the cozy country home was once a bordello where one of the ladies of the evening was murdered by an ungrateful patron.

15. Coincidences, or Red Herrings in the Psychic Nexus: After procrastinating about setting up an appointment to visit Mrs. M in her home, I had finally resolved to go on the day which was the birthday of my late mother. My two consultations in practice (Montclair, N.J.) on days immediately before this date, oddly enough, originally came from the same remote area where Mrs. M lived, and where I had never been before. These patients were completely familiar with Lake Trilby (fictitious name), where Mrs. M lived, and even gave me directions on how to get there. Of course they knew nothing of my forthcoming trip, researches, etc.

The credibility of Mrs. M was generously affirmed by another coincidence. It developed that a cousin of Mrs. M's husband lived in the town next to mine and the cousin's wife was well known to my wife. Later, by force of circumstances she was nominated by my wife to a position on the local school board. The cousin and his wife were very close to Mrs. M and her family, and without their knowing what I was seeking they completely supported Mrs. M's credibility. At the time of my questioning, the cousin and his wife had no knowledge of Mrs. M's previous UFO-entities experiences. It is not unlikely that many "coincidences" that are observed in the emotionally charged investigations of UFO cases are actually part of the psychic (telepathic) nexus (13) and have no direct relation to the UFO event itself, but might act as a red herring.

Discussion

A psychiatric-paranormal survey of Mrs. M raises many questions that might throw light on the otherwise inexplicable UFO-entities experience. The credibility of the leading experient is supported. There was no evidence for psychosis, delusions, dishonesty, lying, fabrication, or exaggeration.

Could Mrs. M's UFO experience have been solely the product of psychodynamic forces? This critique is unanswerable. Clinically, that is unlikely, because of the involvement of other witnesses, including her dog's response, and the physical evidence noted the next day. If her UFO experience was solely psychopathologically predetermined, we would need a positive concentration of emotionally significant events and, for such a unique experience, a precipitating cause, something more specific than the tangential fact that the episode occurred on the wedding anniversary of her parents. Furthermore, there was no past history for any striking UFO experiences or interest in such events.

Her previous psychodynamic structure, however, is helpful in explaining the quality of her reaction: the way she manages anxiety. From what we know of the mother-in-law, we can speculate that it would be unusual for her to have had a folie a deux reaction develop acutely during the UFO experience. This is not a clinically plausible explanation for what happened. The mother-in-law, according to Mrs. M, was never hypnotized, never had any emotional or psychosomatic illnesses, nor major dissociative reactions. Furthermore, upon questioning of Mrs. M, it did not seem that the mother-in-law was hypersuggestible.

Although the existent psychodynamic data are inconclusive, and it would be desirable to have had many additional sessions with Mrs. M, there might be clues in the psi events of her life. These data, which were prominent in the interview, might be analogous to data in other reported UFO cases (14) that were studied via combined psychiatric-psi techniques.

What is the significance of the various alleged psi experiences happening before the UFO event? After the UFO event? Could the UFO experience itself have been a psychic experience with projected telepathic hallucinations and materialization from the experient? If so, this would be a unique and more spectacular event than anything I have ever come across in studies of gifted paragnosts and telepathists.

Could Mrs. M (and her mother-in-law) have been psychically attuned to these events by the UFOs and entities, whereas other people would not perceive them? Could Mrs. M see or have experiences with another dimension that most others are oblivious to, or perhaps only dimly aware of? What is the source of the psi (?) force — human or UFO-

191

engendered — that could be common to both, and how much of its employment, if any, is dependent upon the psychobiological nature of the experient? Is Mrs. M different from other close-encounter UFO witnesses, and if so, in what ways?

What purpose is served by the UFO-entities' form of dramatization? What is the meaning behind the communication? Is it part of some stratagem that is related to psi and to the other odd experiences like the possible MIB, phone calls; or is it all coincidence? Why was Mrs. M "chosen"? Was she conditioned for her UFO experience via past dissociative behavior as later illustrated by her quick affinity for a deep hypnotic trance? Was her UFO experience a paranormal psychodynamic interaction and the product of entrancement? Was she prepared for this spectacular event by many previous narrow escapes from death (e.g., molestation as a child, fearful early experience with ether anasthesia, fear of suffocation in an asthmatic attack, auto near-disasters, etc.)? How reliable and how relevant to the UFO experience is her anecdotal evidence for psi, including family telepathy, finding lost objects, premonitions, and psychodynamic, quasi-religious or psi hallucinations (e.g., the white-cloaked grandfather), unusual rapport with wild or hostile animals, and hauntings before and after the experience? What are the UFO implications of having a permissive family attitude for psi?

Would collaborative psychiatric research (15), which has been successful in elucidating various behavioral and psychosomatic conditions, be helpful in pinpointing the origin and genesis of Mrs. M's UFO experience and in defining the UFO — psi interface? For example, was Mrs. M's decision to become a Mormon influenced by her experiential, psi and UFO background factors, or were her later religious proclivities an inevitable part of her life style and of the same stuff as the formative (and UFO?) experiences that influenced Mormonism's founder Joseph Smith? It would not seem unusual for such an awesome event as Mrs. M's UFO-entities experience to invoke a religious type of reaction. Other contactees have had this type reaction.

Judging from clinical experiences, there are probably many other significant events that we do not know about and which Mrs. M did not or could not (repression) recall, but which would be helpful. Because of insufficient data, it is impossible to state if there was an apparent augmentation or awareness for psi following her UFO experience. However, it is hard to escape the conviction that in some way psi is definitely related to the UFO-entities event, that all is not coincidence, and for all that one knows, the statement by Mrs. M about herself at one point in the interview, that she has a "mission in life," might be as good an explanation as any.

More Questions and Conclusions

If Mrs. M's UFO experience was "designed" to inspire her with a missionary zeal, as has happened to other contactees, why has it not "worked" for her in this way, and for what deeper reasons other than to avoid notoriety has she avoided telling many people about her experience? What is the relationship between her two previous and later UFO experiences and this one? Perhaps much more data than were derived from one consultation would supply sufficient clues to better define the issues.

If this study, including all the alleged psi, were analyzed without the history for the UFO experience, it would not be unusual. Through the years I have studied many people who are healthy (and otherwise) who have had life-cyle-psi experiences on the order reported here. Thus, psi per se should not be overestimated. Situations like this, as in the instance of Mrs. Stella Lansing, the lady who has photographed many UFO's on motion pictures, are best followed over a long period of time. Undoubtedly, other clinical experiments could be devised. However, there is always the difficulty of applying suitable clinical controls that would help in assessing the credibility of the contactee and the validity and interpretation of the experience.

Perhaps the New Berlin landing and repair case, as well as other similar reports, would justify speculation about what might be found if psychiatric studies, including paranormal surveys, were a routine and necessary part of the evaluation of contactees.

NOTES AND REFERENCES

1. Bloecher, T.: author of **Report on the UFO Wave of 1947,** copyright 1967; "Report on UFO Landing and Repair by crew, New Berlin, New York, November 25, 1964," submitted to FSR (and published in Vol. 20, Nos. 2 and 3 — Editor).

2. Bowen, Charles, Editor: **The Humanoids,** Neville Spearman, Ltd., London, 1969, and the Henry Regnery Co., Chicago, 1970 and 1975.

3. There were no indications of major psychopathology or impairment of health, from Mrs. M's answers to the Cornell Medical Index Questionnaire, The Rotter Incomplete Sentences Blank, and the computerized Minnesota Multiphasic Personality Test. Her positive traits on the latter test were described as "adventurous, frank, individualistic, socially forward, enthusiastic, generous, fair-minded, verbally fluent." The test also indicated that her feelings are easily hurt and that she reacts against others who suppress her individuality or independent thinking.

4. One bright sunny summer day, when Mrs. M was approximately twelve years old, she was lying on the ground and noticed "an odd silvery object with no vapor trail, that rapidly moved from horizon to horizon, within thirty seconds. There was no sound. It was so odd that I told my parents.

No one else knew about this." This event occurred before the out-of-body experience (see note 8).

Another time, when coming home from her second year at college, at 3:00 p.m., on a clear day, in Cortland, New York, Mrs. M came upon many excited people who: "... with the police, had been watching a cigar-shaped vehicle, large and silvery. It came straight down, assumed a vertical position, and little chips came out. It was very low, had a hardly audible drone. After a while it assumed a horizontal position, the chips went back in, and it shot away at a terrific speed, at an odd angle." Although she didn't witness this event, she was impressed. She never read anything about UFOs, other than occasional newspaper articles.

Although she has had no personal experiences since the New Berlin landing, she recalled: "There was a rash of sightings in January and March of 1974. Truckers stopped at the foot of the hill and by my house, and at dawn lots of people were watching peculiar colors, which circled around like the flashing light on top of police cars. There was also reported interference with automobiles. I myself heard peculiar hums and loud noises at the time that some neighbors were seeing odd things in the sky."

5. Schwarz, B.E.: "UFOs in New Jersey", **The Journal** of the Medical Society of New Jersey, Vol. 66:460, 1969.
6. Schwarz, B.E.: **Parent-Child Telepathy:** A study of the Telepathy of Everyday Life, Garrett Publications, New York, 1971.

7. An out-of-body experience that I recently studied pertains to Karen, a young woman who recalled: "A group of friends got together. They had a stone house in the Ponoco Mountains (Pa.) I wanted to be at the party very much but couldn't go. I was ill in Blairstown, New Jersey, and fell asleep, but I dreamed I was at the party. I walked in the front door and all the people knew me. One man was on the floor and I almost tripped on him. He said, 'Sorry, I didn't see you coming in.' The next day I went up to visit my friends and the man recounted the same story and how I practically tripped over him. I left my body. The dream was real colorful. The man was certain that I was there in fact, when this was not the case, and many others could prove it. He was the one who brought up the experience."

This woman had one other striking out-of-body experience but never any unusual psi or UFO episodes. Some contactee events seem superficially similar to out-of-the-body reactions: e.g., the possible materialization of humanoids or creatures, traveling to another planet, or the reverse, where ufonauts allegedly appear transparent, can glide through walls, etc. The study of out-of-the-body and some contactee experiences and their interacting influences might seem to be a neglected but rewarding area for research in ufology.

8. Keel, J.A.: **UFOs: Operation Trojan Horse,** G.P. Putnam Sons, New York, 1970.

9. In the early days of her contacteeship, Mrs. Stella Lansing recalled how on one occasion cars drove around the main street of her home town. This went on for a length of time and she was taken by the unreal, empty expressions on the unrecognizable faces of he drivers. Although a small town, where she would usually see familiar faces, this time was different; they were all unfamiliar. Even though this data has the drawbacks of any

anecdotal material, such a depersonalization reaction is not uncommon clinical acompaniment to states of anxiety and depression. One might wonder if some of these examples could work the other way also, and have a valid paranomal or UFO-related nuclear connection. It is a fruitful area for careful investigation.

10. As has been true with several other extraordinary contactees I have worked with, I was impressed with the case of rapidly inducing a deep hypnotic trance, or the tendency for the contactee to almost become spontaneously entranced (see my "Berserk: A UFO-Creature Encounter", published in FSR Vol. 20, No. 1). Perhaps this is analogous to Frankel's observation that the patient "experiences the major part of his symptoms when in a state that is comparable to marked hypnotic responsiveness. The spontaneous intrapsychic events (UFO?) somewhat like hypnosis, could have been evoked in the first instance by the experience of intense fear. This postulates that the event could have been a defense mechanism in which dissociation and distorted sensory perception played a major role. Stated in another way, it is suggested that marked hypnotic responsiveness might be highly important, not only in the treatment of certain clinical problems, but also in their etiology." (Frankel, Fred H.: Hypnotizability and Therapy, a paper presented at the American Psychiatric Association's 127th Annual Meeting, Detroit, May 6-10, 1974, and printed in **Psychiatry,** Vol. III, No. II, June 11, 1974, Audio Digest Foundation, 1930 Wilshire Blvd., Suite 700, Los Angeles, Ca. 90057). The subject of contactees and hypnosis would be excellent material for an extended study or article.

11. Eisenbud, Jule: **The World of Ted Serios: "Thoughtgraphic" Studies of an Extraordinary Mind,** Morrow, New York, 1967.

12. Schwarz, B.E.: Beauty in the Night, **Flying Saucer Review,** Vol. 18 (No. 4) 5-9, 1972.

Chapter 10

Berserk: A UFO-Creature Encounter

"The unknown of today is the truth of tomorrow. "

— Flammarion

One September Sunday afternoon I received an unusual phone call from Allen Noe (1), Trustee of S.I.T.U.,† and Stan Gordon, Director of the Westmoreland County UFO Study Group (WCUFOSG). They told me of an exciting and bizarre UFO-creature epidemic that included 79 documented creature cases and two dozen more in process of analysis, then raging in a six county area of western Pennsylvania. My curiosity was thoroughly aroused and I made plans to visit Greensburg in November.

Matters were advanced on October 27, 1973, when during a UFO field trip to Mrs. Stella Lansing's (2-4) in Massachusetts, I received a telephone call from my office in New Jersey to contact Stan Gordon immediately. It concerned a multiple-witness landing-creature case with dangerous overtones.

From Gordon's telephone description of the details I learned that much of the data, including an episode of a presumed fugue for the possible contactee, was taped out in the field. I gave first-aid advice and made arrangements for my visit the following week (November 1-3, 1973). At that time, thanks to Gordon and his group's generosity and co-operation, I listened to all their tapes in connection with this episode and conducted a psychiatric interview of the leading figure as well as interviews with members of the study group and others, including direct contact with ten-year-old fraternal male twins and their siblings, telephone interrogation of a state trooper, and the farmer-contactee's parents. I also read Gordon's excellent written collations.

The local newspaper carried an article on this case, but in this report pseudonyms will be used for the farmer, the witnesses, the police official, and place names.

Introduction

At approximately 10:30 p.m., Thursday, October 25, 1973, Stan Gordon received a call from Trooper Byrne of the State Police. Something unusual had happened on a farm not far from Greensburg. The

---

† Society for the Investigation of the Unexplained, founded by the late Ivan T. Sanderson.

UFO Study Group field team left shortly to investigate the situation. At police headquarters the initial witness, farmer Stephen Pulaski, + stated that Trooper Byrne had also heard something in the woods and that Byrne saw a glowing area at the location where a UFO was reputed to have landed.

Stephen was questioned by the Study Group on the telephone about what had happened, and arrangements were made to meet him and his father at the shopping mall, from where the group could go to the scene of the sighting. The group arrived at the mall at approximately 12:45 a.m., on Friday, October 26, 1973. In the team was David Smith, a physics teacher and a radiation expert in Civil Defense; Dennis Smeltzer, who majored in sociology; George Lutz, Jr., a former Air Force pilot officer, and the co-director of WCUFOSG; David Baker, a photographer, and Stan Gordon. When they arrived, Stephen related the entire experience.

I — Landing and Creatures

At approximately 9:00 p.m., Stephen and at least fifteen other witnesses, including relatives and neighbors, noticed a bright red ball hovering over the field at a fairly high level. Stephen and two neighbor boys (ten-year-old fraternal twins) decided to go up towards the field. Stephen took along a 30.06 rifle. As they were approaching closer, Stephen mentioned that his auto headlights became dim. They could see the object slowly descending towards the field. The three of them walked up over the crest of the hill and saw the object sitting directly on, or hovering just above, the field. As the object was approaching, Stephen's male German shepherd (third generation inbred), at the house, became very disturbed. The object was now bright white and was illuminating the area. The witnesses estimated the object to be about 100 feet in diameter: "It was dome-shaped, just like a big bubble. It was making a sound like a lawn mower."

As they were observing the object, one of the twins yelled that there was something walking along, silhouetted by the fence. Stephen could not see them well (he wears glasses for myopia). Since the first rifle slug was a tracer, he fired directly over the heads of the two figures that he thought at first were bears. As soon as he fired, and was able to see clearly, he knew that the creatures were something strange.

Both creatures were similar in appearance, but one was about 7 feet tall and the other a little over 8 feet. They were observed to be higher than the fence posts which were over 6 feet high. The larger creature's left hand touched and followed along the fence posts. Both creatures

---

+ Referred to as Stephen hereafter.

were completely covered with long, dark grayish (5) hair and they had greenish yellow eyes (6). Their arms hung down almost to the ground. The smaller creature seemed to be taking long strides, as if trying to keep up with the larger one. The creatures were making whining sounds. almost like that of a baby crying. They seemed to be whining back and forth to each other. A strong odor was also present — something like that of burning rubber.

Stephen then fired a second bullet over their heads, realizing that they were different from anything that he had ever seen and also that they were slowly walking towards the trio. He finally fired three rounds directly into the larger one. One of the boys, now quite scared, ran back towards the house. When the creature was hit, it made a whining sound and moved its right hand up towards the other creature, almost touching it, at which time the glowing lighted object just disappeared in the field and the noise from it also stopped.

The creatures, after having been shot at, slowly turned around and walked back towards the woods. Stephen and the remaining twin noticed that on the field, where the object had been, there was a glowing white area, so bright that you could read a newspaper by it. About this time, Stephen's eyes (and those of one of the twins) began to bother him. The bull and the horses would not go near the area after the incident.

II — Trooper Arrivers — More Action

Stephen was reluctant to go to the police to report the incident, but then thought he had better. After the officer heard about the experience (and came to the farm), and at about 9:45 p.m., Trooper Byrne and Stephen got into the patrol car and drove up the dirt road about 100 yards from where the UFO landing was and stopped just below the corn field, near the woods.

The headlights of the trooper's car were shining towards the field and Stephen said the glowing ring was still visible. At first the trooper thought it was from the headlights, but when he moved his car the ring was still visible. The trooper also shone his flashlight into the bright ring and the beam could hardly be seen. They walked down to a double-stranded electric fence, where the trooper noted that the bottom wire was broken. He asked Stephen about it, who stated that to his knowledge it was not broken before.

Then, about 50 yards to the right they heard a loud walking noise in the woods. The sound of something large appeared to be coming towards them. They could hear trees being torn and breaking. When they moved, the noise would follow, and when they stopped it would continue a few seconds and then stop. The trooper saw a small saddle in

198

the field and about 100 yards to the left there was an illuminated area about 150 feet in diameter. The house was about 250 yards away from the craft and a mercury lamp was in the area, but neither could reflect into that locale. According to Stephen, the trooper was already in the car and they were both quite scared.

The trooper said he wanted to walk up towards the lighted area. But, as he and the trooper got within about 200 yards of it, Stephen stopped and told the trooper: "I don't get paid for being brave. I'm not going any further." The trooper started ahead on his own and then decided it was better for him to go back since Stephen was very excited and might mistake him for something else. He then told Stephen that he would go back to the barracks and call Stan Gordon, who would come up if there was something to it.

At this point, when they started back towards the car, they again heard the movements in the woods. By this time they had been in the area about half an hour. The trooper said that when they got back in the car he was going to turn off his headlights to see if the glowing area would disappear. The trooper got into the car. Stephen then noticed a brown object coming towards them and he wanted to shoot his last round to see if anything would happen. The trooper said it was OK to do so. Stephen then fired his one remaining bullet.

While the trooper was standing at the patrol car door, he noted how Stephen was very upset, perspiring, and pale. Stephen's actions and appearance began to get the trooper worked up. Stephen suddenly yelled that something was coming out of the woods towards them. They both jumped into the car and the trooper drove about 50 yards out of the field when he came to his senses and realized that he was in the safety of the car. He turned the car around and shone the high beam of the headlights into the woods. No sound could be detected at this point.

Later, the trooper described a soft glowing area about 150 feet in diameter. In the glow he could make out small plants. The glow extended about a foot up from the ground and the trooper guessed that if you bent down you could probably read a newspaper by the light. The trooper would not say definitely that it was a circular area, since they were on a slanted strip of land. He said that he did not know for certain if the light was from his headlights or not. He felt that when they were in the area of the glow, the temperature might have been a little warmer than the surrounding area, but he couldn't be sure of this because of the excitement. He also said that the dogs around the farm were kicking up a fuss and that no animals would go near the area where the glow was, even though they were moving around it. However, Stephen stated that when the trooper turned the car around, the glowing area disappeared.

199

When the trooper looked around, he couldn't see the glowing area any longer. (The next morning when he went out to check over the area, he couldn't find anything unusual.)

III — Study Group Arrives: Furore

It was about 1:30 a.m. when the Study Group arrived at the secluded farm and made their way up the long dirt road which went into the field. Two boys stayed behind in Stephen's truck. The team started to move up the field where Stephen told them the object and the ring had been. There was no ring apparent when they arrived. First they checked the area for radiation. Stephen had been checked at the shopping mall before they left for the scene. No unusual level was observed in either case.

While the team was looking over the field, at approximately 1:45 a.m., both of the Pulaskis (father and son) yelled to them. The group ran down to the truck where they were standing and they related how they had seen the entire farmhouse area light up with a glow. The glow had disappeared when the group arrived, but George Lutz and Mr. Pulaski, Sr., went down to the house to look around. They radioed that nothing was found.

The team and the two Pulaskis walked up from the truck towards the area where the creatures were observed. It was about 2:00 a.m. Suddenly the bull (in a nearby field) was scared by something. Stephen's dog also became alarmed and started tracking something. The dog kept looking at a certain spot by the edge of the woods, but the group didn't see anything. George Lutz was asking Stephen some questions when all of a sudden Stephen began rubbing his head and face. George Lutz asked him if he was OK, and Stephen then began shaking back and forth as if he were going to faint. George Lutz and Mr. Pulaski, Sr., grabbed Stephen. Stephen, aged 22, is over 6'2" tall and weighs around 250 pounds. He then began breathing very heavily and started growling like an animal. He flailed his arms and threw his father and George Lutz to the ground. His dog then ran towards him as if to attack, and Stephen went after the dog. The dog started crying. George Lutz and Mr. Pulaski were calling to Stephen to come back, that it was all right, and that they were returning to the car.

Then, Dennis Smeltzer suddenly said, "Hey, Stan, I'm starting to feel lightheaded." Dennis became very weak and felt faint. His face was pale.

Dave Baker and Dave Smith went over to help Dennis. Then Dave Baker began to complain about having trouble breathing.

During all this, Stephen was running around swinging his arms,

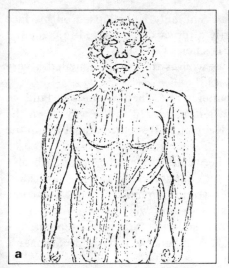

Fig. 1. Study Group artist Bob McCurry's reconstruction of creatures sighted in nearby communities: (a) above left, Latrobe Pa., August, 1973. (b) above right, Beech Hills, August 23, 1973, 2:30 a.m.; (c) below left, Luscon, August 26, 1973, 5:00 p.m.

201

and loudly growling like an animal. Suddenly he collapsed on his face into a heavily manured area. Shortly afterwards he started to come out of it and said, "Get away from me. It's here. Get back."

Just then Stephen and Stan, as well as the others, smelled a very strong sulphur, or chemical-like odor (7).

George Lutz said, "Let's get out of here." Then he and Mr. Pulaski, Sr., were helping Stephen along when, suddenly on the way down the hill, Stephen pointed and yelled: "Keep away from the corner! It's in the corner!"

Stephen kept mumbling that he would protect the group. He also mumbled that he saw a man "in a black hat and cloak, carrying a sickle." He told Stephen, "If Man doesn't straighten up, the end will come soon." He also said, "There is a man here now, who can save the world." Stephen said that he could hear his name — "Stephen. Stephen." — being called from inside the woods. When he collapsed, Stephen's glasses fell off.

On the way down, as Stephen was coming out of his confused state, his father handed him the glasses and Stephen asked whose they were. Stan asked Stephen if he could see OK, and he said, "Just fine."

The group asked Mr. Pulaski if his son had ever acted like this before and he said never. He told them that Stephen had been taking nerve pills (8) since an accident about three years ago.

The group felt that Stephen was part of a contactee syndrome that was involved with future predictions, etc., and they were concerned that Stephen could physically harm himself or others and that professional help was needed.

More Information and Discussion

How can the presumed UFO-and-associated-creatures sighted be related to Stephen's fugue? Although such a brief study as this is not comparable to data derived over an extended period, the uniqueness of Stephen's experience and what we did learn about him from psychiatric study warrant speculation. What might apply to him might also hold for others and provide clues for future studies of such examples.

The unusual circumstances, and the fact that the various segments of events at different times were witnessed by thirteen people, indicate the reality of the experiences. In all instances it seemed that Stephen and the others were truthful. There was no evidence for dishonesty, lying, sociopathic behavior, use of hallucinogenic drugs or alcohol, in connection with this experience or previously. The reports of the various witnesses, family members and neighbors were compatible. Part of the action was tape recorded as it was happening. Specifically, it would seem in "reality" that there were lights which were first low in the sky and then descended to nearly land, or hovered closely above the ground, and which had an associated lawn mower sound; that the UFO might have dimmed the truck's lights; that the brightness of the UFO's lights inflamed the eyes of the two witnesses; and that the action and stench associated with the creatures caused presumed behavioral reactions for the people involved and for dogs, horses, a bull, and cattle. Stephen's story was essentially the same whether given to the UFO Study Group, the trooper, or to me (BES). It was fully corroborated by independent interviews of the other witnesses by the Study Group and by me.

Because Stephen is an experienced hunter, and presumably a good shot, it would seem likely that he did fire three rounds into one of the creatures with the apparent effect of the creature's moaning, lifting its upper extremity, and walking back into the woods with its companion. This happening is confirmed by one of the twin boys who was with Stephen at the time. As in other alleged creature situations (9), it is amazing that after all the action there is such an overall paucity or even a total absence of tangible evidence for the events. In this case there are only broken branches, possibly a strand of interrupted wire, and five rifle shells found on the ground at the site. Although the search was not exhaustive, there were no "bigfoot"prints, blood, hair, scorched earth, or other evidences — unlike some other cases studied. What happened to the creatures? Did they just disappear? How could the source of light, which appeared to be on, or just above the ground, have disappeared without any trace or any indication of its source? Where do these things come from and where do they go?

Stephen's acute fugue with furore is apparently out of context for him. A study of his past life revealed no evidence of any previous similar dissociative, disorientated behavior, nor any character traits like sleep-walking, sleep talking, fainting, amnesia, trance-like states, etc. Furthermore, there is no past history for convulsive disorder, brain injury, or disease, that could cause temporal lobe seizure or automatism analogues to Stephen's reaction to the creatures. The information derived from Stephen, his parents, neighbors and several physicians indicates that the fugue was a specific reaction to the UFO-creatures experience — a solitary, outstanding event in Stephen's life. During the interviews Stephen had no memory of what happened during the fugue.

Farming and coal mining are hazardous occupations. While working in the mines, Stephen had had injuries, including a recent alleged trauma to his right eye, fractures and sprains of the left ankle. Three years ago he had a serious back injury. He had no permanent disability, however, and was never diagnosed "accident prone". Stephen recalled how following his back injury, his physician allegedly told him that he would not live beyond young adulthood. This gloomy prognosis must have disturbed Stephen and, coupled with other events in his past life, made him a good candidate for being (as one physician wrote) "scared to death." Nevertheless, he worked hard and was a "going concern" without any history of fugues or psychosis.

It can be assumed that the trauma and terror, precipitated by the UFO landing and the creatures — by the fact that one of the creatures failed to be killed by the shots fired at close range — nearly unhinged Stephen. The fugue was precipitated when the Study Group was with Stephen on the scene, and about the time of the sudden appearance of the stench. The stench might possibly have been subliminally detected by Stephen and the others just before the fugue, but it was during and after all his going berserk that it was noticed. At that point, all the cascading aspects of the dangers were suddenly realized and he was overwhelmed with anxiety. He lapsed into the fugue, and acted out violently until he collapsed face down upon the manure-strewn ground.

During this part of the psychiatric interview Stephen dangerously tottered between varying planes of entrancement and frequently had to be brought back to consciousness as he supplied more details. "Was it a dream? I heard a crying noise. I could see a man in a black robe, carrying a scythe. Behind this man was fire and in front of him was a force, and in this force were the creatures. They were calling, 'Stephen, Stephen!' One was laughing. It was a tantalizing laugh, and making me mad. My hands were clenched tight. Behind us was a big light. In this light something was telling me to go forward. 'Go forward. Come on!' It was edging me on.' I could see myself as crazy, as a man so powerful that I wasn't scared of anything. The creatures kept calling me and the light kept saying: 'Go, my son, you can't be hurt.' I think of a mother sheep calling her little lambs. As I walked to the edge of the woods, the creatures kept wailing. I looked at them and all I could think of was death and the faceless form in the black robe who was commanding these things to kill me — it was hate . . . a hatred for everything. I knew that these things came from this force and if they got to the light they would be destroyed. The tension was so terrific that I passed out. Then I heard, 'He is here — He is here.' But who is He? Somebody was putting a puzzle in my head. My hands and ankles were hurting. Somebody was telling me that these people are going to destroy themselves. I kept seeing the date 1976 — 1976. It popped out of my mouth: 'If these people don't straighten out, the whole world will burn.'"

When Stephen was asked his opinion about what happened, and why he, a Pennsylvania farmer and coal miner, was chosen for this

Composite sketch of scene of incident, based on Bob McCurry's reconstruction.

experience, he answered: "I'm living in hell now. What I'm telling you happened before. This is how the earth was destroyed. It will be very soon, and this world will be gone. Somebody better find out before long or the world will end. We're destroying the world. What's the fire? What's going to happen is burning. Is there someone smarter than us that is playing upon us, laying a picture or puzzle out for us? It seems stupid but it seems like I *have* to tell the President of the United States, because somebody else has to know. It seems that somebody else is also being told at the same time, but they're not going to do it. They're scared. I don't know what happened in the field, or what these guys told you, but I felt like an animal. If you could find the one who would believe me — 1976 is not far off. I don't believe America is going to live to be 200 years free, because that's been getting to me too. And the world will go. Man will destroy himself."

Might the truest explanation for Stephen's fugue be found in the psycho-dynamics of his past life? Stephen is the oldest of three siblings, the youngest being ten. Life has always meant intense struggle to survive. He claims that since the age of ten he has practically run the farm himself (his father was away from home, driving a truck). In addition to all the chores, Stephen had his school work. He was also involved in frequent fights. He recalled once beating up a bully so badly that the youngster could not return to school for three weeks. One of his few pleasures in high school was being a first-string tackle on the football team; at the time he was 6'2½" tall, and weighed 250 pounds.

Stephen related his story in a serious and somber way. There was little fun in his life. For example, his first memory of his mother was when he was at puberty and she was pregnant with his youngest sibling. In commenting about his desire to be a veterinarian, he said it was only because of the money he might earn, and had nothing to do with humanitarian aspects. He described his father as a rather brutal man given to sudden outbursts of temper. The father nicknamed Stephen "Pooch." Stephen was frequently punished when the father was angry at the younger children, and the punishment was swift and severe: punching in the mouth and beatings. The mother never intervened. Stephen also recalled his father telling how the grandfather was banged and cut up by the Mafia and had to go into hiding for fear of his life. Violence became an important part of Stephen's life. He recalled the time he was driving through a town and saw a fight. He stopped his car, jumped out, started punching. He said that the combatants were amazed that he, a stranger, would subject himself to such risk. He then recalled an episode, with some relish, where an older neighbor made remarks about Stephen's girlfriend (and later wife). When the man entered the house, did $1,700

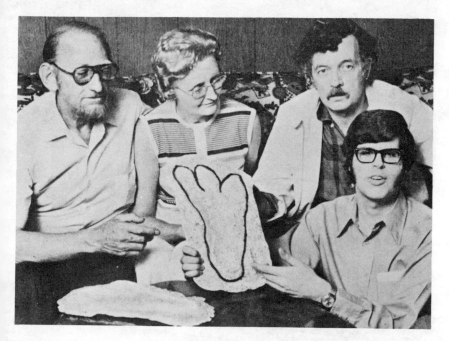

Stan Gordon, of the Westmoreland County UFO Study Group, with plaster case of "bigfoot" print. Behind him, left to right: Robert Jones (SITU member); Mrs. Noe; Al Noe.

damage, and it was known that it would be some time until the police arrived, Stephen, as a last resort, grabbed a rifle and made elaborate plans to shoot the man in the leg and finally to kill him. Tragedy was narrowly averted by the timely arrival of the State Police. His life amibition to enter the military forces was thwarted by an injury to his right leg. Stephen summed up his life by saying: "Everything I tried never ended up right."

Stephen appeared intelligent. Although he was not well read and seldom went beyond the Pennsylvania *Farm Journal*, he could clearly describe various life experiences and his accounts were well thought through and hung together. He had no previous all-consuming interest in UFOs, supposed monster lore, horror films, or such. He was a Roman Catholic but apparently not very devout. His wife is Protestant. His father is of Polish descent and his mother half English-Scottish-Irish and half French. Stephen had no previous interest in religion, prophecy, werewolves, the occult, or any esoteric philosophies. Life meant a grindstone and reality.

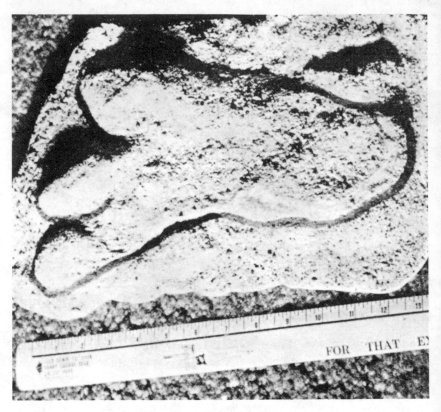

Cast of "bigfoot" print, 13 inches long.

One enigmatic experience happened approximately five to six weeks before the alleged UFO-creature episode, shortly after Stephen and his wife moved to their apartment and had a telephone installed with a private, unlisted number. They received a mysterious phone call in which a man's voice told Stephen that he would be killed if he didn't get out of town in one week. This threat was not taken lightly. Also, shortly after this incident he claimed that the starter wires were pulled on his car. He could account for neither of these experiences. They are mentioned in this report because of the recurring motif of violence through so much of his life and, of course, because of the violent episode under study.

Perhaps these various background factors gave Stephen ample permission for violent acting out as a means of coping with otherwise overwhelming situations. Thus, it was no wonder that Stephen, who could usually succeed by brawn if nothing else, was terrorized by the creatures when they failed to succumb to his shots. It is not unusual under such circumtances for mechanisms of psychic containment — suppression and repressions — to break down completely, and for the patient to lose contact with reality, and for psychosis or fugue to ensue. Furthermore, it is not unusual at such time for the patient to regress via a mechanism of hostile identification with the aggressor — and to take on the posture and characteristics of the aggressor. In this way, the one who was terror-stricken by the trauma (or what associately reminded him of it, or what precipitated the original trauma) defends himself from his own anxiety and fears, and perhaps in Stephen's case, of being unable to kill or *lex talionis*, his fear of being killed in return: "I'm going into those woods to kill them or they'll kill me." This might have accounted for his fugue-like state, when the appearance of the approaching creatures was imminent — either real or otherwise. Stephen lost control and was carried away by his unconscious, and mimicked what he observed the creatures to be: he growled, clawed with his outstretched hands, and made violently flailing movements, which decked one of the investigators, and his father, and culminated in Stephen's collapse. The excitement of what had happened, which was then being relived when the Study Group arrived, was pressed to the breaking point by the appearance of the stench which might have heralded the possible re-entry of the creatures. This was more than Stephen could handle.

In the minds of the Study Group members, the fugue (and as it sounds from the tapes) might have conformed to Stephen's transfiguration or possession by the creatures. That possibility is highly speculative; it can neither be proved nor disproved. His vivid "possession" by the creatures was also similar to some spectacular seance situations in which the entranced medium assumes the alleged personality, expression, voice, etc., of the deceased. However, in those situations other elements are operative, such as histrionics derived from subliminal clues or possibly telepathy from the living, or for that matter, disembodied entities. It is of interest that these creatures, as well as the study group's and artist's reconstructed drawings of other creature cases studied by the UFO group (see Figure 1, for Study Group artist Bob McGurry's reconstructions of creatures in nearby community) might have some resemblance to medieval paintings as werewolves (10). Could the myth of the werewolf (11) as it survives today in the dreams and associated alleged psi phenomena have a germ of truth in past and forgotten UFO-creature cases? If the clock were turned back four centuries, would Stephen be diagnosed as suffering from lycanthropy (12)?

There is an element of psi in many UFO sightings. Stephen's experience has so many bizarre aspects, such as the UFO lights coming and going without any clearly discernible source; strange appearances and disappearances of the creatures with minimal evidence for their continuing existence, that one wonders if the common force in all these events was a UFO-induced psi-effect, and if this influence could in some way, either independently or in conjunction with the psychopathology, have effected the changes in Stephen and accounted for his fugue. Could the UFO and the creatures have materialized or dematerialized into another dimension? How does one prove this? What explanations are there? If materialization were possible, then this could account for many strange happenings and it would not be unusual to anticipate many wild and unheard-of science-fiction-like yet "real" effects.

For example, Pierre van Paassen (13) (the newspaper man) wrote how his German shepherd dogs savagely fought with a poltergeist black hound, until one shepherd dropped dead. If this was so, then why couldn't this be possible with the UFO-associated creatures? As a matter of fact, Stan Gordon and the Study Group have in their files instances where creatures may have killed chickens, ripped off the hindquarters of a St. Bernard dog, and torn the throat of a pet deer. If these experiences are projected (materialized?) by such an unknown force — invasions from another reality — the appearance of the creatures with the UFO could not have been better designed to inspire terror, nor could they have chosen a more suitable subject than Stephen as their Frankenstein to produce a more predictable result. Although one of the creatures was shot, it didn't collapse and there was no tangible evidence of its existence or wounds. Unlike the relatively infrequent examples of the creatures maiming other aminals, the Study Group has no evidence of injuries to human beings. Perhaps this inexplicable fact is similar to the weird events where under favorable conditions and trained observers the entranced Polish medium Kluski allegedly materialized a large bird of prey, a lion, and an anthropoid ape. Like the UFO creatures, these experiences also had associated stenches and in no instance did they harm any present at the seances (14).

The sensational, bizarre, and potentially dangerous significance of the UFO-creature cases, as in this instance, makes it mandatory that the greatest care and responsibility be exercised in collecting and reporting the data.

Careful analysis of each such encounter as Stephen's would seem essential in order to determine whether there is a tenable cause-and-effect relationship or whether it is a coincidence, a hitherto unrecognized expression of florid psychopathology, or some intention from the "UFO force" that one is unaware of and incapable of understanding at this time.

The ideational contents of the warning in the fugue are similar to many reported contactee prophecies and, in Stephen's case at least, might be viewed as part of his psychodynamic makeup. It is more likely that the ideas which were ostensibly from the Man in Black with the sickle actually came from Stephen himself, when confronted with the major life-death threat, rather than that they were implanted from elsewhere (UFO, etc.). In this case there is evidence for the former and not much for the latter, other than a similarity to the oft-repeated gloomy prophecies of contactees, as noted by Keel (15). All these cases of supposed prophecy and other psi phenomena might be profitably studied by the psychiatrist for psi and psychopathology.

The fugue prophecy might be a caricature or projection of Stephen's ambivalence towards his father and of his ready involvement in many fights with victory or defeat, life or death at stake. The portrayal of good and evil was dramatically highlighted in this cruel exchange. It was what Stephen saw and heard — no one else. The group contended with, shared and suffered the reactions to the horror; therefore, it is likely that Stephen's cosmic prophecy of doom and salvation was a projection of his own horror of the moment and of past emotional experiences. This is more likely than the unprovable assumption that it was directly related to some unknown force associated with the UFOs and creatures. But who knows? The latter possibility cannot be completely disavowed when considered with the many documented UFO-psi cases in the worldwide literature.

Perhaps the acceptance of this assumption is similar to the reasoning that favors the ET hypothesis,: viz., because the phenomenon is not explainable by any known technology of Planet Earth, it must come from a different planet. This approach seems to leave out of consideration the vast and impenetrable possibilities of psi. It is analogous to the specious, misinformed reasoning that the psychiatrist sometimes deals with in his consultations, e.g., it is erroneously assumed that because there is no "organic" cause, such as physical signs implicating the patient's cardiovascular system, etc., that the cause must be emotional. The psychiatrist does not make a diagnosis on negatives or absence of evidence. He must have a plausible series of facts, experiences, pattern of reactions, etc. ET versus UT — who knows?

This case is but one of many that Stan Gordon and the Westmoreland County Study Group have documented. More might be speculated about various intriguing aspects, but suffice it to say that this case demonstrates (1) the here-and-now implicit danger to those witnesses who are involved in such an experience, (2) perhaps more so, the dangers to those who study such people, (3) the challenging need for collateral, psychiatric investigations, and (4) the urgent need for a bold but responsible stance in finding out all we can about the UFO-creature relationship.

NOTES AND REFERENCES

1. Noe, Allen, V.: "ABSMAL Affairs in Pennsylvania and Elsewhere," **Pursuit,** Vol. 6 (No. 4): 84-89, Oct., 1973.

2. Schwarz, B.E.: "Stella Lansing's UFO Motion Pictures," **Flying Saucer Review,** Vol. 18 (No. 1): 3-12, Jan./Feb., 1972.

3. Schwarz, B.E.: "Stella Lansing's Movies of Four Entities and Possible UFO," **Flying Saucer Review,** Special Issue No. 5, UFO ENCOUNTERS.

4. Schwarz, B.E.: "Stella Lansing's Clocklike Possible UFO Formations", **Flying Saucer Review:** (for future publication) submitted November 5, 1973.

5. Most of the members of the Study Group, and the witnesses, are thoroughly familiar with the appearance of bears, which are most infrequently seen in the area.

6. The creature's eye colors seem to be a distinctive feature of many reports. The greenish cast may be due to the possible existence of a **tapetum lucidum,** which is found in dogs and some nocturnal animals. For example, cats' eyes glow in a beam of light because of this special tissue, which reflects the light forward and improves the night vision. When the eyes are red, it might be due to the retinal reflex. Whatever the origin of the creatures: e.g., if they are materialized, or have existed in dark caves, completely undetected, etc., it is amazing that witness accounts seem to be consistent on these points, which conform to an anatomical reality that most witnesses would not ordinarily know about.

7. At approximately this time George Lutz was using his carbide lamp which emits the familiar odor of acetylene ($CaC_2 + 2H_2O \rightarrow Ca(OH)^2 + C_2H_2$) which was not confused with the presumed creature stench.

8. In my telephone interview with him, the father did not know the name of Stephen's drugs. At the time of the incident, Stephen said he was not taking any medication. Emergency room visits to his local hospital were for sprain of the left ankle (Feb. 19, 1973) which was recently fractured; for a piece of glass in his eye from an exploding light bulb (April 25, 1973); and situational anxiety in the coal mine where he injured his eye May 29, 1973). He was given a prescription for a mild tranquilizer (Vistar-il, 25 mgs.), and referred to a neurologist. But, first, on his own, he saw an opthalmologist (May 25, 1973) for the alleged eye injury and the physician found no evidence for ocular injury. "The one abnormal finding was a best corrected visual acuity of the right eye of 20/50." The neurologist saw Stephen on July 11, 1973 because of "severe orbital headaches and right temporal pain." The neurologist noted that the patient had previously seen four or five physicians about glass in his right eye. All except one could not find anything. The neurologist's examination revealed the central nervous system to be objectively intact; and an opthalmological exam, aside from conjunctivitis of the right eye, to be within normal limits. He made the diagnosis of severe anxiety neurosis with pain in the right eye. The patient was treated over a period of time with "sedation, analgesics and reassurance." He improved considerably

and returned to work. Here again, is data that might have contributed to Stephen's fugue. He was very vulnerable to any injury or, in particular, ocular disturbance (UFO-induced "eye burn"?).

9. Noe, **op. cit.,** Keel, J.A.: **Strange Creatures from Time and Space,** a Fawcett Gold Medal Book, Greenwich, Conn., 1970, 288 pp.; Clark, J., and Coleman, L.: "Anthropoids, Monsters, and UFOs," **Flying Saucer Review,** Vol. 19 (No. 1): 18-24, Jan./Feb., 1973.

10. Hill, D.: "Werewolf," in **Man, Myth, and Magic: An Illustrated Encyclopedia of the Supernatural,** Marshall Cavendish Corp., New York, 1970, Vol. 22:3008-3012.

11. A fascinating account of the werewolf as it survives in modern man's dreams, with similarities to the data in this report, can be found in pioneer psychoanalyst-parapsychologist Nandor Fodor's **New Approaches to Dream Interpretation,** Citadel, New York, 1951, Chapter 4, "Lycanthropy as a Psychic Mechanism": pp. 146-159.

12. Superficially considered, hypnotic studies, including an attempt at regression (or a sodium pentothal interview), might seem attractive but they were contra-indicated because during this interview with the Study Group, as well as with me, Stephen frequently gave indications of becoming entranced while recalling certain aspects of the creature-MIB sequence. He had to be forcefully called back to consciousness and there was a clear-cut danger of violence under the prevailing conditions and without any opportunity for follow-up treatment, etc. Although of no statistical significance, it is an odd fact that five outstanding male contactees whom I have studied or known about were all loners, or "touch-me-nots." They all seemed to be in excellent physical condition and the kind who would not be trifled with. They all seemed to have good mechanical ability (e.g., could repair motors, etc.) and they were adept in the use of firearms; and, with one exception, they had had past experiences with what might be considered excessive violence (see **FSR Special Issue** No. 2 BEYOND CONDON: 46-52, June, 1969; The **Journal** of the Medical Society of New Jersey, Vol. 66 (No. 8): 460-464, August, 1969; **FSR Special Issue** No. 3 UFO PERCIPIENTS: 20-27 September 1969; FSR Vol. 18 (No. 4): July/August, 1972).

13. van Paassen, Pierre: **Days of Our Years,** Hillman-Curl, Inc., New York, 1936, pp. 248-251. For additional allied phenomena and references see Schwarz, B.E.: "Human-Animal Paranormal Events," **Journal of the American Society of Psychosomatic Dentistry and Medicine,** Vol. 20 (No. 2): 39-53, 1973.

14. Fodor, Nandor: **The Unaccountable,** Award Books, New York, 1968, pp. 121-125.

15. Keel, J.A.: **Operation Trojan Horse,** G.P. Putnam Sons, New York, 1970.

Chapter 11

The Twilight Side of a UFO Encounter

Brent M. Raynes

Seldom are the paranormal mechanics of a UFO encounter as visibly demonstrated as they were in this particular incident, an incident which contained many classic manifestations.

My attention was alerted to this situation at about 6:30 p.m. on Tuesday evening, October 28, 1975, when I received a telephone call from my associate, Mrs. Shirley Fickett of Portland, Maine. Mrs. Fickett excitedly briefed me on an interesting new UFO sighting that had taken place in the early hours of Monday, October 27, near Oxford, Maine. It involved two young men, whom we shall call P, 18, and W, 21, who shared a trailer in Norway. (To protect the witnesses from possibly undesirable feedback we do not use names or even initials.) At about 7:30 p.m. I telephoned W's mother as the young men did not have a telephone at their place. Mrs. W. informed me that the young men were there at her house at the moment and that earlier in the day, when Mrs. Fickett had called them, she suggested that they check the automobile and the young men with a compass, which they did. They found that the needle spun wildly in reaction to the car, and both young men, and even seemed to register a slight reaction with her and her husband. She also told me that they had seen UFOs that evening and, when I indicated a desire to do so, encouraged me to drive up. As soon as I had made arrangements with my friend James Carey of Windsor, and we decided to meet at the Androscoggin County Sheriff's Department in Auburn, where the W family had phoned in a report on the event. I copied the details from their file on the call, and noted that they had telephoned in the data to Dr. J. Allen Hynek's Center for UFO Studies.

At about 9:45 p.m. we arrived at Mr. and Mrs. W's residence in Oxford. The two young men were there, quite visibly shaken and upset, and Mr. and Mrs. W displayed concern over their conditions. Within perhaps a minute of stepping inside the house we were asked if we would like to see a UFO. Naturally we said we would. And as James Carey later wrote for inclusion with my records: "The young man, W, pointed skyward and told us that the bright light in the sky was a big UFO, another we were told was another UFO, and in another section of the sky was still another, all bright and visible to everyone concerned. I am an amateur astronomer, and I told him that what he was concerned about were in fact not UFOs at all, but heavenly bodies, and that he should not be alarmed as these would not in any way harm him since they were natural objects, each in its place since the creation of the universe. He was angry with me, and went into the house. I went to my car and got my star maps. I showed him that his first "UFO" was in fact Jupiter, the largest planet in our solar system, the second "UFO" was Betelgeuse in the constellation of Orion, and the third was the planet Mars."

I followed W as he entered the house and quickly set up my tape recorder. I explained to him that I wanted him to describe for me everything that he could remember and that I would then review it with him. We stepped into the living room to conduct the interview. About an hour later P. joined us and I questioned him about the various things that W had described to me. At this point I also had them both hold my pocket compass, but no reaction was registered. Also, shortly after arriving, I checked the car (1971 *Plymouth Satellite*), but again I found nothing abnormal in my readings. While we were there, Ben Twitchel of the Civil Defense in Oxford arrived with a geiger counter and checked the automobile over, but indicated that he had gotten nothing other than normal background readings.

Meanwhile the details had begun to solidify. Both W. and P. worked at night jobs. (W. at poultry processing plant, and P. at a wool mill). Hence their being up at 3:00 a.m. on October 27, when this experience unfolded, was not unusual. They had been inside listening to music when suddenly they heard from outside a sound similar to an explosion of some sort, so they rushed outside but saw nothing unusual. As they stood outside, W. suggested that it would be nice to go for a short ride, and P. abruptly recommended a drive down to nearby Lake Thompson. With P. driving, they had planned to drive about four miles south down Route 26 and just a short distance past the Oxford Plains Speedway stadium and then cut across to a road that would take them a couple of miles to the west into Oxford. They would then head southwards down the western side of Lake Thompson. But instead of taking this route, they had driven only about a mile down Route 26 when, according to their testimony, the car turned on to a back road to Oxford, completely under its own control. P. had a firm grip on the steering wheel, but there was nothing he could do.

This road is a more direct route to Oxford, about five miles long, passing by Webber Cemetery and Allen Hill. The ride seemed unusually smooth and they estimated that it took only about two minutes to go over it. A song that was playing on the radio at point of entrance was still playing at point of exit.

They continued on through Oxford and down the eastern side of Lake Thompson. About a mile south of Oxford, they passed a field with a group of cows sitting on the ground, all shaking their heads from one side to the other. This struck them as unusual since this had been the only sign of life they had seen on the strange ride down from Route 26.

Just a short distance further they were passing a large cornfield to their left where there were two white lights shining out on to the road. They thought that someone was sitting out in the field in a truck. They slowed to a stop and suddenly the thing began rising. They then considered that it was probably a helicopter, so they turned the motor off and rolled down the windows, but there was no sound. The object also had an assortment of other lights around its body that were green, blue and yellow, but they were extinguished when it rose up just above the tops of the trees that lined up in a row by the road in front of the field. It was only about 20 or 30 feet from the car and seemed very large and elongated, cylinder-like in appearance.

P. restarted the car and hit the gas pedal. They rolled up the windows and locked the doors, with the object giving pursuit. As they were continuing south about a mile down the road, they were aware of the "brightest lights I've ever seen" (W's description), their next fully conscious recollections were of being on the right side of the road, at a complete stop, a mile south of the cornfield site, situated on the left side of a gravel road that empties on to the tarred road they had been travelling. Their windows were rolled down some and their doors unlocked.

They glanced at each other and both saw something strange in the eyes of the other. To W. P's eyes were "all just orange" while to P., W's eyes were orange except for a dark area in the center where the pupils are.

The UFO was still visible in the sky to the east, so they continued south into West Poland where they turned around and headed north along the same road that they had just come down. At about two miles the object was no longer visible. W. suggested that they turn back and so they did. Then by an unexplained impulse, as they were going back, again headed south, P. turned into a gravel road leading down to Tripp Pond, which is located to the east of the southern part of Lake Thompson.

There, off to the east, at about a 20 or 30 degree elevation above the horizon, was the cylinder-like UFO, giving off a bright white appearance. It was hovering, and W. estimated that it was perhaps 500 feet distant from the car.

Meanwhile, upon their turning into the mouth of this road, the car motor died and could not be restarted, and the car radio faded out.

216

Within a few moments the object seemed to move in an up-and-down fashion, and then rose up into the air to about an 80 degree elevation, in a south-easterly position, and remained there for the remainder of the encounter, which was approximately an hour and a half. W. estimated that the UFO was 500 yards from the car at this point.

Within 45 minutes to an hour of their being stuck on this road, two disc-shaped objects with green, red and blue lights appeared in the sky, spotted by P., and W. estimated they seemed to be about a quarter of the size of the "mother ship," which they both agreed was the size of a football field. The discs put on a spectacular "air show" type of display wherein they performed aerial motions in time with one another. In falling-leaf fashion they descended to Tripp Pond, "skimmed across the water," and then flew upwards at right angles, like ascending a pair of invisible stairs, except that these stairs would be going upwards in one direction, at angles, and then suddenly reverse the direction.

Then they noticed a strange "dark grey" and "thick-looking fog" rising out of the pond.

Tripp Pond is approximately a half mile from where they sat at the entrance of this gravel road, but during this experience it appeared to be only 20 or 50 feet from them. One section of the pond seemed to be all water as far as they could see, like an ocean, and there was an island, which one of the discs seemed to fly over during its maneuvers.* In reality there are hills in the distance behind the pond and no islands are visible.

At any rate, the "fog" soon engulfed their car during which time a voice boomed in over the radio announcing that it was going to be a clear and bright sunny day. The "mother ship" was the only thing visible to them above. The car started when P. tried again at about 6:30 a.m. and at about 7:00 a.m. they arrived at the W. home. They had intended to keep to themselves everything that had happened, but immediately upon setting foot inside the house they were overcome with a number of odd symptoms. They both felt light-headed, their eyes burned, their throats became sore, they couldn't talk coherently, they suffered lack of balance and co-ordination, their teeth became sore and even loose, they

---

*George Yeaton Jr., Civil Defense director for Farmington, Maine, saw a cylindrical object with green, red and orange lights hovering low over an island in Rangeley Lake at about 4:30 a.m. on November 5, 1975. The object projected a "bright light" on to the island and fully illuminated it for about 15 seconds, during which time his car radio went dead. He was less than a mile from the island. Not long after extinguishing the light beam, the object "zipped off at an unbelievable speed." (Source: Portland, Maine, **Sunday Telegram**, November 30, 1975.) The similarity between these two separate events is noteworthy.

had difficulty in breathing, and they experienced "chills" despite heavy clothing.

At one point they were both startled at the same instance as a mental impression came to them in waves — "no language" as best they could describe it — wherein they were told; "We're not done with you yet. We're coming back for you."

Mr. W. noticed that both young men had yellow discoloration on the skin immediately surrounding their eyes. P. observed in the bathroom mirror that his tongue had a "brownish-white" sort of "scum" on it, and that it was "really cracked." (W. recalled: "When we came to, it felt like it was a desert inside my mouth. It was so dry.")

The experience seemed to contain symbolic elements of sorts. For example during my initial investigation of October 28, W. remarked: "What was weird was when the big one went straight up, the clouds seemed to follow it. It just took off, and all this time not a car went by. We didn't see a person, or an animal, or a bird ... nothing! And when the cloud disappeared two ducks went by and then two geese went by and then two ducks again went by. They were going in twos, and we noticed the cows were getting up in twos."

Neither young man recalled seeing the moon during this experience. Mrs. Linda Carey, Mr. Carey's wife, consulted the *Farmer's Almanac* and found that the moon was in its last quarter and rose at 11:01 p.m. on October 26, and set at 1:30 p.m. on October 27. Was the "mother ship" actually the moon? In view of the curious distortions of reality, that must be considered.

The after effects also included strange secondary hallucinations. At about 4:00 p.m. on October 28, W. and P. visited the Tripp Pond site and on several occasions saw what appeared to be white snow flakes coming down around them and overhead black cubes and spheres flying in the direction of the pond, while silver spheres whizzed in all directions. W. alone witnessed a red face-like outline as well as what looked like a beak of a giant bird that flew across the sky and dived into the pond.

On the night of October 27, P. was watching television in the living room of Mrs. W's home when he saw a black cube-shaped object "tumbling" in the air. It seemed to disappear through a wall. A few minutes later what looked like "golden wires" appeared all over the television set. They vanished without a trace after a few moments also. Even though W. was in the living room at the time, he saw nothing of this.

That same day W. was alone in his parent's home when he saw an ash tray rise into the air about a foot and then drop back down on to the table.

At about 8:00 a.m. on October 28, something walked across the roof of their trailer in Norway. Shortly afterwards P. went into a very deep sleep. This sleepy condition was repeated again about 4:00 p.m. on October 28, during their visit to the Tripp Pond site, where they both suddenly became very tired and fell asleep in W's 1971 *Chevrolet 10* van.

About an hour before our arrival on the night of October 28, at about 8:45 p.m., three knocks sounded from the front door. W's oldest sister, 22, opened the door. No one was there. P., standing near the kitchen sink about eight feet from the door, heard a male-sounding voice say the letters "UFO". No one else heard it.

My second visit was on November 1. By that time a number of noteworthy developments had erupted.

On October 29, at approximately 9:00 a.m., there came a knocking on the front door of the trailer in Norway. W. opened the door (he was alone), and outside stood a stockily built stranger who had a crewcut hair style, wore sunglasses, and was dressed in dark blue clothing. He asked W. if he was the one who had seen a "flying saucer," and upon getting the affirmative he told W., "Better keep your mouth shut if you know what's good for you." With that the stranger scurried away and around the corner of a nearby building, never to be seen again.

On October 30, at about 8:40 p.m., I was conversing on the phone with my friend James Carey, discussing this case, when the operator cut in to inform me that someone was attempting to place an emergency call to my number. We hung up and within moments my phone rang and it was Mrs. W. She was very upset and told me that her husband was behaving in an "irrational" manner. He had developed an obsession to visit the UFO sites that night but Mrs. W. was fearful of this so she hid the car keys from him.

Her voice quivered as she told me: "I talk to him and then he'll sit there, and sit there, and then he'll say 'What's the matter?' and we just discussed it and he'll be saying 'What's the matter?'"

I suggested that she let me speak to him, but she replied that he did not want to speak with me. Then I told her that perhaps it would be best to let him drive up to the UFO sites, but he responded that he no longer wanted to. Also as we were talking he told her that he knew she was going to have difficulty reaching me.

Not long after our conversation ended, Mrs. W. went to the bathroom, suffering from a sudden and severe headache that began in the left temple, within probably less than five minutes. A UFO-type light had been outside, but when the headache ceased it was gone.

Mrs. W. noticed that Mr. W. was restless throughout that night, but he recalls no dreams. And when I confronted him with his actions he could not account for his unusual behaviour.

Looking back at the experience of October 27, W. said that he had been functioning as his normal self, he feels that he would most certainly have been very frightened, but both he and P. were in an emotionless sort of state as this UFO activity transpired.

Regarding their friendship, the two young men explained that W. had just been discharged from active military service (US Navy) about a month and a half before the UFO incident of October 27, and P. was visiting in the area with his mother and stepfather when they became acquainted. They were both amazed that they had experienced many identical things. Within a week they moved into a trailer and shared expenses. And it was at this point that P. began to have ESP insights. For example, one night about a week before the UFO incident P. told W. that they should not go out that night for a ride as something bad would happen. W. ignored him, and they and two friends were involved in an auto accident.

W. told me that on occasions in the past he had seen the outsides of houses in which he psychically knew the appearance of the interior, and upon stepping inside it would be just as he had visualized in his mind, despite the fact that he had never been inside those buildings before.

Chapter 12

The Maine UFO Encounter: Investigation Under Hypnosis

Shirley C. Fickett

The case of W. and P. was brought to the attention of the International UFO Bureau in Portland, Maine, on October 28, 1975. A friend of mine called from Lewiston, Maine, stating that a brief account of the incident had appeared in *The Lewiston Daily Sun.*

From the Eastern bureau headquarters, I contacted the paper as well as the Androscoggin County Sheriff's Department, which had also been notified of the UFO encounter experienced by the two fellows during the early morning hours of October 27. The Sheriff's Department supplied the unlisted number of the W. family, and upon calling I talked extensively with Mrs. W. about the case. Upon learning that the young men were experiencing continuing physiological after effects, I realized the implications that the two had undergone some very traumatic experience.

It was November 11 before I could get to the W. residence for a taped interview. Both fellows were present and talked freely of their UFO encounter. We were all curious about the lost time element when the UFO beam of light hit the car, sliding it sideways and rendering the two unconscious. It was decided that hypnosis was the best course of action to follow in order to try to pull together the missing facts.

At about that time, through mutual friends, I met Dr. Herbert Hopkins of Old Orchard Beach, Maine, and discovered that among other talents he was a hypnotist and used this therapy on some of his patients. He had five years study on the subject to his credit as well as a background of psychiatric study. I made arrangements with him for a number of sessions to learn if W. could be regressed, and to see if we could learn what occurred during the blackout. After the first session, Dr. Hopkins said he would do the hypnosis free as a scientific adventure, as well as to cut our costs. W. was chosen as the subject for study since he was the elder, and served as a spokesman whenever an interview was conducted.

P. was present for the first hypnosis session as were W's parents and myself. However, after that session P. refused to be present, and he gradually withdrew. He refused to discuss the subject, and not long after that he moved to Oklahoma with family members where he remains to this writing. During the November 11 interview he remarked that he was terribly shaken by the ordeal. The remaining hypnotic sessions were all attended by the W. family and myself, taping them for the records. Gradually, over a period of time, the enigma of those lost moments of unconsciousness began to unfold under the skillful and gentle technique of Dr. Hopkins.

Session 1, December 2, 1975

Dr. Hopkins explained how hypnosis works, what to expect from it, and that the sessions could not last any longer than thirty minutes once Mr. W. had been put under. I will exclude dialogue here to save space, and cover only the highlights of the most important findings. Since Dr. Hopkins did not know the complete story, and had heard only a sketchy account from me, he did not have too much to work with in the first two sessions. Later I gave him a full report of what W. knew in the conscious mind. After that the probing of what had occurred became easier.

In the first session, Dr. Hopkins performed an arm levitation excercise after W. was under, whereby he tried to push the arm down, but to no avail; by this means he knew his subject was under full control of the trance state. As Dr. Hopkins brought the subject to the point where the light hit the car and they passed out, W's excitement became apparent by his breathing, and it was at this point the session was terminated.

Session 2, December 10, 1975

At this session a complete description was given by W. of the earthly-appearing man who approached him October 29 and threatened him not to divulge any further information about the UFO encounter. Again, there was further review of what happened on the conscious level in order to bring W. to the point where the light hit the car. This session ended with W's statement that he was outside the car at the point when it was in the process of skidding sideways after being hit by the light from the UFO. He was reluctant to give any more information and he was then counted out from the trance.

These first two sessions each lasted approximately fifteen minutes or so. The ones that followed lasted about thirty minutes, and revealed much more.

Session 3, December 17, 1975

This time W. was in a more emotional state than at any time other than the final session. Dr. Hopkins guided his subject back through time, bringing him to the area where he concluded session 2 when the car was hit by the light. After much probing W. stated that he was standing on a floor suspended above, looking through a window and observing the car sliding sideways with his friend still within. Further questioning revealed he was standing in a room approximately fifteen feet high and thirty-five feet in diameter. There was one door in the room and the walls caved inwards as they rose. There was no furniture, and at this point W. was alone.

It was soon established that a non-human being came in to join W. Although it was not human, we learned from W. that it was a living being, but not of this world. At this point, as the doctor instructed W. to observe the creature and relate what he saw, it was obvious that he was under great stress, and his breathing became labored, but he continued. His voice trembled slightly as he described the being as about four and a half feet tall, wearing a garment that "looked like a sheet," and having a face that was not at all human. Under questioning W. was having much difficulty finding words to describe the face of his visitor, and emotion rose once more, making it impossible for him to forge ahead. The session was brought to a halt at this point.

After the hypnosis, it was brought to Dr. Hopkins' attention that ever since the UFO encounter, W's eyes had been bloodshot continually. The doctor examined his eyes and confirmed that they were still in that condition.

Session 4, December 23, 1975

It should be pointed out that during this taped session there was an alternation of high-frequency sound within the tape that did not show up in the other recordings. There was no electrical equipment within the room that could account for this.

W. seemed much calmer as Dr. Hopkins slipped into the area where he had left off in the previous session. It was stated that the creature walked on feet, had hands and arms. It had three fingers that were webbed. (In a later session W. stated there were four fingers, but the doctor established that one appendage was a thumb, not a finger.)

This was the only time W. would discuss the shoes worn by the creature in spite of repeated questioning about it later. He stated the shoes looked as if they were made of paper.

As Dr. Hopkins went to explore the face of the creature, we learned that the skin was white, the head was shaped like a mushroom, and that it had two eyes (later W. stated these were slanted, large and white in color, and were unblinking). The nose was small and rounded; no mouth could be observed.

The creature began relating to W. by what he, W., refers to as "brain waves" (speaking telepathically). By this manner he was told not to be afraid, that he would not be harmed. When asked by the doctor if the creature told W. who he was, he said "No." When asked if the creature inquired who W. was, the answer was: "He already knew my name."

Next, W. said he was escorted to another room where he met four more similar beings. This room was described as being like a hospital room with what appeared to be an operating table. It had equipment and machinery. Two needles-full of blood were extracted from W's arm (at the elbow of the right arm). After this, they tried to make him lie down on the table for an examination. He rebelled, hitting one of the creatures in the face. In response, it just looked at him, and showed no signs of retaliation. At this point W. was beginning to breathe deeply and show signs of uneasiness, so once more he was brought back to consciousness.

Session 5, January 14, 1976

After a slight review of the previous affairs, Dr. Hopkins took W. back once more to the subject of the appearance of the creatures. Their garments were black in color. (Because W. had stated they looked like sheets, we had assumed they were white ... This was a surprise.)

The sleeves of the garments were flowing, and extended to the hands. The gowns were long. Their arms appeared short compared to the body structure, and W. did not notice whether they had fingernails or not, although he observed their fingers were different lengths, and that they had joints like ours but were thinner than the human finger. Their garments seemed to be made of paper (here Dr. Hopkins named all manner of materials, but nothing seemed to fit but paper). There was no hair on their heads.

Attention was next focused upon the room and the table within. After hitting the creature, W. had finally relented and lay down to be examined. The table was white and soft. There were bright lights overhead, and W. stated that an instrument was used for the examination. When asked if it hurt, the reply was negative. The subject had once more been under hypnosis for the alloted time and was thereupon counted back to consciousness.

Session 6, January 21, 1976

The questions began concerning the feet and shoes of the creatures, but for some reason the only thing W. would relate was that

224

some of them were wearing footgear and some were not. That was all he would say in spite of continued questioning on the subject. When asked whether or not the beings had ears, W. could give no answer. He did not relate that they had no facial hair. He was asked to draw a picture of them upon awakening.

Now came interrogation about the examination. The machine used was square with gauges on the side, knobs in the middle. This had an extension on it about four feet long, and at the end of this was a smaller machine which slid over W's body as it was maneuvered, but did not come in contact with the body. W's clothing was all removed (the beings assisted). This bothered W. but, although the room felt cool he was not cold. Dr. Hopkins named all the parts of the body when asking if they were examined: eyes, nose, mouth, ears, chest, etc. Each time the answer was "Yes." Travelling further down the body, the question was asked; "Did they examine your genitals?" When this was confirmed, the next question was; "Did they do anything to them?" The answer to this was in the negative. So the questions went on to all the other parts of the body. It appeared there was a thorough going-over, on the part of the intruders, from head to feet. A small sample of hair was taken and put into an empty container. There were no other machines used, and no wires were attached. It was estimated that the examination took about forty to forty-five minutes in all.

After his clothes were put back on (this time without any help), W. stated that the beings began to communicate with him mentally, saying they had been watching him for some time and wanted to study him. They stated they would be seeing him again and he was given a shot of something. This was administered in the right arm near the shoulder. He was told that it might make him a little tired. When asked if it did, he stated "Yes, about a week later!" After this, W. was escorted back to the room where it all began, and related that next he was back in the car with his friend P.

Before awakening W., Dr. Hopkins went on to a few more questions, asking if there were a lot of test tubes in the hospital room. The answer was yes. We learned that a fingernail sample was taken and bottled. There was more questioning as to what was done with the blood samples. W. stated that after the samples were placed on a table awhile, they were taken from the room by one of the creatures. Upon being asked how he felt upon returning to the car, W. related that it felt like there was glass in his eyes. The doctor asked if this told pretty much the story of what happened while W. was unconscious, and the answer was affirmative.

Once more the hypnosis was terminated. Upon awakening, W.

The creature as described by "W", drawn by Shirley C. Fickett

The creature, drawn by "W" following the hypnotic session on February 21, 1976

stated he felt there was something he was supposed to do. He was told, and escorted to the kitchen table where he drew a picture of the beings he'd observed while aboard the UFO.

Later Dr. Hopkins asked if we could have a couple more sessions to tie up some loose ends.

Session 7, March 9, 1976

More questioning about the first room. The window size was about one and a half feet. The floor was shiny. Walls a shiny grey, and the ceiling the same. W. felt a slight vibration and there was an odor as though something had burned. There were no pictures on any of the walls. More stress was laid on the area where the creature was hit. Upon impact, he was not knocked down but just stepped backwards, he made no noise, and the others did not react. His skin felt harder than ours, there was no discoloration, and no mark remained where the impact was made.

The creature seemed surprised when hit and when asked if they appeared to be friendly, W. stated "Yes." There was no indication that the beings communicated among themselves, for there was no sound between them. A button was missing from W's denim sleeve, which he said they put into a jar after cutting it off.

After W. returned to the car, it appeared that P. had no recollection that his friend had left him.

Throughout the hypnosis sessions there was complete consistency of both the conscious and subconscious mind, during the questioning by Dr. Hopkins.

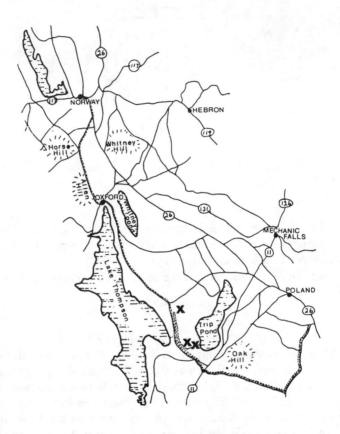

Area where the witness saw the UFO. X indicates the place it was claimed the light shone on them from the object. XX where they stated they observed UFOs over the lake.

W. said very little in this session but was more disturbed than at any other time. Dr. Hopkins suspected it was due to the line of questioning. This dealt in the main with the question of when the beings told W. they would return. W. stated he was given a time when they would see him again but when asked when this was, he would not answer. After persistent questioning on this point, W. became very upset, trying desperately to say something but at the same time giving the impression that something was holding him back. He trembled and shook his head indicating alternately yes, then no. Dr. Hopkins stated there was great conflict going on within. He was asked if he had been made some sort of promise and the answer was "Yes," but the nature of that also remains deep within the subconcious mind. W. was so upset that the questioning was brought to a halt and the session ended.

And so we have an account of what occurred during the blackout when the car was hit by the beam of light, with the exception of the promise made to W. and the matter of the return to the beings. Perhaps it is just as well that that remains in the shadows of W's mind.

Chapter 13

Comments on the Psychiatric- Paranormal Aspects of the Maine Case

Shortly after the Maine UFO Encounter, Brent Raynes telephoned me. Since it was impossible for me to leave at once, I suggested some nearby colleagues who had ample facilities at their disposal. However, since this didn't work out and I was becoming curious with each new report from investigators Mrs. Shirley Fickett and Brent Raynes, both of whom had corresponded with me for some years before the incident, I could resist no longer and drove to Mrs. Fickett's home in Portland, Maine, on January 16, 1976.

Mrs. Fickett reveiwed past and current developments, and showed me all her material. I had previously listened to audio tapes of the hypnotic sessions that Herbert Hopkins, M.D., had with W. The following day, W., the contactee, arrived with his parents at noontime, and in the presence of Mr. and Mrs. Fickett, Brent Raynes (and his parents who came later), it was possible to go over the whole experience and conduct a psychiatric-paranormal survey. Although this technique of airing material in the presence of everyone (exclusive of P., the other young man who was with W. the night of the experience) had its drawbacks, there were advantages. For example, it was possible to observe the interaction between W., his parents and the investigators, etc., and also to weave back and forth over many features of the story. The obvious drawbacks to this quasi public method were compensated for by seeing W. and his parents individually and privately. During the eight-and-a-half hours spent with the family, I photographed all the people and we attempted an experimental paranormal audio taping (1).

W., aged 21, was a U.S.N. veteran of the Vietnam war, who received an honorable discharge. A high school graduate, he seemed to have average intelligence, and was open and cooperative, with one understandable proviso, that anonymity be maintained. W. gave no evidence for any undue trends of thought or preoccupations. Two and one half months after the contact W. still seemed frightened and puzzled by his unusual experience. His account dovetailed with what he had told Mrs. Fickett and Brent Raynes. There was no evidence from W's past history, or from interviews of his father and stepmother, for dishonesty, lying, falsification of, or loss of memory, previous sociopathic or dissociative behavior, or of excessive interest in flying saucers, detailed knowledge of the Betty and Barney Hill abduction case (2), or the Pascagoula incident (3), etc. This was also the situation for W's parents. They were distressed by what had happened to W., and as reported, the father even developed an episode of entranced and strange behavior (4). The father wanted help for his son (and himself) and had to fathom the meaning of what happened. He completely trusted his son, and his family shared that attitude with Mrs. Fickett, Brent Raynes, Dr. Hopkins and myself.

The hypnotic sessions penetrated W's amnesia and yielded material that W. was unaware of. Only gradually did he learn what had happened aboard the UFO. It is interesting that, like the Hill's case and the Hickson-Parker case, W. had a physical examination. But superficially and technically considered it seemed so absurd that one wonders if this wasn't also staged by the UFO forces in order to create a particular impression. While entranced, W. recalled hitting one of the entities who was solid (5) and who did not retaliate.

Many of W's symptoms following the encounter, when he entered his parent's home, might be explained as the physiological expressions of anxiety. Although weightlessness can be a symptom of anxiety or depersonalization, it is not a common complaint, and in view of the possible teleportation this symptom should be kept in mind. The battery of physiological tests (6) that were used with the astronauts could be applicable here and might yield valuable clues. The complaint of sore and loose teeth is not common, but it would not be an unusual reaction for someone to develop when frightened and clenching his teeth. If the eyes were indeed orange (7) it is unusual. I've never come across that history in seeing thousands of patients through the years. Although seriously disturbed patients in mental hospitals can present bizarre symptoms, they don't develop orange eyes. Floyd Farrant, my ophthalmologist colleague, also could not account for this. However, he said that when he uses flourescein in his work, the eyes become transiently orange. Could W (and possibly P) have had an eye examination with fluorescein dye? The orange eyes are also reminiscent of what is reported for many of the UFO-related Big Foot encounters, where they eyes are described as a glowing yellow or orange.

Possibly the sightings and events aboard the UFO were sufficiently awesome to induce the terror and the psychosomatic sequelae of sleepiness. Electroencephalography might give clues to the particular stage of sleep induced, or define a normal rhythm that is usually associated with a trance-like state. Other information might show temporal lobe concomitants to W's (and later to his father's?) fugue, changes in photic sensitivity (e.g., a factor in his headaches), etc. Although I've done electroencephalograms on gifted paragnosts (and on one person involved in an outbreak of presumed poltergeist activity) there were no scalp lead changes when successfully performing. That doesn't mean that UFO contactees might or might not have findings unless serial tracings or specialized techniques are used.

Although perhaps not unlike some of Mrs. Stella Lansing's seemingly allegorical experiences (8), there are the bizarre symbolic features of the twosomes of cows shaking their heads, and the ducks and Canadian geese alternately flying in twos. Was this reality, illusion, or hallucination? It seems similar to later events that occurred in the home and the pond, where W. and P. saw black cubes and spheres, and silver spheres. W. alone saw the beak of a giant bird. At times he saw things when others didn't, and this was also the case for P, who saw at W's home a black cube and golden wires, which W. didn't see. Many of these percepts are similar to what Mrs. Lansing has filmed on numerous occasions. Also, although there was no one else with him, W. reported seeing an ash tray suddenly levitate. Other psi and puzzling aspects of the case include the "fog" (9) that engulfed the car, possible telephonic and mail effects, telepathy, precognition, various poltergeist effects, and a man in navy blue. What a field day for a team of investigators!

The question could be asked, what psychodynamically significant events, if any, might have gone on that might have set up the contactees for their experiences? Although it would have been desirable to have spent more time with W. alone, it was learned that he was upset, when he was in the Navy during the Vietnam war, and his parents were divorced. His father choked up when he confided that W's natural mother attempted suicide and had been hospitalized twice. It was strange that the stepmother didn't volunteer that she was not W's natural mother. The stepmother seemed to be a warm person who related well to W. She wanted the best for her family. She, like W's father, had been married previously, but unable to have children of her own, she and her first husband had adopted two children. W. was thus the second oldest of four natural siblings and of two young adoptive siblings. Of all the children, only his older sister, age 22, was involved in the UFO sequelae, for when she once opened the door after hearing a knock, she discovered no one there. The father, but not she, heard spelled out the letters "U-F-O." Were these events psychic projections from the unconscious of the protagonists and aimed at specific people and not others? If so, why and what is their origin? Paragnosts Jacques Romano and Joseph Dunninger were masters of telepathy, who could produce analogous presumed psychic effects when they were properly worked up, so that would not be an unusual situation, but again, why these people, at this time and place? What are the psychic dynamics (10)?

Approximately three months prior to the contact, W. and his family were jolted when they learned that the stepmother had an advanced malignancy which would need immediate and prolonged treatment. It should be noted that in some other contact situations prior to their experience the protagonists, like some gifted paragnosts, were keyed up to a near-crisis proportion, for the future seemed to hang in the balance. It has been mentioned that while in the service W. had already lost his mother through divorce, and apparently she was a taboo subject. Now W. was threatened with the loss of his warm and giving stepmother, and also his plans for marriage were marred. The reverberations echoed throughout the family; however, it is obvious that such tragedies are not that unusual, and when similar situations exist elsewhere, they are rarely, if ever, accompanied by UFO-psi sequelae as happened here. It is regrettable that there are not suitable clinical controls to aid in the evaluation of such factors. However, the highlights touched upon here suggest how this might be a fruitful area to explore.

In contrast to W's parents, P's family denied the validity of their son's reality and even called him a liar. Perhaps this lack of understanding drove him out of the home. P. moved west and it was impossible to obtain any further information. It might be wondered how well he will fare in the future, because of hypothesized previous similar home experiences (11) and the way that his UFO contact was handled (mangled?).

On speculating why these young men were "chosen" it should be noted that it might not have been an accident, for in their short acquaintanceship both W. and P. were drawn together by their interest in the occult. Could the affinity have set the stage for what later happened? Motivation and suggestion are powerful forces. They can be contagious, and in spontaneous psi examples or in some seances they seemingly further the phenomena. The psychic nexus is part of a continuum — it can go back in time and peer into the future. Although as far as we know, both men had no previous consuming interest in UFOs, there was a background for psi. Perhaps a more prolonged and detailed study of W. and P. could uncover more psi data and better define the UFO-contact/psi interface. Before a collective unconscious effect is proposed, all the specific individual influences, interactions and experiences of the protagonists and their families should be worked out.

Psi could also account for the supposed EM effects. The alleged feats of Uri Geller (12) and other gifted mediums (13) support this viewpoint. Perhaps a study of many gifted contactees will reveal the hypothetical, anatomical, biochemical, or psychic substratas that energize and set off the critical interaction with the UFO. My experience indicates that W. has much in common with other contactees and gifted paragnosts I've studied, i.e., an apparent superabundance of energy, individualism, often being a loner, tendencies toward dissociation and perhaps much pent-up tension — people who give the impression that if their energies are not sufficiently channelled they would be ready to explode. Whatever the final reason, it is also a fact that in some of the families I've studied there is a permissive attitude for psi, sometimes going over three generations, or by history even longer.

Unfortunately not much is known about P. Although W. had no past dissociative behavior like sleepwalking, fugues, excessive daydreaming, etc., it should be noted that like so many contactees in my experience, and unlike most people in general, he was an excellent hypnotic subject and had amnesia for what he recalled during entrancement.

Not much was learned about W's family history. His father's father was of German descent; his mother came from a long line of New Englanders, some of whom were clergymen, and there might have been a witch or two in the background. W.'s mother was of Irish extraction and came from the midwest. Aside from her mental illness (recurrent depressions and suicide attempts?), not much is known about her. According to the father, W.'s natural mother had no knowledge of her son since the divorce. The father did not know if the former wife remarried or not. In the interviews, it appeared that W.'s relationship to his mother was glossed over. His private responses indicated unrequited longing and curiosity. Possibly this repression could have been displaced and have added force to the outlet in his contact and related psi experiences. Although touchy, this is also a necessary area for further probing.

W. recalled a possible psi episode when he was in the Navy. While stationed in Norfolk, Virginia, he once met a stranger on the street, called him by name, and told him things about his life. Although W. could not immediately recall other similar psi examples, he said this experience was not unusual. Coupled with the psi aspects of the UFO experience, this faculty might indicate that W. possesses the potential of being a powerful medium. However, this does not explain how, if psychic ability is an indispensable factor for a UFO experience, it took the specific trappings: i.e., the supposed EM effects, the terror, the medical examination, etc. Is the brilliant display of psi — via the UFO symbolism — the message? Could it be as simple as some contactees proclaim: that the purpose of the contact is to alert man to the existence of forces and powers that exert control over this destiny, and that these forces can vastly expand man's awareness and free him from the materialism that

Figure 1. Photograph taken by Shirley Fickett at the UFO site. Two strange artifacts resembling UFOs, are seen, similar to those Mrs. Stella Lansing has obtained on many occasions.

235

endangers his present-day culture: Or the opposite could be: if man can't learn to cope with such forces as his own hostilities and aggressions he will be destroyed by them. Like all powers, psi can be used for good or evil, depending on the values accorded: e.g., myths, dogmas, superstitions, and the belief systems that surround us (14). Whether these forces and effects come from projections and condensations of men (or UFO entities) — individually or collectively — in complex ways analogous to how thought and feelings can be transferred in psychodynamic telepathic drawing experiments (15), is impossible to determine. Whatever the explanation, and the cause and effect relation, the paranormal aspects appear to be central in this case. Mrs. Fickett, Brent Raynes, and Dr. Hopkins had to cope with factors that ethically prohibited their pursuing matters further, but they are to be complimented for their care, consideration and diligence.

Under utopian circumstances it would have been advantageous to have had collaborative psychiatric study of W., P., and their families, so that the loose ends to their experiences could have been pinpointed and fitted together. Facts could replace speculations. In psychotherapeutic techniques the more time that is spent, the more that is learned.

Complex human matters cannot be approached in a simplistic way. In future cases it is hoped that more physicians can be recruited to aid in the investigations and that it will be possible to have thorough physical examinations, appropriate laboratory studies, including electroencephalography, etc. At the least, as much attention should be paid to the human part of the equation as is given to the other data. Perhaps something of practical benefit could come from ufology. No study of any close sighting, landing or contactee case is complete without plans for a long-term follow-up, an adjunctive medical, psychiatric-paranormal survey, and the contributions of the various social sciences.

The thirty-minute attempted paranormal tape recording made in the presence of everyone during the visit did not yield anything. However, in their studies Mrs. Fickett and Brent Raynes took pictures of the UFO site. Mr. Raynes obtained some unusual photographic effects, but artifact seemed to be the likely explanation. Mrs. Fickett's pictures of the alleged landing site showed some strange aritifacts resembling UFOs which were similar to what Mrs. Stella Lansing has obtained on many occasions. (figure 1).

NOTES AND REFERENCES

1. Schwarz, B.E.: "Commentary on the Roberts Mystery," **Flying Saucer Review,** Vol. 21 (No. 6) 18-19, 1976. **Also, on a more recent** audio tape Mrs. Lansing obtained a halting man's voice, perseverating: ". . . please believe me," and then later, "Please believe me, **Mrs. Lansing."** This was associated with jamming of the tape recorder, and was photographed on motion picture film by Mrs. Lansing. Experimental presumed paranormal tape effects in connection with ufology can also be found in: "Follow-up on Betty Hill," submitted to FSR for publication, 1976.

2. Fuller, John: **The Interrupted Journey,** Dial Press, New York, 1966.

3. Blum, R., and J.: **Beyond Earth,** Bantam, New York, 1974.

4. For similar entracement with a fugue and its possible dangerous complications, see Schwarz, B.E.: "Berserk: A UFO Creature Encounter," FSR, Vol. 20 (No. 1): 3-11, 1974.

   Also, a situation that I have followed over a period of time and which Stan Gordon and the Pennsylvania Center for UFO Research, of Greensburg, have thoroughly investigated, involved a series of spectacular psychic effects, MIB phenomena, and recurrent fugues, during which the quasi contactee behaved as if possessed, and demonstrated, on many occasions, dangerous, violent acting out.

5. Similar indications of the solid (materialized?) nature of the UFO or entities are given in a Venezuelan case, where the protagonist stabbed the UFO-associated dwarf and found that the blade "glanced off the body as though from steel," (Creighton, Gordon and Bowen, Charles (ed.), **The Humanoids,** Neville Spearman, London, 1969, pp. 93-94) and in the instance where Gary Wilcox threw a rock at the craft and it bounced off (see FSR, Special Issue No. 3, 1969, pp. 20-27, "Gary Wilcox and the Ufonauts."); also, the famous Kelly-Hopkinville sighting as reported in Hynek, J. Allen: **The UFO Experience, A Scientific Inquiry,** Henry Regnery Co., Chicago, 1972, pp. 150-155. In **The Edge of Reality** (Hynek, J. Allen, and Vallee, Jacques, Henry Regnery Co., Chicago, 1975, pp. 129-142), Dr. Hynek recounts the example of Mr. H., who with three other hunters had noticed what they thought was an airplane come down and crash. The craft, or whatever it was, had four occupants beside it. In the course of matters, Mr. H. fired a shot and hit one of the forms in the right shoulder: "When the individual was struck, he spun around, down to his knees, and he got up with the other guy's assistance, and looked over and said or hollered, 'Now, what the hell did you do that for?' (p. 136)." This experience indicates a solid effect. For many years afterwards Mr. H. suffered with this horrible secret. Through coincidence or synchronicity it was my fortune to spend several hours with this man. As in other contactee situations, I learned about his many personal and family paranormal experiences.

6. The severity and persistence of many of W's symptoms, as for example his weightlessness and sleepiness, would suggest considering the battery of physiological studies for some contactees that were used for the astronauts (see Driscoll, Everly: "Every Man's Response to Zero-G," **Science News,** Vol. 102 (Sept. 9): 172-174, 1972; and "Inside the Crew of Skylab II," **World Medical News,** Dec. 14, 1973, pp. 26-27).

7. Although not orange eyes, a related eye effect pertains to a contactee under study by the Cleveland Ufology Group. In the midst of her experience, this woman noted a golden spotlight shining out from her left eye. She claimed it was 10-12 inches in diameter and would light up the TV, refrigerator, walls, and that she could read through it. My study of this contactee revealed many interesting psychic aspects for her and other members of her family.

8. Schwarz, B.E.: "Stella Lansing's UFO Motion Pictures," FSR, Vol. 18 (No. 1): 3-12 (Jan./Feb., 1972).

   "Stella Lansing's UFO Movies of Four Entities and Possible UFO," FSR, Special Issue No. 5, UFO Encounters: 2-10, 1973.

   "Stella Lansing's Clocklike possible UFO Formations," FSR, Vol. 20 (No. 4): 3-9 (January 1975) Part I; **Ibid.**, Part II, Vol. 20 (No. 5): 20-27 (March 1975). **Ibid.**, Part III, Vol. 20 (No. 6): 18-22 (April 1975). **Ibid.**, Part IV, Vol. 21 (No. 1): 14-17 (June 1975).

9. In World War I, British troops mysteriously disappeared at Gallipoli, after they were enveloped in a strange mist, according to accounts from New Zealand sources.

   References on mist and UFOs are: Creighton, G.: "Teleportations," FSR, Vol. 16 (No. 2): 14-16 (Mar./April 1965): Galindez, Oscar A.: "Teleportation from Chascomus to Mexico," FSR, Vol. 14 (No. 5): 3-4 (Sept./Oct. 1968); Frederickson, Sven-Olof: "Finnish Encounter on the Snow," FSR, Vol. 16 (No. 4): 31-32 (July/Aug. 1970); Frederickson, Sven-Olf: "More on the Imjarvi Case," FSR, Vol. 16 (No. 6): 22 (Nov./Dec. 1970); Frederickson, Sven-Olof, et al.: "The Strange Force That Moved a Car," FSR **Case Histories Supplement No. 10: 1-3** (June 1972). The apparently related subject of teleportation with its parapsychological and ufological implications, can be found in a 30-item bibliography featuring studies by Fodor, Sanderson, Jessup, Creighton and Galindez; see Galindez, Oscar A.: "A New Teleportation Near Cordoba," FSR, Vol. 19 (No. 3): 6-12, (May/June 1973); also see Bowen, Charles: Car Teleported by UFOs in Rhodesia," FSR Vol. 21 (No. 1): 18-20 (June 1975); van Vlierden, Carl (transcribed by Bowen, Charles) "Escorted by UFOs From Umvuma to Beit Bridge," FSR, Vol. 21 (No. 2): 3-10 (August 1975); and the Travis Walton case in the APRO **Bulletin,** Vol. 24 (No. 5): 1-5. (Nov. 1975); **ibid.**, "Walton Takes Polygraph Test," Vol. 24 (No. 6): 1-3 (Dec. 1975).

10. Some of my psychiatric studies touching on the paranormal aspects of ufology can be found in FSR, Vol. 17 (No. 2): 4-9 (March/April 1971); Vol. 17 (No. 3): 21-27 (May/June 1971); Vol. 18 (No. 4): 5-9, 17 (July/Aug. 1972); Vol. 19 (No. 1): 3-6 (Jan./Feb. 1973); Vol. 19 (No. 2): 18-23 (March/April 1973); Vol. 21 (Nos. 3, 4):, 22-28 (Nov. 1975). Also, see, Proceedings of the Eastern UFO Symposium, Jan. 23, 1971, Baltimore, Maryland, pp. 8-12 (sponsored by APRO, Tucson, Arizona); Proceedings of the 5th APRO UFO Symposium, June 15, 1974, Pottstown, Pa., pp. 14-18; Proceedings, MUFON 1974 UFO Symposium, Akron, Ohio, June 22, 1974, pp. 82-95. A fascinating case from the New York-New Jersey megalopolis dealt with possible landings, occupants and sightings, involving different witnesses near the Stonehenge apartments. See Bloecher, T., Hopkins, B., and Stoehrer, J.: "Digging Holes in the

Ground, Occupants Sighted in New Jersey,'' **Skylook,** No. 100, pp. 3-7, (Mar. 1976). My cousin whose medical office is close by, told me about a medical secretary at the local hospital and her related sighting with possible telephone harassment. I also saw four of the Stonehenge protagonists in cursory psychiatric and paranormal surveys, and unsuccessfully attempted some movie experiments. EU, the day doorman, and a leading experient, has had lifelong high-quality psi: e.g., possible precognition — he claimed foreknowledge of the UFO activity — apparitions and telekinesis.. His son and wife also had unusual presumed psi experiences. EU and the apartment electrician shared a close daytime sighting. They noted how the top floor of their apartment was unique, and might have resembled the stereotyped concept of a conventional UFO by its circular shape, dome, and flashing lights on the sides. EU wondered: "Is there an attraction to this building?" It might have been more than just the building. If hoax can be excluded for the episodes of the little man digging a hole, this series of UFO events in the heart of the metropolitan area is unusual. From the earliest years to the present FSR has had many excellent articles on the general and psychological psi aspects of ufology.

11. Robinson, David B. (ed.): **Experience, Affect, and Behavior, Psychoanalytic Explorations of Dr. Adelaide McFadyen Johnson,** The University of Chicago Press, Chicago, 1969.
12. See Creighton, Gordon: "Uri Geller, the Man Who Bends Science,'' FSR, Vol. 19 (No. 5): 8-11 (Sept./Oct. 1973); Puharich, Andrija: **A Journal of the Mystery of Uri Geller,** Anchor Press, Doubleday, Garden City. N.Y., 1974; and Geller, U.: **Uri Geller, My Story,** Warner Books Inc., (Paperback) New York, 1975.
13. Fodor, Nandor: **Encyclopaedia of Psychic Science,** University Books, New Hyde Park, N.Y., 1966.
14. The masterful writing of John A. Keel and many FSR editorials and articles through the years fully explore these challenging possibilities.
15. Schwarz, B.E.: "Psychodynamic Experiments in Telepathy,'' **Corrective Psychiatry and the Journal of Social Therapy,** Vol. 9 (No. 4): 169-214 (1963).

Chapter 14

The Man-In-Black Syndrome . . . 1

Followup on the Maine UFO Encounter

Flying Saucer Review recently published the account of a spectacular possible teleportation, involving two young men in the state of Maine (1-3). David Stephens, one of the protagonists, has been involved in some bizarre follow-up experiences which, hopefully, will be fully reported later. This account will be confined to an unusual Man-in-Black (MIB) experience that involved Dr. Herbert Hopkins, the skilled physician who conducted the hypnotic sessions with David Stephens. Dr. Hopkins is a 58-year-old family physician who lives in a beautiful coastal resort town of Maine.

For the purpose of this report I will try to present the happenings that involved him and other members of his family, using a narrative style based not only on quotations obtained from Mrs. Shirley Fickett's original letters and tapes sent to me shortly after the MIB visitation, but also telephone calls and direct interview with Mrs. Betty Hill who was also involved in the case, numerous telephone and written communica-

Herbert Hopkins, M.D.

tions between Dr. Hopkins and me, and taped interviews with Dr. and Mrs. Hopkins, plus a brief meeting with his two sons and daughter-in-law, at his home in Maine, from 1:00 p.m. to 7:30 p.m. on December 1, 1976. Relevant aspects were also confirmed on interview of Mrs. Hill in Portsmouth, New Hampshire, on November 30, 1976, and an interview of Mrs. Fickett in Portland, Maine, on the morning of December 1, 1976.

I. Dr. Herbert Hopkin's Experience with a Man in Black

"September 11, 1976. Time: 8:00 p.m. Saturday. This was the first time I had been alone in the house for an extended period of time. My wife and children had gone to an outdoor movie, which I dislike.

"The telephone rang and I answered it. A man's voice identified himself as the vice president of the New Jersey UFO Research Organization (4), and he told me he would like to talk to me about David Stephens case. He asked if I was entirely alone and if it would be convenient for me to see him. I told him to come right up and I would talk to him. I did not even ask his name, which is very uncharacteristic of me, and also I never see anyone alone since my home and office have been broken into twice and since there is a great deal of illicit drug activity in this town at the present time — even the murder of a pharmacist.

"Immediately I went to the back door to turn on the light so that he could see his way in from my parking lot. Just as I turned on the light, I saw this man dressed in black coming up the porch stairs. I saw no car, and even if he did have a car, he could not have possibly gotten to my house that quickly from *any* phone. Strangely, at the time I did not think of this but opened the door for him without even asking who he was. I do not do things this way ordinarily. He did not introduce himself, but simply came in. He was about 5 feet 8 inches tall and weighed perhaps about 140 pounds. He wore a black derby, a black jacket, black tie, white shirt, black trousers and shoes. I thought, 'He looks like an undertaker.' I was struck immediately by his immaculate attire. His suit had not a wrinkle and fitted him like a clothing store dummy. It didn't fill out his legs and arms. The crease in his pants was perfect and razor sharp. The suit looked as if he had just put it on. Everything about him seemed to be super-perfect. He asked if he might sit down and I said 'Yes.' As he sat down, the crease in his trousers even at the knees did not flatten but stood out.

"He removed his hat and I saw that he was completely hairless and had no eyebrows or eyelashes. He had a smooth face with no hair follicles. He had a small nose set low, and small ears, set low. His head and face were of a dead-white color and his lips were a vivid red in stark contrast to his white face. His eyes were not remarkable — couldn't tell the color, I must have been 12 feet away from him. I remained calm and unafraid as I appraised him. I wonder why? As he asked me about the Stephens case, I noted that he spoke in an expressionless, monotone, scanning speech. His voice — he spoke English, flawless, with no accent, but no sentences, no phrases, just a series of words (5). His voice was completely neutral and passive.

"After I told him about the Stephens case, he said, 'That's just what I thought.' As I was telling him about the case, he idly put the backs of the fingers of one hand against his lips (he wore grey suede gloves), I noticed that the bright red of his lips had become smeared and the backs of his gloved fingers were stained red! This character was wearing lipstick!

"I thought, 'This is some kind of a queer.' His mouth was a perfectly straight slit, which he hardly opened. I didn't see any teeth. His head seemed to blend into his collar. He had a receding chin, and he did not move his head at any time; he didn't turn his head, nod, or anything. His head was perfectly stationary with the upper part of his body. As a matter of fact, I'd say with his entire body, except his legs.

"He then told me that I had two coins in my left pocket, which was true, a dime and a penny. He told me to take one of the coins and hold it out in the palm of my open hand. I took the penny because it was the larger of the two coins. Perhaps a 25-cent piece would have been better. I placed the shiny new penny on the palm of my extended hand and looked towards the strange man. He said, 'Don't look at me, look at the coin.' I did, and the shiny new penny was now a bright silver color. He told me to keep looking at the coin; as I did so the coin slowly became light blue in color, and then it began to become blurred to my vision. My hand was in sharp focus, but try as I might I could not seem to focus on the silver-blue penny. It became more blurred, became round like a little blue fuzzy ball, and then became vaporous and gradually faded away. All the time this was going on I felt and heard nothing. I looked at him and said, 'That was a neat trick (6).' I felt eerie at this and asked him to make the coin return. He said, 'Neither you nor anyone else on this *plane* (not planet) will ever see that coin again.'

"He then asked me if I knew why Barney Hill died, and I told him that I assumed it was the result of a long illness. He told me that this was not the case, that Barney Hill died because he knew too much. He then asked me if I knew how Barney Hill had died, and I told him I understood that he died of a heart attack (wrong information, I was to find out later) (7). He then told me that this was not correct, that he had died because he had no heart, just as I no longer have a coin. This frightened

242

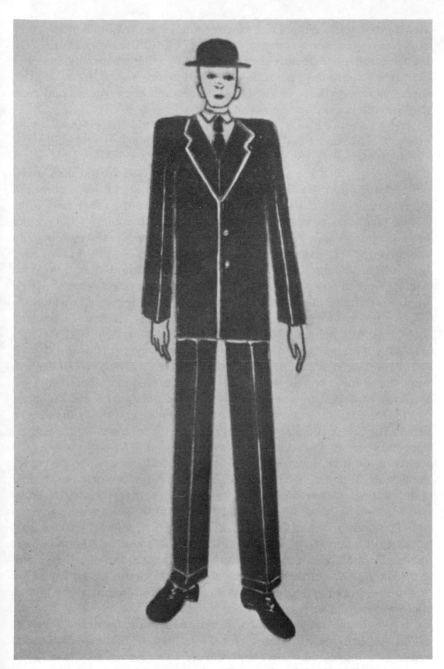

Dr. Hopkins' strange visitor, based on a sketch by Shirley Fickett.

me. He then told me that I had tape recordings of the Stephens case and also correspondence relating to this case. I said that this was true. He then ordered me to destroy the tapes and any other correspondence and literature I might have pertaining to UFOs in any way, or I would suffer the same fate as Barney Hill. He said he would know when I had done this, but did not say that he would come back.

"As he spoke his last words, I noticed that his speech was slowing down. Slowly, and a bit unsteadily, he got to his feet and said, very slowly, 'M y e n e r g y i s r u n n i n g l o w — m u s t g o n o w — g o o d-b y e.' He walked in four steps to the door and I opened it for him. He clung tightly to the railing as he went down the steps, one foot at a time — one foot down, then the other next to it, before taking the next step — not one foot after another. I watched him as he very unsteadily and slowly walked to the corner of the building and the driveway. He was so unsteady I thought he might fall. I saw a very bright light shining up the the driveway and thought that it must be coming from his car — but there was no light there when he arrived. The light was definitely brighter than automobile headlights and was bluish-white in color. I immediately rushed to the nearby kitchen window and looked out to watch him, but I didn't see or hear anything and the light was gone. I rushed out to the front porch but saw no car leaving.

"He walked in a different direction from the driveway—180 degrees opposed to the direction that he came in. I can't remember seeing his shadow. And walking out that way there is no way he could get out because the house is on one side of the driveway and the hedge on the other. The hedge is dense and he'd have a hard time getting through it, especially in his weakened condition. When he didn't appear there, I went out the front door on to the front porch and stood there looking for some time, watching the driveway, waiting for him to come out, but he didn't appear, and no car left the driveway. Two or three cars passed by on the street in the meantime, and I didn't think to look up.

I was much shaken and left all the lights on. The interview took only a matter of minutes. Oh, I don't know — twenty minutes. At no time was there any odor. When the man came to my house, the dog (half shepherd and half collie) barked, then put his tail between his legs, and hid in the closet (unusual behavior). A mother cat and four newborn kittens and a Persian cat were apparently not affected.

"When my two sons and wife returned from the drive-in movie, about one and one-half hours later, I told them of this experience. My oldest boy suggested we examine the driveway for marks and he got a flashlight. We went out and found in the very middle of the driveway a series of marks that looked like a small caterpillar tractor tread. The

244

marks were about four inches wide and continued for only about a foot and a half. There was nothing except this single set of marks. No automobile could have possibly made them because the driveway is too narrow for a car to get over far enough so that its wheels would be in the middle of the driveway. Also, they were too deep and distinct to have been made by a motorcycle, and, also, they did not continue for any length greater than that mentioned above. The marks were gone the next day (no one had used the driveway in the meantime).

"We went back inside and my family urged me to do as the man said. I erased the four tapes and then physically destroyed them in the fireplace. I burned some articles on UFOs and believe I had cleaned out everything. I called Shirley Fickett and asked her to contact the *National Enquirer* and tell them not to publish anything (on the Stephens case). Oh, how I hated to destroy those tapes. They weren't hurting anyone, but I wanted to be safe and I was really terrified at this point. I slept well that night, but a week later I had recurring nightmares in which I would see this creature's face getting bigger and closer. The nightmares stopped after a week and have not returned. We have had a lot of trouble since with the telephone (8) being cut off, clicks followed by background sounds indicating that there was an open line to another telephone somewhere, but never any voices. Also, people kept breaking in on phone calls. At the present time, however, the phone has not been disturbed any more. I hope this is the end!"

Mrs. Madeline Hopkins, R.N, the physician's wife, and their two sons and daughter-in-law, verified the account. Mrs. Hopkins recalled how surprised her two sons and she were when they returned home: "All the lights were on — on the porch, the front room, everywhere. I said that something was going on, so John (son) came in to find out. We saw my husband at the table which had a gun on it. I asked what went on? He started telling us the story. I said, 'Well, what good was the gun if he made a penny disappear?' I wish I had been there. But then, if I had been there, I don't think he (MIB) would have come."

II. Strange man and woman visit Dr. Hopkins' son and daughter-in-law

Dr. Hopkins continued: —

"Here is a transcript of the strange case of John and Maureen Hopkins, my eldest son and his wife.

"Friday, September 24, 1976. Time of phone call 7:30 p.m. (dark). Weather: clear, dry and cool. Air quiet. Phone answered by Maureen. Conversation: name given as Bill Post. Party calling knew her name, and called her by her name, said he was the friend of a friend who knew John, but did not state who that person was. He stated that they were from Conway, New Hampshire, and were at King's department store in Biddeford. He asked if they were busy and if they were alone, and he wanted to know if he and his companion could come to visit. There was a pronounced buzzing on the phone and the man's voice sounded distorted. He wanted to know where they could meet and asked, 'Isn't there a McDonald's (fast food restaurant) close by you?' He said he was at King's shopping centre and that he could get there in 5 minutes. This would be impossible even under ideal conditions; also, this was a Friday evening and the traffic on U.S. Route 1 was very slow and congested in this area. It would take at least 25 to 30 minutes at this time and under these conditions to get from King's to McDonald's. He said he would recognize John's white van. (John's white van was disabled, in the garage, and he was using his mother's green Chevy, which the man did not know about.)

"It took John 3 minutes to get to McDonald's as it is quite close. When John drove into McDonald's a young man walked over to him and said, 'Hi, John.' The window was down and he extended his hand into the car to shake John's hand. He had previously described his car to Maureen over the phone and said it had temporary New Jersey plates on it. John recognized the car as described and noticed that it did have temporary New Jersey plates (9), but the plates were devoid of any letters or numbers, merely saying: 'Temporary, N.J., 1975.' The man asked John where could they talk, and John suggested their mobile home. John asked the man to follow him, but they got separated due to a traffic light changing. John slowed down and saw the man's car cutting across the parking lot, going in back of the building, and coming out the driveway and stopping right in back of him. Evidently this person was very familiar with the territory and knew how to take a shortcut and to circumvent the red light. The car followed John to his mobile home.

"The man had a female companion. They were both Caucasian and appeared to be in their mid-thirties. He was about 5 feet 8 inches tall, medium build, about 160 pounds. He had dark hair, but short and smoothly slicked down, a style not seen for many years. He wore a tan, short-sleeved shirt with matching buttons, open at the collar, no tie. His trousers were dark brown, neatly pressed, and had wide cuffs. Style of shoes was not noticed. He wore dark-rimmed glasses. His nose was small with two nostrils, brown normal-appearing eyes, medium-size ears set far back. His voice was high-pitched and had a nasal quality. His complexion was light. He was very talkative without really saying much of anything, and he was quite fidgety.

"His woman companion was about 5 feet 8 inches tall, 150 to 160 pounds, with a pronounced potbelly. She had small firm breasts set very low, below the costal margin, and wore no bra. She wore a plain white blouse, black and white checked skirt of an unknown material (seemed it may have been plastic), nylon stockings, black shoes, the slip-on type with small heels which we do not see now. She talked very little, with a whining voice. She had excessive makeup by today's standards, including very red lips. When she stood up, she seemed quite off-centre in relation to the way her legs seemed to join her hips. She walked with very short steps as did her male companion, and leaned forward as though she might fall. She wore no glasses, and her blue eyes appeared to be normal: her nose had a sharp pointed ridge. She had small ears set well back, and very light blonde hair pulled back in a bun. Both presented a rather old-fashioned appearance, perhaps of 20 or more years ago.

"When John and the strangers arrived, Maureen was looking at a Jacques Cousteau underwater TV show which was still on. The man commented that the type of submarine being used was elementary. He downgraded it and indicated that the underwater work being shown was child's play.

"Then while Maureen was in the kitchen, and he was alone with them, John asked them to sit down. The man turned to the girl and said, 'Yes, Jane, I guess we can sit down for a little while, can't we?' John asked them if they would like something to drink (non-alcoholic), and the man answered, 'We don't drink, take drugs, or anything.' John then said that he meant soft drinks like Coca Cola. Both accepted Cokes but did not even taste them.

"The man asked John if he watched TV much and what he watched. The man and his companion seemed startled when John told them that both he and his wife watched TV frequently. It was difficult for John to explain to them that he and his wife did most things together. The man said that he knew where John's father lived and asked him if he talked to his father very much and what they talked about. He kept at this point, asking: 'Well, did you talk about anyting else?' He never got to the point of the three-letter-word I choose not to mention.

"He then said, 'The sky is very clear tonight,' and said, 'You are going to be in amateur radio [no equipment visible, but John, like his father, was involved]. What are you going to use your transmitter for?' When John told him, he asked, 'Is that all?' He asked what kind of literature John and Maureen read. John told him that they read many different things but did not elaborate, and the visitor answered, 'Yes, I know.'

"John went into the kitchen where Maureen was preparing something to eat and asked her to come back with him because he did not want to be alone. Reluctantly she joined them. The man asked John what he did and John told him he was a musician, and the visitor seemed puzzled. While questioning John, he kept pawing and fondling his female companion while repeatedly asking John if it was all right to do this and if he was doing it right.

"John left the room to answer the phone, and the man asked Maureen to sit beside him on the couch, but she refused. While John was on the phone, the man also asked Maureen how she was made. She said, 'Oh, what do you mean?' He said, 'I mean, how are you built?' She answered: 'Well, I guess I'm built just like any other girl.' Then he asked her if she had any nude pictures of herself so he could see how she was built and to study the pictures. She was upset and refused, saying 'Certainly not,' that she had none. John returned to the room and that was the end of that part of the conversation (10).

"The man said to John: 'You are going to New Jersey.' John did have plans to go to New Jersey, but he had not said so to this couple. The man told him to forget the route that the Automobile Club had given to him and that he would tell him how to get there. He then told of a detailed and complicated way to get to New Jersey, which avoided turnpikes and other well-travelled ways and, instead, used all out-of-the way back roads and numerous detours. Later, out of curiosity, John tried to check out some of these roads and found some of them discontinued, some of them rerouted, and some of them no longer considered back roads but now improved main roads.

"That was the end of the visit. The female stood up and said she wanted to leave. Her male companion also stood up but did not start to leave. She repeated to him several times that she wanted to leave, but he did not move. Finally, she said to John, in apparent desperation: 'Please move him; I can't move him myself.' He was standing closer to the door than she was, but not blocking her exit.

"John finally said, 'Well, I think you'd better go now.' and tried to calm her down. There were no obstacles — he, she, and the door were in direct line, and apparently the only way she could go to the door was to go directly to it through him: he had to move. The man seemed to want to sit down again, but suddenly left, followed by the female, walking a perfectly straight line, exactly over the spot where he had been standing. They didn't even say goodbye.

"My oldest son had not been able to sleep for a week prior to this visit and for a week after that. I prescribed some Dalmane for him. He said it didn't do much good. However, there was no apparent effect on my other son, wife, or daughter-in-law. Approximately a few weeks after the visit, the man telephoned and spoke to Maureen. He apologized for

FLYING SAUCER REVIEW

fsr

Volume 23, No. 4, 1977   70p

Chilling encounter with
a weird visitor and his
lop-sided, pot-bellied companion.
See . . .

THE MAN-IN-BLACK SYNDROME page 9

Pauline Bowen's impression of John and Maureen Hopkins' strange visitors.

anything he might have done that seemed inappropriate or out of place, or if they didn't like the way he acted. He was sorry for that and said it wouldn't happen again. He asked if they could please talk some more. However, Maureen just cut him off by saying she didn't want anything to do with people like them (11)."

REFERENCES AND NOTES

1. Raynes, Brent, J.: "The Twilight of a UFO Encounter," **Flying Saucer Review,** Vol. 22 (No. 2): 11-13, July, 1976.
2. Fickett, Shirley, M.: "The Maine UFO Encounter," **Flying Saucer Review,** Vol. 22 (No. 2): 14-17, July, 1976.
3. Schwarz, B.E.: "Psychiatric-paranormal Aspects of the Maine Encounter," **Flying Saucer Review,** Vol 22 (No. 2) 18-22, July 1976.
4. As far as I (BES) am aware, there is no New Jersey UFO Research Organization. Possibly this title was chosen because I am the only New Jersey link to David Stephen's case.
5. Edwards, P.M.H., Ph.D.: "The Interpretive Dilemma" (Part One), **Canadian UFO Report,** Vol. 4 (No. 1): 13-15 (Fall), 1976, (Part Two), **Ibid,** Vol. 4 (No. 2): 10-11 (Winter), 1976-1977.
6. The exact circumstances of the disappearing coin were described to Walter B. Gibson, at his home on February 17, 1977. In addition to being a magician himself, Mr. Gibson had written numerous books and articles on his friends Houdini, Thurston, Blackstone, and Dunninger, and had also authored 282 novels on The Shadow. He could not think of any explanation for the "neat trick." Although in my researches of gifted sensitivities I have never seen dematerialization (or materialization!), I have witnessed some impressive demonstrations of negative telepathic hallucinations by Jacques Romano (**The Jacques Romano Story**, University Books, Inc., New York, 1968, pp. 3-4).
7. Mrs. Betty Hill visited Dr. Hopkins and his family and reassured them that "Barney's death was a stroke and not a heart attack."
8. I had recorded Mrs. Fickett's and Dr. Hopkin's telephone conversations on September 16, 1976 and September 20, 1976 on my Lanier Edisette dictating equipment while simultaneously making written records. When my secretary was preparing to type the protocols, I was shocked to hear her say, "Nothing came through, except a slow, low-pitched, unintelligible growl." This could not be remedied by using four other tape recorders that I had access to, and also a variable-speed special taping apparatus utilized by the electronic inventor Donald Selwyn of the National Institute for Rehabilitation Engineering, Pompton Lakes, New Jersey. My office equipment has seldom given trouble. When there has been some difficulty, it was easily localized and repaired. In this case a large part of the recording having to do with the MIB description was ruined.
   On December 27, 1976, at 9:00 p.m., I had telephoned Betty Hill and compared notes about the latest developments in the David Stephens case (see reference 11) and Dr. Hopkin's MIB experience with the particular reference to Barney Hill. When I hung up, I learned that an upstairs fuse had blown which knocked out many circuits in the house, including my

consultation room lamp. Since I couldn't find the trouble, an electrician was called the next day and he could not understand why the fuse had blown since none of the circuits had overloaded (see "Talks with Betty Hill, FSR, Volume 23, Nos. 2, 3, and 4, 1977).

When I was checking one of the fuse boxes in the cellar, the office phone rang. I ran upstairs and found there was only a dial tone. The phone was out of order, and the next day the telephone repair man was called. When the phone was in order again, and I tried to call Dr. Hopkins, more than an estimated twenty-five times over a period of four days, to make arrangements for my visit with him, I either got no answer, or there was a busy signal. Dr. Hopkins later told me that someone was at home all that time and his phone was not in continuous use.

Joseph Dunninger and Walter Gibson

251

Finally, on December 14, 1980, I received a technical report from Donald Selwyn on the tape of September 20, 1976: "The tape could not be understood when played from the original casette. It was too slow at normal speed and the pitch range was so low that nothing could be understood. The only information I had been given by you (BES) was that the conversation had been recorded directly from the telephone line by you and that the cassette recorder you had used was not operating on batteries but was powered from an AC outlet. You had no idea what might have caused this abnormal recording; you stated the recorder operated normally before and after this particular cassette and this was the only problem cassette you knew of. The voices on the tape were greatly reduced in speech rate and pitch, to a pitch approximately equal to normal pitch divided by a factor between 3.2 and 4.15. Most of the tape was recorded at a relatively constant speed; wow and flutter were a problem only near the end of the second side of the cassette, for a very short period of time, and that might have been due to the tape being near the end and thus not being stabilized by the tape reserve now gone from the feed reel in the cassette. One very unusual and interesting effect was noted during the analysis and the restoration (re-recording) processes. In some portions of the tape, sustained but rapid-fire two-way conversation were taking place, with back and forth interchanges, such that one person's voice was 1.7 to 1.50 octave lower than the other person's voice. Or, the second person's voice was .75 to 1.50 octave higher than the first person's voice; or else both voices were displaced part of this amount, each in the opposite direction, for the stated net difference. Had the tape speed varied (during recording or during playback, then **both** voices would have changed pitch by the same amount and in the same direction. I know of no explanation for what apparently did occur — one voice going lower in pitch and the other higher, on a consistent and continuing basis, throughout rapid two-way conversation. For these taped portions I was able to properly restore one or the other speaker to normal pitch, but not both, or in some parts I set a pitch in between allowing one speaker to be low and the other high, but both understandable, as a compromise."

Financial considerations prevented voice stress analysis, however, Mr. Selwyn remarked that: "Dr. Hopkins may be been under a great deal of stress, due to the subject matter and his own words — but not yourself, it would seem."

9. The Montclair Police Department and the Motor Vehicle Registration Office stated that temporary New Jersey license plates are good for only 20 days, and, as Dr. Hopkins surmised, they have letters and serial numbers. Thus, if the observation is correct, the plates that were devoid of numbers or letters, and had a date of 1975, would be hard to account for through official sources.

10. I have touched upon some of the sexual aspects of the UFO cases elsewhere **(Flying Saucer Review,** Vol. 17, No. 2: 4-9, March/April, 1971; **ibid**; No. 3: 21-17, May/June, 1971; and "Talks with Betty Hill," **Flying Saucer Review** Vol. 23, Nos. 2, 3, and 4, 1977). However, mention might be made of one unreported situation which had some parallels to the experience of Maureen and John Hopkins and which involved a leading Ohio UFO investigator, Mrs. Geri Wilhelm. Space precludes detailing many of

her group's UFO sightings and investigations and presumed related poltergeist effects. However, as a background to the Hopkins's experience, three things that happened to the Wilhelms involved: (1) the electric oven being maximally (and dangerously) heated when the switches were in the "off" position; (2) Mrs. Wilhelm's observation or hallucination of a little man in a silver suit, who was not seen by her husband who was with her at the time, but who was later seen independently by her daughter who knew nothing of her mother's observation; and (3) Mr. Wilhelm's once being run off the highway by an MIB-like pursuer who tried to crunch him into a trailer truck and then into a gulley.

I visited the family on September 11, 1974, and checked out their accounts. Whatever the meaning of so many of their odd experiences, two events might be relevant to the Hopkins MIB case. One evening after an appearance on TV about UFOs, Mrs. Wilhelm received a call from a man with a German accent. He told her about HG, a famous scientist, and said Mrs. Wilhelm should telephone him. She did so, and noted that HG also had a German accent. He made many lurid and grandiose claims about himself and UFOs. Although the telephone recording of the first caller was intact, the HG conversation, as it was later discovered, did not record. "It sounded like I was talking long distance. There were bee-beeps and high-pitched noises. We were frequently interrupted as he was being called to other phones. I could overhear him talking a different type of language — real gibberish. He sounded angry and strange." HG was insistent upon meeting Mrs. Wilhelm, and she finally compromised on a nearby bowling alley.

Being an adventurous person, she went off in high spirits but left the recording by the telephone with a note for her husband, in the event anything might happen to her. HG said that an Apollo XVI patch would be his calling card, and that she should bring "a little money, so that we can sit and have a drink," and he mentioned a strange name of a type of drink. Mrs. Wilhelm walked over to the bowling alley and met HG, who showed her his Apollo XVI patch. He said, "I'm really not HG. I'm possessing the body of HG. I'm making it do what it is doing." Mrs. Wilhelm related: "I got him a beer and myself a coke. I got him another beer and he told me how beautiful I was and said that since his wife had been killed in an accident, he'd like me to give up everything I have on earth and marry him, and go to his planet. He said he had kept one space in the saucer that was leaving and that it would arise from Tylersville at 8 o'clock that evening and that he would be flying over the townhouse where I lived." Mrs. W. recalled that when she went to buy the second beer for HG, there was another family sitting in the booth behind them and that the World Series was on television. The lady asked HG who was winning and he answered with, "What is the World Series?" The lady said, "What do you mean? Anyone who lives in America knows what the World Series is." When Mrs. Wilhelm got back to the table, the lady told her about the conversation and said, "Where is this man from? He has to be from out of this world. He's sincere, but he really doesn't know. He told me he's too much in love with you to care about the World Series."

When HG discussed the subject of God and his alleged inhabitance of the planet Terrapin, the creatures, etc., Mrs. Wilhelm became upset and left by a side entrance. She thought of going to the front where the parking lot was and get the license number of his Mazda car. However she was fearful that if she did that, she might never see her husband and two children again, so she walked directly home.

When Mrs. Wilhelm returned home and told her husband about what happened, she said it was odd because at the time of Geri's interview with HG their four-year-old daughter came downstairs, sat on her father's lap, and told him that her mother was at the bowling alley with a man who had a ring on his left hand. This was strange because Angel had no idea where her mother was going nor that the man had a ring on his left hand. Mrs. Wilhelm said HG reminded her of the "perfect example of a German Reich type of person that Hitler said would be the superior race: he was a little over 6 feet tall, had white hair, had big blue eyes, and wore a wedding ring, plus another ring that looked like a college ring."

Mr. and Mrs. Wilhelm thought the experience was a hoax, even if it was well planned, until that night when she and another investigator received calls from different people near Tylersville Road saying that a saucer-shaped craft was rising out of the woods. The time was 8 o'clock, as HG had said.

"The feelings I had were of evil when I was in his (HG) presence. I'm thankful for the fact that I believe in God, and I had Him with me at all times."

A friend and associate UFO investigator of Mrs. Wilhelm, BR, who knew about the HG incident, once called and asked HG to tell her about what happened. However, he refused to talk about it. Discreet inquiries by additional Ohio UFO investigators discovered that HG's listed house number was not correct, that according to his fellow workers at the factory, where he was well thought of, he had no previous interest in UFOs; and because he was of a rather introverted and shy nature, the above-cited experience would have been completely out of character. Even up to my most recent telephone follow-up (February 22, 1977) this information has remained unchanged. However, the varied psychic and telekinetic effects in Mrs. Wilhelm's home and family life persist. After I interviewed Mrs. Wilhelm in the presence of her mother, Mrs. Sherrin, and two other friends, and listened to the HG telephone-recorded tape, I was aware that here again was an opportunity (note p. 26, **Flying Saucer Review**, Vol. 17 (No. 3): 21-27, May/June, 1971) to interview a parent of a leading UFO experient. I wasn't disappointed because after conducting a psychiatric-paranormal survey, Mrs. Sherrin, who had a responsible job in a photograph studio and seemed to be a straight-forward lady, free of any relevant UFO psychopathology, recalled how approximately a year and a half previous to my interview, she received a call, one January evening, from her favorite Aunt Lorraine (mother's sister): "She was four years older than I. We were like sisters. We talked about different things we had done in the past, places we had been together, just sort of reminiscing. I was home alone. This went on for about half an hour, but when I hung up, I thought 'It was Lorraine! But she's dead. She was killed instantly in an automobile accident six or seven months ago! I even get chills now, talking about it. In fact I was so upset, I dialed her number but nobody answered."

My question that uncovered this example was prompted by a hunch based on a previous 'telephone voice from the dead' case (see Schwarz, B.E.: Telepathic Humoresque, **The Psychoanalytic Review**, Vol. 61 (No. 4); 591-606, 1974-75, example 12, pp. 600-602, and of another case, where after an APRO symposium (Pottstown, Pa., June 15, 1974) a middle-aged couple told me (and the woman later wrote) about some of their UFO-psychic, M.I.B. experiences, including a bizarre telephone call. From a: "Roger — and I had a brother named Roger, the eldest of three children, who had died a few days after birth. I never knew of him until I was in my thirties. I never told anyone about him except my husband and daughter. The grave is unmarked, and those who knew of his birth and death at the time (who were very few) are either dead or, most certainly, have long forgotten. The phone rang, and my husband answered. He said it was a man asking for Beverly:

Beverly: Hello.
Man: Hi, Bev. This is Rog.
Beverly: Who?
Man: Roger.
Beverly: I am afraid you have the wrong Beverly.
Man: Oh, no I don't. **You're** the one I want. I know that.
Beverly: But I don't know any Roger.
Man: Yes you do. **Think**, Beverly. Think — way, way back.
Beverly: Tell me your last name or I'll have to hang up.
Man: You know that as well as I.
Beverly: I don't know you, and I'm going to hang up unless you tell me who you are and what you want.
Man: (Long pause, sigh). Oh, Beverly, I do so want to talk with you.
Beverly: I'm sorry.
Man: (Another long pause). All right. I'm sorry Beverly.
Beverly: It's all right. 'Bye.
Man: (Pause). G o o d b y e. (In long, drawn-out sounds).

The woman continued: "The man's voice was always quiet, calm, well-modulated, not exactly a monotone, but close and quite strong with emphasis on words I underlined. The wrong thing about all this is our phone is listed under Campbell's name, not mine. And how many wrong numbers can be dialed and a name like Beverly asked for and a Beverly lives there? My family said that I turned white and shaky and was extremely unlike myself during and after this conversation." These examples for whatever they are worth, should not be dogmatically construed as proving anything, but they merely indicate the uniqueness of some of the UFO-related material, which is begging for a prolonged, detailed psychiatric-paranormal study of the experients and their families.

11. During the Hopkins family's stressful post-MIB period, there were some new developments with David Stephens, the young man who, with his friend, had the alleged teleportation and who was studied hypnotically by Dr. Hopkins. Mrs. Shirley Fickett wrote me on September 20, 1976, that Friday night (September 17) David visited her and reported an intensification of activity: "His friends are seeing these things (UFOs). Lights came on and stayed on; TV doing the same; the refrigerator door opened and slammed itself; the outside door then opened and didn't stay shut. Someone said something about UFOs and the kitchen table slid out 5 to 6

inches from the wall. Four people saw this:"

Mrs. Shirley Fickett also wrote me: "It was on September 17, 1976, that I received a call from Mrs. Herbert Hopkins, stating that her husband had experienced a visit from an unearthly 'man in black,' who told him to rid his property of all UFO material. Dr. Hopkins was upset and did not speak to me on the phone. Later that afternoon I went to his residence and he carefully related the incident of the night before. I wrote down his exact words and forwarded them to Dr. Schwarz.

"On September 13, 1976, as Mrs. Bea Stephens, David's mother, was cooking a spaghetti supper, she reached for a bowl in the cupboard above the boiling water on the stove. The bowl slipped from her hand and the water burned her abdomen. She was home alone at the time and rushed to her physician. When she and her husband, who had previously been at the store, returned home, he looked up at the ceiling and noted spots where the water had hit and also three 7s on the cupboard, above the refrigerator. The numbers gradually faded away, but on September 17, 1976, I received a call from the Stephenses telling me that the number 7 in reverse had appeared on Bea's abdomen among the markings from the burns received on the 13th. The following day I was visited by the Stephenses, and Mrs. Stephens let me photograph her abdomen. However, the photo did not come out. During the visit, Mr. Gene Stephens drew a picture of the 7s on the cupboard door, which I (Shirley Fickett) have redrawn (see Figure 1, a)."

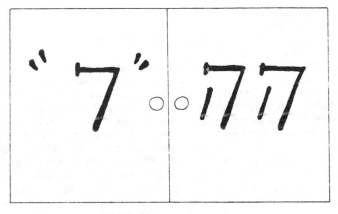

Figure 1a

This data was independently confirmed by a letter from Mr. and Mrs. Gene Stephens and also a drawing by Mrs. Stephens of the reverse 7 on her abdomen (see Figure 1, b). It is of more than passing interest to compare Mrs. Stephen's periumbilical reverse 7 which corresponded with the 7s on the cupboard doors with Michel's spectacular case where the doctor developed a geometrically perfect triangle in the umbilical region shortly before his son also developed a triangle in the same region (see Michel,

256

Aime:The Strange Case of Dr. "X", **Flying Saucer Review, UFO Percipients**, Special Issue No. 3: 3-16, September, 1969).

Another thing: David was stopped by the police because his one headlight was out, and he was asked for his driver's license, which he didn't have. The police radioed Augusta and the reply came back that David Stephens was deceased as of last October 27, 1975). David was told he was an imposter, and he resisted arrest. Help was called and three men showed up. David panicked and was jailed after a fight. They kept telling him that he was not David Stephens. Finally, after three hours, they let him go, after taking finger prints. Later he checked and there were no records of this imbroglio!, nor of other things that occurred that night! (For a similar case of missing police records, see footnote on the Hackettstown case, pp. 8 to 9, **Flying Saucer Review,** Vol. 18, (No. 1): 3-12 Jan/Feb., 1972).

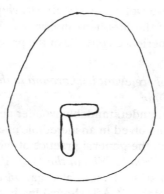

Figure 1b

The Man-In-Black Syndrome . . . 2

Follow up on the Maine UFO Encounter

Doctor Herbert Hopkins is the medical man who was consulted by Mrs. Shirley Fickett and Brent Raynes when they were investigating the Maine teleportation/contact case involving witness David Stephens and a friend (see *Flying Saucer Review* Vol. 22, No. 2). It was he who hypnotically regressed Mr. Stephens and recorded the sessions.

In the first part of this present article an account was given of the bizarre man-in-black visitations that were experienced, first by Dr. Hopkins himself, and secondly by his son and daughter-in-law.

As a result of these weird encounters Dr. Hopkins, very disturbed, destroyed the tapes of the Stephens interviews. We now take a look at the doctor, and his experiences outside of the present case.

III. Possibly relevant background to the MIB visit

1. Brief Curriculum Vitae

The reader might understandably wonder about the credibility of a person who has been involved in an incredible encounter. Dr. Hopkins is a physician involved in the general practice of medicine, specializing in allergy. He is listed in *Who's Who in the East,* 10th Edition, 1966-1967. Besides belonging to several medical organizations, he is a graduate electronics engineer of the RCA Technical Institute, studied for—but did not apply for — ordination as a minister of the Christian Advent Church, as well as, more recently, an ordained Spiritualist minister. He has been involved in private research on electro-acoustic and electronic systems and is vice president of the General Sound Corporation, and President of Hopkins Sound Technology, Inc. He has many patents and has written his own applications for patents. His stereo speakers, which are listed in an authoritative text on the subject, are used by leading recording companies.

He was an honors student at the Christian Advent College of Aurora, Illinois. While there, he did research in physics. He later transferred to the Univerity of Illinois Medical School on a scholarship (Ivy League Award). His more recent research activities have included a theory of anti-gravity and free energy. He has taken many courses through the years, including specialized techniques in hypnosis. Aside from a transient asthmatic condition, he has enjoyed good health throughout his life. He is of old English and German stock and is married, his wife acting also as his office nurse. They have two sons; one an accomplished and successful musican; and the other a skilled auto mechanic. There has never been any question of sociopathic difficulties, use of habit-forming, addictive, or hallucinogenic drugs, delirium, etc.

These facts and opinions are supported by examination of relevant documents and interviews of the doctor, of various members of his family, of Mrs. Fickett, and Mr. Raynes. Through coincidence or synchronicity, this data is further supported by the fact that Dr. Hopkins is a medical school classmate of my brother-in-law, George P. Balz, M.D., Clinical Professor of Rheumatology at the University of Cincinnati, who recalls HH fondly, as a brilliant, well-thought-of student. Coincidentally also, Dr. Hopkins is physician to the eminent Maine dowser, Henry Gross, who was written up by Kenneth Roberts (12-14) as well as studied by me (15,16). Mr. Gross and his late wife Olive, as well as their daughter Clara, spoke highly of Dr. Hopkins. His intelligence, emotional stability, and inventiveness appear superior in all respects.

Possibly these manifold unique attributes give clues why Dr. Hopkins and not the others who were involved in the Stephens case was chosen for the MIB visit. He has proven expertise in physics, electronics, medicine, philosophy, religion, and apparently highly developed psi capacities. Possibly he could bring a better understanding to the Stephens experience, which might be undesirable to the UFO force, whatever that is. For, had he not destroyed his evidence, he might have given further thought to the Stephens experience, pursued the case, and tapped meanings that have eluded others. Could he, a highly developed sensitive, which made him open for this event (materialization?), have also posed a threat to the UFO forces and been the reason for their inducing his abrupt withdrawal? Certainly his MIB encounter succeeded in ending all publicity, but it also, fortunately, made it possible for me to prepare this report for the serious readers of FSR. Whatever the final interpretation of his experience, we are deeply in Dr. Hopkins' debt.

2. Developing awareness for Psi

Although my visit was too short to document various anecdotal paranormal events reported to me by Dr. Hopkins, it should be noted that in other psychiatric-psi surveys of people who claim close UFO, or UFO-related, encounters, the psychic aspects were often striking. In organizing and sketching some of these possible psi experiences, the writer is confronted with the problem of how to compress these accounts into readable form, while not omitting significant deatils, for psi is a continuum, and a cutoff point between people and events is hard to establish. However, possibly some of Dr. Hopkin's life experiences will throw some light on his MIB encounter.

Dr. Hopkins had no particular knowledge or interest in psychic phenomena until recent years. Having an inquisitive, philosophical-scientific type of mind, he enrolled in a Silva Mind Control course because it "was supposed to increase one's ability to concentrate, increase one's attention span, and make one more aware, etc." He was so impressed by it that his wife then took the course, and he repeated it five times. Once, after the course, a lady they met in class asked them if they had ever been to a Spiritualistic church. They said no, that they knew nothing about it. However, shortly afterwards, he and his wife attended out of curiosity. Although he was reared an Episcopalian, had attended a Christian Advent College in Illinois, and had converted to Catholicism when he married his wife, he felt that these teachings left him dissatisfied. He had many friends and patients among the clergy of these different denominations and others, but he never received satisfactory answers to his queries: "Why am I here? Where did I come from? Where am I going?

At his first session at the Spiritualist Church, although his wife and he "tried to blend in with the woodwork, because we didn't know what kind of kooky thing this was," they were surprised to hear the spirit messages and then were shocked when the minister recited a host of details about Mrs. Hopkins' background. The process was then repeated with Dr. Hopkins. The minister told the physician that he was a gifted sensitive himself. He then went on to predict a series of events including the Hopkinses attending many more meetings and finally Dr. Hopkins becoming an ordained Spiritualistic minister himself. Needless to say, Dr. Hopkins was astounded and protested that he had no intention of doing any of that. However, after various "happenstances" and unusual events intervened over a period of time, he became an ordained Spiritualist minister. He even established his own church, which meets in his home and is attended by a handful of intellectuals.

Dr. Hopkins might have wondered if much of his previous life was in some way a preparation for these later developments, for he recalled with clarity two particularly outstanding possible psi events.

3. Veridical nightmare

The day before Thanksgiving, 1949, while in medical school in Chicago, the doctor and his wife went to Aurora, Illinois. That evening he had a nightmare: "I saw a black *Dodge* car. It was not a brand-new one. It was on fire and there were five people in it, screaming and trying to get out — unsuccessfully. I was horrified. I then found myself in back of the car looking at the license plate, and the numbers seemed to burn themselves indelibly into my hand. I awakened with a start, and Madeline asked me what was wrong. I told her of my dream. She said it was just a nightmare, and I should forget it. I tried to go back to sleep; then finally I got up and wrote down the license number and put it in my pocket. The next morning when we went downtown for breakfast, we drove past a garage and there was a large tow truck with a chain and hook. Hooked onto the chain was a black *Dodge* car burnt to a crisp. I backed up so I could see the license plate. I compared it with the number written down on the paper in my pocket: it was identical! That spoiled our appetite for breakfast. My wife was shocked. That night there was a special edition of the paper, and we read that a Dodge car with five people in it had burned and all the occupants had died in the car. They gave the names of the people, but I did not know any of them. They meant nothing to me. . .they were total strangers. I thought that over for a couple of days and went back to school on Monday.

The nightmare was preceded by an episode in anatomy class where one of the students accidentally cut a ureter, which he should not have done, and he commented to the effect that it wouldn't make any difference to him (the deceased) now. However, another student said he wasn't so sure, and that led to a discussion. Dr. Hopkins said: "I was the most dogmatic of the group, for any psychic phenomena or seeing yourself after death and things like that were absolutely hogwash. I could not accept that under any circumstances because it could not be scientifically proven. It was quite a heated discussion. That is why I did not say anything about my dream to the other fellows. I didn't want to be embarrassed by telling them what had happened and having people say, 'See, I told you so!'

4. Possible precognition

"Nothing happened for many years, and then in 1957 we bought this house and were living here. My wife's brother-in-law was recovering from a subtotal gastrectomy and was with us, also my wife's mother, my younger brother, and my wife's niece. There was no way I could get out of the house without being seen. They were all up that night, but I was dead tired from a rigorous schedule of surgery and house calls plus office work; so it must have been a little bit before eleven that I went to bed and had a dream. Because it was a dream filled with firm, unshifting, unquestionable detail, colors, sights, sounds, smell, everything complete, everything was just that real, I knew it wasn't a dream. There was a peculiar, all-pervading consciousness about it.

"I saw this car: a two-tone green 1956 *Buick* special. It ran into something that I did not see. There were three people in the car, two girls and a boy. Then I found myself looking at the license number of the car, and I noted it and remembered it. I also noted that the incident occurred in front of 70 East Grand Avenue. I awakened with a start. Madeline asked me what was wrong. 'I didn't hear any crash: what are you talking about? You must have been dreaming.' I said, 'No. This was real. A car hit something. I heard it. It happened right in front of 70 East Grand Avenue.' She said, quite correctly, 'Well, if it happened there, how could you possibly have heard it? All the way up here!' Again I tried to go back to sleep but I couldn't.

"Finally I wrote down the number that I had seen on the car and I fumed, fussed, squirmed, and twisted, but I couldn't get to sleep. Finally, after 20 minutes my wife said, 'Well, if you are that concerned about it, I'll call Paul.' Paul Belrose was the man at the desk in police headquarters at night. He was a patient and a close friend of ours. If he had been a stranger, she would not have called. She asked Paul if there had been an accident on East Grand Avenue. And he said, 'Excuse me, please, there is a call coming in. Hold the phone while I take it, and I'll be right back to you.'

"A minute or so later he came back on the phone and said, 'Yes, Madeline, what was that you were telling me about? An accident?' And she said, 'Doc had a dream that there was an accident in front of 70 East Grand Avenue involving a two-tone green *Buick*. It hit something he couldn't quite see, but the car backed up and drove off.' Madeline continued, 'Doc's quite shaken up about it and can't put it out of his mind.' Paul said 'Guess what? I'm shaking too. That was the call that just came in! (More than 20 minutes after HH's dream.) But I don't have all the details. A woman called from 70 East Grand Avenue and said she saw a green car hit a pole and she saw some young folks in it but she didn't know what kind of car it was and she didn't see the license plate.'

"So we provided the license number and the description of the car, and that there were two girls and a boy. We said that the car had driven off toward Pine Point and in the general direction of Portland and South Portland and that it would be picked up by the South Portland police and that the kids would be arrested. Madeline told him that and Paul said, 'I'm going to notify the South Portland police, and if I hear anything I'll call you back.'

"I felt relieved and went to sleep. About an hour later the phone rang and it was Paul Belrose from the police desk. He said, 'I have something to tell you that's going to shake you up. The South Portland police have called me and they stopped a 1956, two-tone green *Buick*, with that license number with a damaged front bumper and grill. There were two girls and a boy in it. The car had been taken without the owner's knowledge. They were under arrest, exact details, detail for detail.'

"You know I witnessed the whole thing, well before it happened. Now I have no knowledge of the time that the accident happened when the car burned in Auroroa, Illinois, I don't know whether I dreamed that at the time it happened, before, or afterwards. I don't have that information because the time was not given in the newspaper write-up, and I really didn't notice the time that I awoke, so the information on that is uncertain." (It could have been telepathic) (17).

5. Possible paranormal experiences with mother after her death

Dr. Hopkins could recall no psychic experiences for his mother or father. However, a series of events happened after his mother's death at age 82, three years ago. He was quite close to his mother, who was living with him and his wife. His father had died some years before. Both Mrs. Hopkins and the doctor recalled how, after his mother's death, the lights would frequently go on in various parts of the house, and each would think that the other had turned them on, which was not the case.

On one occasion, out of habit as when his mother was alive, the doctor checked her room. Madeline had placed two pillows side by side when she had made up the bed. The doctor, as was his mother's custom, placed the pillows on top of each other and on the way out, smoothed out the cushion on his mother's rocking chair. The next morning Mrs. Hopkins asked him if he had disturbed the bed and he told her what he had done, explaining he didn't know why he did it other than it just made him feel better. The wife then wanted him to look in his mother's bedroom because the bed was in disarray as if someone had slept in it, and there was a deep imprint on the top pillow with a profile of a head. Also, the cushion on the rocker appeared to have been sat on. They gave no more thought to this experience, but the following night when he glanced into the room he thought he could see his mother sitting in the chair. It faded away and he went to bed.

Then one evening, a week later, Mrs. Hopkins was watching the news on the television downstairs. At seven o'clock she shut off her TV and went upstairs to get her uniform for the evening office hours. She got part way up the stairs and heard the TV, but she was sure she had shut it off. So she went downstairs again and found that indeed the TV was shut off. Going upstairs again and looking through the bannister railings on her way up, she could look into her mother-in-law's room. Because of the way the TV in that room was tilted, she could clearly see the screen and it was on. She went downstairs again to ask if her husband had turned it on. The doctor said he had not been up there and did not turn it on himself, so they went up together and found that the TV

263

was on and that it had been turned from Channel 13 to Channel 8, in time for his mother's favorite program at seven o'clock, *What's My Line?*

The doctor was curious about how long the TV might have been on (thinking they might have left it on accidentally) and felt the set. It was stone cold. If it had been on even for five minutes, it would have built up some warmth in the enclosure of the cabinet. He turned off the set by pushing in the pull-out, push-in switch of the kind that precluded the possibility of the dog or cat brushing against the knob and accidentally turning the set on.

One Friday night, when the Doctor had assembled a group of intellectuals interested in "picking up communications," his deceased mother's presence was not only "sensed" but the double latched doors to the meeting room suddenly opened wide, cool air came through, and when one of the group rose to close the doors, the doors closed and clicked shut spontaneously.

6. Potpourri, including possible paranormal tape from Dr. Hopkins' late father

Although Dr. Hopkins was familiar with alleged psychic photography, he had never tried that himself. And when Henry Gross once said that he thought the doctor could be a good dowser, he tried it with Henry and was successful. He never repeated the event. Another time as the mood hit him, he sat down and put his tape recorder on and said: "Please, Spirit, help us. Please guide me. Dear Spirit, soon help me. Dear helpful Spirits, dear guiding Spirit, spirits of the so-called dead, please help me. Please guide me. Please speak up that I may hear you clearly on this tape."

When he played the tape back, he was shocked to hear, as was confirmed by his wife, the voice of his late father, which came between and over his phrases. The voice said: "Please help me — please guide me. Help (18)." He never repeated this event because, "I hadn't the time nor the inclination (19)."

Notes and References
12. Roberts, K.: **Henry Gross and His Dowsing Rod,** Doubleday & Co., New York, 1951.
13. Roberts, K.: **The Seventh Sense,** Doubleday & Co., New York, 1953.
14. Roberts, K.: **Water Unlimited,** Doubleday & Co., New York, 1957.
15. Schwarz, B.E.: Physiological Aspects of Henry Gross's Dowsing, **Parapsycology,** Vol. IV (No. 2): 71-86, 1962-63.
16. Schwarz, B.E.: **Psychic Dynamics,** Pageant Press, Inc., New York, 1965.
17. Precognition, possibly the rarest of psi abilities, might be better understood

if viewed as part of the psychic nexus. It is part of a continuum, as is well illustrated in the Hopkins case, with it's long-standing and variegated manifestations of psi and synchronicity, possibly evolving into the explosive psi-laden UFO experience and MIB encounter. Further examples of the psychic nexus can be found in my "Precognition and Psychic Nexus," **Journal of the American Society of Psychosomatic Dentistry and Medicine,** Part I, Vol. 18 (No. 2): 52-59, 1971; Part II, Vol. 18 (No. 3): 83-93, 1971; and in "Psi and the Life Cycle," **ibid.**: Vol. 21 (Nos. 2, 3, 4), and Vol. 22 (Nos. 1, 2, 3, 4), 1974.

18. Discussion of some of UFO contactee Mrs. Stella Lansing's presumed paranormal tapes can be found in Commentary on the August Roberts Mystery, **Flying Saucer Review**, Vol. 21, (No. 6): 18-19, April, 1976. Interestingly enough, in comparison with Dr. Hopkins' plaintive voice on the paranormal tape Mrs. Lansing had a similar experience on November 8, 1975. I had been visiting her at the time, and although we attempted various filming and recording projects, we did not immediately play back the tapes and did not know what was going on. However, the next morning she informed me that shortly after I left her home "I (S.L.) put the reel recorder in the rewind position and it stopped. The motor was 'on' but it wouldn't play. It took from 2:30 until 3:10 a.m. until it played. And then it didn't end until 4:00. I filmed to show that the switch was on and the extension cord plugged in. There were funny noises. Something like typewriters, or electrical switches. A voice from the speaker kept saying: 'Please believe me, please believe me.' I recorded this on the cassette machine which was next to the reel recorder."

It was hard to define the circumstances, but Mrs. Lansing filmed the machines, and it appeared that the jamming and the placement of the switches were as she described. She had the reel-to-reel on in the "play" position hoping to make a recording because of a recent case experience of mine which I had told her about and where some spectacular recordings were allegedly made in that paradoxical position. We tried this particular experiment also because the night before, when she was alone, she again taped a direct voice saying, "You believe," many times over. Later, when she edited the tape we made together, she heard interpolated between her speech and my talk various phrases that had no apparent relationship to our talk and which occurred apparently randomly: "My name is Melinda ... I'm from the Spirit world ... run out of film now ... run out ... energy gone ... I can't stand it any more." Although I heard the "Please believe me," and at one point, "Please believe me, Mrs. Lansing," in a deep, halting doleful voice, I did not have an opportunity to check out the other statements. However, it is of interest that at the early morning time when I left, perhaps with disappointment for not achieving results and also wearied by Mrs. Lansing's chain-smoking and night-owl vitality, that the voice said, "I can't stand it any more," might have clearly reflected my unexpressed feelings.

19. Perhaps unconscious resistance to psi is the key to developing an awareness for this ability. In many UFO reports the conscious — not alone unconscious — resistance to psi accounts for the omission of much relevant possible paranormal data. The subject of resistance to psi is brilliantly explored by Jule Eisenbud, M.D., in his **Psi and Psychoanaly-**

sis (Grune and Stratton, Inc., New York, 1970), and J.A.M. Meerloo, M.D., in **Hidden Communion and Unobtrusive and Unconscious Communications** (Garrett Publications, Helix, New York, 1964).

The Man-In-Black Syndrome . . . 3

Herein continues the discussion of the alleged paranormal experiences of Dr. Herbert Hopkins, the physician who became involved in the investigation of the Maine UFO encounter/teleportation/contact case reported by David Stephens and a friend (see FSR Vol. 22, No.2).

It was Dr. Hopkins who conducted the hypnotic regression of David Stephens and recorded the sessions. It was the tapes of these sessions which were destroyed after the doctor had suffered a bizarre yet sinister man-in-black visitation described in Part I of this article.

7. Alleged psychic healings and related subjects

For his healing commission as a Spiritualistic minister, Dr. Hopkins turned in sixteen cases. None of the people he helped were aware that he was a physician, and no one paid him a fee. Some of his cases included a woman who had a chronic draining perforated eardrum, a woman who had non-union of a fractured thigh bone with insertion of a metal plate, a case of intractable, severe migraine, a woman with widespread dermatitis, a woman who had a lumbar cast because of three fractured vertebrae, and two patients with far advanced malignancy.

Alleged extraordinary results were obtained in all these cases through the mediumship of the physician-Spiritualist minister. In almost all of these cases the people were under the care of their personal physicians, some of whom were known to Dr. Hopkins. However, in no instances were the physicans aware of Dr. Hopkins' role.

My short visit to Maine precluded possible interviews of the afflicted people who claimed the cures or their physicians, and it was impossible to examine the data, including the X-rays. I hope, however, that at some future time this can be done, and if warranted, a report prepared for a medical journal. It is readily acknowledged that there are all kinds of claims for psychic or "miraculous" healings, but in most instances unfortunately the documentation is so poor and there are so many technical objections that the data is worthless. However, whatever the final interpretations of the Dr. Hopkins' cases, the cures were "real," both to him, a skilled physician, and to the people who were helped.

266

It is hoped that his study can be undertaken with safeguards that protect Dr. Hopkins from people expecting "miracles" and yet which adhere to tough scientific standards (20). Perhaps it might shed some light on the possible modus operandi of poorly documented alleged UFO healings (21) and alleged healings by the late Brazilian peasant Arigo (22), as studied by physician Andrija Puharich, and the even more controversial fraud-tinged Philippine psychic surgeons (23).

It is stressed that Dr. Hopkins disclaimed any knowledge of this and related literature, and as a matter of fact was surprised when I asked him about the possible relationship of the disappearing coin and his earlier healing of a fractured case, where a metal plate allegedly disappeared, as confirmed by X-rays.

When Dr. Hopkins and his wife were asked about possible tele-somatic (24, 25) experiences (telepathically precipitated psychosomatic reaction), they could at first recall nothing. Then, as is often the case in interviews of this kind, Dr. Hopkins remembered how, at the end of the Silva Mind Control Course both he and his wife had to "work" ten cases successfully. "Both Madeline and I, as well as the majority of others got ten out of ten on the first try. The case card is filled out with all the data known regarding some particular individual with a serious disorder; minor disorders are not used. For testing, three people sit together — the monitor holds the card, the scribe who writes down what the psychic says about the patient. The monitor is handed the card in a sealed envelope with a cut-out (a window that shows the name, address, age and sex of the patient). The monitor reads only this information to the psychic taking the test and without removing the card from the envelope, to prevent telepathy. The cards are carefully screened so that the monitor does not get the card of someone he or she may know or have heard about. The psychic then goes into the so-called Alpha State which is taught by Silva Mind Control and then proceeds to give the physical description of the patient which is recorded by the scribe. Then the physical and emotional problems are described by the psychic and recorded by the scribe. After this is all done, the sealed envelope containing the card is opened and the answers are compared with the facts as stated on the card. If the information given essentially matches that on the card, as well as other information not on the card which may be later verified, the psychic is given 'one point.' Ten points results in the award of a certificate.

"Madeline's first 'case' was that of a Mongoloid child (male). She said she had a sudden sensation of feeling very cold and uneasy and complained that she had goose-pimples all over. Then she blurted out — 'Oh, that child — there is something wrong — it is going to die soon.

Oh, it is a Mongoloid — take it away quickly!' Because of her state of agitation she was 'awakened' to give her release from this case. The envelope was opened and on the reverse side of the card was the single word Mongoloid!'

Before leaving the subject of alleged beneficial paranormal influences of disease, comment might be made about possible telepathic or clairvoyant perception of illness. Throughout the years Dr. Hopkins has often made out-of-the-ordinary diagnoses where he just intuitively knew what was wrong with his patient. In particular, he recalled one clinically excellent example where he told the attending surgeon and his colleagues that his acutely ill patient had an inflamed Meckel's diverticulum. This diagnosis is almost never made clinically, and it is frequently confused with appendicitis. However, because of the patient's worsening condition, the surgeon decided to explore the abdomen, and found just what Dr. Hopkins said he would. With good humor Dr. Hopkins remarked that his colleagues have often said, "When Herb says the patient has such and such, don't argue with him."

8. Out-of-the-body Experiences (OOBE)

Dr. Hopkins felt that with time he would be able to induce out-of-the-body experiences which he characterized as disappointing: "I can go someplace and see remarkable things, but when I come back it is more or less like a dream and I forget a good part of it. It is like trying to recall a dream in totality." He could cite no specific examples other than saying that everything was quite mundane. He had never had a spontaneous experience. Nor had he attempted OOBE with a patient (26).

When I interviewed Dr. and Mrs. Hopkins, the wife recalled a spontaneous example where she left her body and visited a patient of her husband's who was quite ill with multiple sclerosis: "Gretchen couldn't come up for her injections so she asked if I could go down and give it to her. She was lying on the couch and couldn't get up or do anything that day. Anyway, about supper time I said, 'Gee, I've got to do something about her.' So I sat down and started meditating and saying: 'Now, Gretchen, you're going to feel better and you are going to make your supper. You are going to do the dishes.' About fifteen minutes later she phoned and said, 'Madeline, the funniest thing happened. While I was lying on the couch, I saw you standing by it with your hands out, and you told me to get up, make my supper, and do the dishes, and that I'd be alright.'"

Mrs. Hopkins recalled an involuntary OOBE that she had with her husband. She was upstairs and he was downstairs, reading a medical journal, late at night. She said: "I floated down and read the title of an article he was reading, then floated upstairs and re-entered my body. I sat up again, physically intact, and came downstairs. In the meantime my husband had turned the page, and I told him that I saw what he was reading a little while ago, and asked if he had seen me. He said, 'No.' Then I told him what he was reading and gave the exact title of the article. When he turned back the page to check, the title was correct.

9. Dr. Hopkins' strange encounter with time

Dr. Hopkins does not recall a specific date for this occurrence, but it happened after the hypnosis sessions with David Stephens, and after his visit from the MIB (September 11, 1976). Dr. Hopkins stresses that all the clocks are electric ones.

As told to Shirley Fickett by Dr. Hopkins: "I normally get up at the customary time and don't really depend on an alarm clock. Upon awakening, I looked at the bedroom clock and because of the time, thought I'd awakened several hours too early. I then looked at my watch and that gave a different time: from the bedroom electric clock, by a number of hours.

"I called my wife and asked the right time and according to the kitchen clock, it was a different time from both my watch and the clock in the bedroom.

"Wide awake, I dressed and went downstairs to observe the clock in the family room where the hypnosis sessions with David Stephens had occurred. The family room clock was four hours ahead of the kitchen clock which also proved to be an hour fast. . .(Watch was slow).

"I then tried to establish some correct time and went to the laboratory in the cellar to discover that the clock was not as far ahead as the clock in the family room. We had nothing to go by to establish time and I then went around and re-set all the electric clocks as well as my watch."

About this incident Dr. Hopkins observed that maybe someone was trying to get through to him and to try and prove that there is no such thing as time.

10. Credo

When Dr. Hopkins had finished critically reviewing this manuscript, he sent me a gracious letter with some comments and a most meaningful and revealing paragraph about himself. "I ultimately found what I was looking for in Spiritualism as long as I could keep away from some of the emotionalism involved and from many who claimed the ability of mediumship but who were obviously fraudulent. Indeed I have met some genuine Mediums but they are few and far between. I have taken the tests and have demonstrated mediumship abilities, but prefer not to use it unless backed into a corner, so to speak. Mediumship is simply not something you can switch on or off like an electric light and most of the time it cannot be induced at all. Giving spontaneous 'readings' to everyone or anyone who asks is just so much baloney as far as I am concerned. These are personal feelings that I do not express in most cases for obvious reasons. Nevertheless I am happy to be a Spiritualist for its philosophy and the freedom of thought it encourages without the encumberances of a binding and unthinking Creed. Each man to his own."

Summary

The Hopkins family's MIB experience raises many questions. However, it would seem to be unique because of the high credibility factor for all the involved people, and also because the data was almost immediately recorded by a physician of vastly superior intelligence, sensitivity and presumed psychic talents. It is hoped that, despite the acknowledged shortcomings of the anecdotal data and obvious need for more intensive study, this report will serve to put the spotlight squarely on this too-neglected aspect of ufology, so that other investigators, including behavioral scientists and particularly psychiatrists, using a variety of techniques, will not offhandedly cast such material aside but will show serious interest and probe the manifold, complex, interrelated factors.

It is shameful that aside from Gray Barker's *They Knew Too Much About Flying Saucers* (University Books, New York, 1956), and John A. Keel's many articles in FSR and his *Operation Trojan Horse* (G.P. Putnam's Sons, New York, 1970), after all these years, still so little concerted effort has been devoted to the MIB syndrome, when it could be a practical and accessible area for study. It is noted that 2 years after Barker's book, the *Proceedings of the 1976 CUFOS Conference* (Center for UFO Studies, Evanston, Illinois, 1976) had nothing on the MIB problem. Certainly this is part of the UFO mystery; and if investigators are not to find themselves in the trap of the blind men and the elephant, all parts of of the UFO anatomy must be responsibly explored. Perhaps the terror and confusion, as is evident in the Hopkins case, as much as the conscious and unconscious resistance of various investigators to such way-out material, has accounted for part of this unfortunate stalemate.

In truth, if I over the years hadn't personally known August C. Roberts, a leading figure in the earlier Barker book, and John A. Keel, as well as others, I too would probably not have paid serious attention to their reports and other similar published material, because it would have been easier to ignore this vital human part of the equation to many close UFO sightings. It is long overdue for duly qualified investigators to come to grips with the psychic, MIB, and psychopathological part of the UFO mystery.

Notes and References

20. Schwarz, B.E.: UFO Contactee Stella Lansing: "Possible Medical Implications of Her Motion Picture Experiment", **Journal of the American Society of Psychosomatic Dentistry and Medicine,** Vol. 23 (No. 2): 60-68, 1976.

21. For references to various UFO alleged healings and injuries, see my chapter entitled "Psychiatric Parapsychiatric Aspects of UFOs," in Haines, Richard, F., Editor: "UFO Phenomena and the Behavioral Scientist," Scarecrow Press, Metuchen, New Jersey, 1979.

22. Fuller, J.G.: **Arigo, Surgeon of the Rusty Knife,** Thomas Y. Corwell, New York, 1973.

23. Sherman, H.: **Wonder Healers of the Philippines,** De Vorss & Co., Los Angeles, 1967.

24. Schwarz, B.E.: "Possible Telesomatic Reactions," **The Journal of the Medical Society of New Jersey,** Vol. 64 (No. 11): 600-603, November 1967.

25. Schwarz, B.E.: "Clinical Studies on Telesomatic Reactions," **Medical Times.** Vol. 101 (No. 2): 71-76, December 1973.

26. The following vignette might illustrate the synchronicity-psi interplay culminating in this example with a spontaneous possible psi physician-patient visit. On November 13, 1958, during my studies of the nonagenarian paragnost Jacques Romano (see **The Jacques Romano Story,** University Books, Inc., New Hyde Park, New York, 1968, 243 pp.), I was driving him through the Lincoln Tunnel from his home in New York to my office in New Jersey when he told me several highly specific items about one of the surgeon guests, PC, who would be at my home later that evening. This was startling because I had hardly met PC before, and of course Romano never knew him. Needless to say, of the people at the party Romano "selected" PC for what turned out to be a highly successful "spirit reading." Furthermore, Romano told PC's wife that at that moment her coat was being mended. The doctor and his wife couldn't believe this, so, to satisfy their curiosity, Mrs. C. telephoned her home and immediately verified Romano's assertion. The psychic and psychodynamics became more intriguing when the surgeon later said, in the presence of everyone, that he himself had had many presumed telepathic experiences with patients, and then he recalled one possible precognitive dream of his own from approximately 1940.

In his dream, PC went to the Aqueduct Racetrack and bought a selector's form from Longshot Tex, who told him all the winners. The dream was so vivid and impressive that PC went to the racetrack the next day with his sister-in-law. He told her about his dream on the train. When they got off: "There in the corner was Longshot Tex. He had five cards in his hand. I bought one. I had been going to the races for many years, but I had never seen or heard of him before. There were seven races in the

271

card. He had two choices, first and second. My sister-in-law made a fortune. I chickened out. I couldn't believe it. Shortly afterwards I returned to Aqueduct and asked if anyone had seen Longshot Tex. Finally someone said, 'He's a stranger around here, and we haven't seen him in a long time.'" On three subsequent occasions PC asked about Longshot Tex, only to receive the same answer.

Now, as it happened, PC had chronic, severe, intractable rheumatic valvular heart disease. Years after I met him, he was taken one day to the intensive care unit of the local hospital in severe congestive heart failure. His cardiologist felt that all had been done that could be done and that heart surgery was out of the question. PC, wondering if anxiety could be contributing to his heart arrythmia and clonic calf contractions, called me in to see if I could think of something that would help him. I reviewed his chart and spent some time with him and made some recommendations for an anticonvulsant. His condition was grave and he continued to deteriorate. Finally, his cardiologist told PC's wife that there was only a short time left. The wife, who was a nurse, sought my help because of her husband's imminent death and the expected traumatic effects on the family. She even told me about funeral arrangements.

The night of PC's expected death I had a dream where I was actually at his bedside in the hospital and saw him in vivid color and detail. I knew he had rallied and was going to make it. When I went in the next day to see him, this was indeed the case. His wife and cardiologist were astounded. PC subsequently showed sufficient improvement for later heart surgery, from which he had complications and unfortunately did not recover. In our visits after the crisis he never mentioned the experience, but as I asked him questions, it seemed that I might have correctly appraised the nuances of his improved situation.

Thus, in this case the over determined emotional needs of the physician-patient, his family, and other consultants, including me, might have been intertwined and precipitated the unexpected rally. However, in addition to all the obvious wish-fulfilling psychodynamics and subliminal factors, the interaction of possible unconscious traveling clairvoyance (similar to OOBE; also see "Built-in Controls and Postulates for the Telepathic Event," **Corrective Psychiatry** and **the Journal of Social Therapy**, Vol. 12 (No. 2): 64-82, March, 1966), should not be discounted as a factor in his rally. Could PC, a natural sensitive, the one Romano "chose" years ago for a psychic demonstation, plus PC's (and his family's) psi experiences have made him a suitable candidate for his therapeutic result? This example, minus any UFO angle, is otherwise similar to Dr. Hopkins' previous psi experiences and his development of vulnerability to the MIB syndrome. It demonstrates the need for cautious, careful, detailed probing before jumping to any unwarranted premature conclusions about causation, etc. (See my case entitled "The Revival Meeting" (pp. 221-223) in Possible Geriatric Telepathy, **Journal of the American Geriatric Society,** Vol. XXI (No. 5): 216-223, 1973).

Chapter 15

Talks with Betty Hill: 1 —
Aftermath of Encounter

John Fuller's *Interrupted Journey* (1) describes Betty and Barney Hill's† abduction aboard a UFO, where they were intensively studied and examined by the occupants. Because of emotional psychosomatic complications following this experience, the Hills sought psychiatric assistance and were seen in hypnotherapy by the eminent psychiatrist, Benjamin Simon, who treated them over an extended period of time.

Little has been written about related experiences of the Hills before or after the initial contact in 1962. Fuller wrote an earlier book describing UFO activities in Exeter, N.H. (2), an area 14 miles from the home of the Hills and Simon (3) prepared a short article for a psychiatric journal.

Barney died February, 1969, age 46, of cerebral hemorrhage, the same disease that his father died of. Since then Betty has continued to appear on various TV interviews as well as to lecture to various UFO, university, and scientific organizations.

Earl Neff, Cleveland ufologist, showed me Xerox copies of the Air Force Manual, "Introductory Space Science," Chapter 33, which is used in an elective course, Physics 370 at the Air Force Academy. This chapter explores the UFO problem and contains interesting paragraphs on the Hills. He also showed me Xerox copies of a subsequent edition which is highly diluted compared to the first. However, official government correspondence omitted mention of an original and detailed chapter which was only discovered by Neff's persistent sleuthing.

Beyond such official recognition, the significance of the Hill's experience assumed enormous scientific importance when in 1968 Marjorie Fish (4) constructed a model and analysis of Betty Hill's star map. Betty had seen the star map aboard the UFO, and two years later (1964) she recalled it following post-hypnotic suggestion and drew it during automatic writing. Miss Fish showed that Betty's star map was correct and that some of the stars Betty drew were not known to astronomers in September 19-20, 1961, having been discovered later. Of all aspects of the case, Marjorie Fish's tour de force more than any other has excited the interest of scientists.

---

†For ease in communication Mr. and Mrs. Hill, as well as some other persons in this article, will be referred to by their Christian names.

Having studied people who have had alleged close UFO sightings, contact with occupants, etc., I was naturally curious about Betty Hill, by far the most thoroughly studied, and most famous of those who have had UFO contacts. My curiosity was further whetted when I met Betty and her mother at an APRO symposium in Baltimore, January 23, 1971, and later at an APRO meeting in Pottstown, Pennsylvania, June 15, 1974, when I again visited with Betty and also met Barney's sister Lillian. I learned that Betty had had many unusual experiences that might have been related to her UFO contact. These events might give clues to the kind of person Betty is and how they might fit into the jigsaw puzzle that comprises the UFO mystery.

Betty impressed me then, and more recently when I visited her home in Portsmouth, N.H. (January 18, 1976), and in a study in my office+ (March 11-13, 1976), as a highly intelligent, open, straight-talking, good-natured lady of unquestionable probity. A graduate of the University of New Hampshire and a social worker for many years, Betty has a splendid sense of humor and a good grasp of reality. She graciously consented to these studies and experiments.

The anecdotal nature of much of the experiential data which preceded and followed the UFO abduction is an admitted shortcoming. However, because of the uniqueness of the Hills' UFO capture and the subsequent Fish confirmatory analysis of the star map, it is essential to record material that has been hitherto either omitted or overlooked. Since the person should not be studied apart from the other data, the UFO experience might be more fully understood if all its segments are included. To omit some material because it is subjective or anecdotal, and not the more desirable objective data, is folly and wasteful, and blurs the total picture. Therefore this report describes apparently relevant events that followed shortly after, and long after, the Hills' abduction as well as some possibly related situations that occurred long before the abduction. In a concluding section, a clinical experiment in audio taping is reported.

Home Sweet Home Potpourri

Occasionally, after the abduction, when Betty returned home she would find that although other coats would be in the living room closet, *her* coats would be unaccountably thrown in a pile in the middle of the living room and topped with Barney's scarf.

Other disruptive household events included this recent (1975) situation: Betty returned home and noticed that a kitchen clock had been

---

+ A 10-channel electroencephalogram taken at this time was normal.

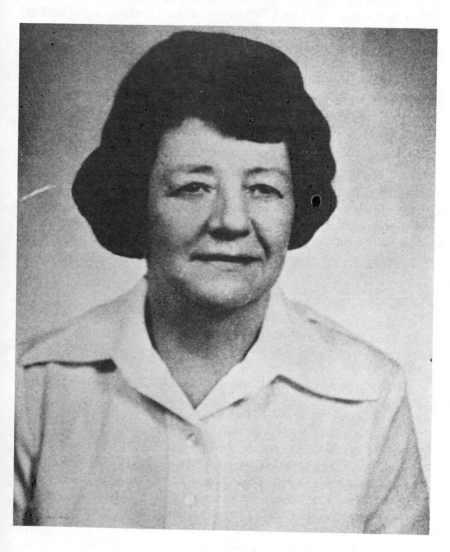

Betty Hill

set back three hours and 15 minutes. It was an electric clock, made by her mother, and although she has four other electric clocks made by her mother, nothing happened to them. Once before Betty had problems with another electric clock. "It stopped running about a week after Barney's death, at 7:20 p.m., which was about the time he died. I left it. Several months later, the clock started running again, but the amazing thing was the fact that the clock started at the exact moment to correct it in time."

Sometimes Betty would come home to find ". . .someone must have adjusted the gas burner, because when I turned it on the flame went up quite high. One time I came home and all the water in the house was shut off. Another time all the sinks had the plugs in and the water was running full force, flooding the house. I have an oil furnace with a circulator pump, and the pump motor has springs in it. I'd come home and find someone had pulled the springs out and I'd hear the clack-clacking. Another time when I came home, the wires were pulled out of the pump.

"Last August (1975) I was gone all day and had the burglar alarm system on. When I came home, the girl who rents the front apartment came down, all excited, and said the police had been there. At two o'clock in the afternoon the alarm had gone off. The police came and looked around but couldn't see anything. When I got home, the side door (the burglar alarm was still ringing) was wide open. Whoever it was must have gone in the side door, tripped the alarm, and then when the police went by must have ducked down, and later ran out and left the door open. That's the only way I could figure it out. [Nothing was missing.]

"One night when I came home (August, 1975), my refrigerator had stopped functioning. I was told a repairman couldn't come for 3 to 4 days or a week. So I cleaned everything out and transferred the food to a basement refrigerator. Two days later the broken refrigerator started functioning, and I've had no problem since. It's like something is done and the electricity starts malfunctioning. Irons, toasters, radios, and TVs shut themselves off. Once I came home, turned on the TV, but there was no picture. I tried it two or three times — still no picture. I called the TV repair service and when he finally came (I hadn't turned the TV on for days), he just turned it on and said: "What's wrong with it? Look at that, you've got a beautiful picture.' So, I'm the only person in the world who has self-healing electrical appliances.

"Things got so bad after Barney died (1969) that my niece and her husband — students at the University of New Hampshire — gave up their apartment and moved into my basement apartment, to keep an eye on the house. But so many strange and mysterious things happened that they couldn't take it. They heard noises in my apartment as if someone was moving around. When they investigated, they didn't find anything. They had a feeling that someone was there. When they went downstairs, they heard a bang: the front door opened, a man walked down the front hall, went out the front door, got into his car and drove away. They checked to see what the bang was, and the clothes pole in the corner of the closet had been knocked over. Apparently the man was hiding in the closet: which was the only place they didn't look. I wondered why anyone would be interested in going in there.

"All kinds of characters have followed me. One of them looked very much like one of the men who went to jail on the Watergate thing — he looked so much like him. He was baldheaded and on the chunky side. I found him in my front hall, and asked what he was doing there. He said he was selling subscriptions to magazines. When I asked where his magazines were he laughed and left. I saw him again in the parking lot at the Welfare Office where I work. He was reading the *New York Times* —holding it up to his face and putting it down, and up again. Then, instead of going into my office, I went upstairs to the ladies room which overlooks the parking lot, and I watched him again. He then came up into the hall, looked around, went down to the parking lot and drove off.

"During the McGovern election campaign I had kids from all over the country come to my house one day. One was a little guy who introduced himself as Donald Simmons. He said he was a law student, but he kept trying to get away from me. Later I learned that Donald Segretti used the name of Donald Simons when he was in NH and closely resembled the man who came to my home."

The blue dress and blue earrings
The first mysterious event happened six weeks after the abduction. On the night of the capture Betty was wearing a blue dress and blue earrings. One night, six weeks afterward, when Barney and she had just come home from an evening out and entered the kitchen, where they have a snack bar, they noticed a pile of leaves. In the leaves were Betty's blue earrings. She grabbed them, put them in her jewelry box, and hasn't touched them since.

Recently (1975) while studying a spectacular contact case in New Hampshire, Betty was intrigued to learn that the chief protagonist was a woman who was wearing, at the time of her alleged UFO apprehension, the exact shade of blue dress and same kind of fabric that Betty had worn the night of her capture.

The iceman cometh?

One afternoon, about three months after the capture, Barney had come home early. Shortly afterwards when Betty came home, Barney was still resting. Betty walked into the kitchen, and there on the snack bar, underneath a newspaper, she noticed "a frozen piece of ice in a pattern — as if somebody had taken a bowl, filled it with water, and frozen it. There were strange marks in the ice." She woke Barney up and questioned him for this nonsense, but he didn't know what she was talking about. Without thinking, she put the ice in the sink and ran hot water over it. As an afterthought she condemned herself for not putting the ice in the freezer and checking the data in the accompanying newspaper. She found this ice would melt only when the hot water was running on it and she and Barney took turns during the evening going to the kitchen to do this.

Tapped telephone

"My line has been tapped so many times. They set up a circuit telephone in the office of a federal agency so that whenever my phone rang it was like a party line. They heard the phone ring, picked it up, and listened in. Twice this happened the same way. For example, when I had a phone call and I later put the phone down and then picked it up again to make a call, my line was open, and I said, 'Hello.' Someone Answered, 'Federal Agency.'

I asked what he was doing on my line, and he said they were trying to protect me. I said I didn't need their protection, that I'd protect myself. I went down to the telephone office and told them to get a truck and take the tap off the line.

"And after that the Air Force tapped my line. Only what they did got reversed. They were getting my calls and I got theirs. My phone would ring, I'd pick it up, and some voice would say, 'I want to speak with Johnny.'

"And I'd say; 'Johnny? There's no Johnny here.'

"That went on for months. At first I thought someone was playing a joke on me, but when I realized that I was tapped into Base Intelligence, I had it corrected. Even when the BBC was here for a filming and a psychiatrist who was with them picked up the phone, he overheard: 'Pease Airforce Base Intelligence.'"

My upstairs tenant

"Maureen Keating, my upstairs tenant, reminded me of other experiences. One was my mail, which she put on the radiator in the front hall, went to the store and when she came home, the mail was gone. At the same time, my cat which was locked in my apartment, was found outdoors.

"On another occasion, someone was in Maureen's apartment and turned on her radio. I thought she was at home, and called up to her. A man's voice answered, saying he was waiting for Maureen to come back, and she knew he was there. Later he left in a blue car. Maureen knew nothing about this, has checked with others for a year, and still does not know who this person is. Also, she does not know anyone who drives a blue car."

More odd happenings

On many occasions neighbors have reported to the police that prowlers were seen looking in the windows. Her phone frequently rings, but when she answers there is no one on the line. A typical episode occurred when Barney was alive, and his cousin Marge, who lives in Baltimore, kept dialing the Hills in Portsmouth. She did this four times until someone came on the line and said; 'The Hills are not home. They've gone to a meeting and they won't be home until 11:50.' Betty added, that the 'someone' even told Marge where we had gone for the meeting, the name of the organization — the whole bit. My guess is that the telephone operator got tired of listening to Marge dialing."

Laurie and the Air Force Manual

Betty's friend Laurie got hold of the unexpurgated pages from the Air Force Physics text that described Betty and Barney's abduction. Laurie sent a copy to Betty. However, it took more than a month to arrive, going from Boston to Indiana, to Portsmouth. In the meantime, a man visited Laurie and introduced himself as an Air Force officer. He threatened Laurie for stealing Air Force property and was nasty. He said he was going to have her arrested and thrown in jail for the rest of her life.

When Laurie's husband came home and heard about it, he was furious. He called the Air Force and asked to speak to the man, but was told there was no one on base by that name. Laurie and her husband never found out who he was. But, whoever he was, he knew that Laurie had a copy of that particular chapter. Laurie had the reputation of being a psychic and she claimed that she had once been tested at Duke University.

Mr. Geist

Barney's son by his previous marriage, Barney, Jr., was in the service, stationed in Panama. Several times between two and four in the morning, when Barney Jr. was on guard duty, he was approached by a tall, swarthy man dressed in white pants, shirt and jacket. The man had a foreign accent; yet Barney Jr., who spoke Spanish, said it was not a Spanish accent. The man said his name was Mr. Geist (ghost), but said nothing further about himself. Mr. Geist quizzed Barney Jr., about Betty and Barney's experience with the flying saucers. Betty did not know if any of Barney Jr.'s friends had contact with this man subsequently or before. However, the military authorities soon found out about this relationship and they questioned Barney Jr. extensively about his father, Betty, and their experience. Other relatives, and Betty's two adoptive children by her previous marriage have never had similar experiences.

Man in Green

"One day Barney's sister Lillian decided to come up from Philadelphia and visit on the spur of the moment. We didn't know she was coming. I picked her up, brought her to the house, and went to work. Between 8:30 a.m. and 2:00 p.m. three men came to the door. The first said hello, and that he had come to check the gas meter downstairs. Lillian said, 'Fine, go ahead.' Shortly afterwards a second one came and said, 'I've got to check the gas meter.' She thought that was strange since someone had been there, but maybe he hadn't done the thing correctly, so she said, 'OK.' He went down. Finally, a third man came and said, 'Oh Lillian, your brother told me you would be here to let me in.' She locked the door in his face, since she then realized something was wrong, for Barney did not know she was here (surprise visit). And that really scared her. Lillian went out and sat on the front steps until Barney got home from work. The men were all dressed in green shirts and green pants.

"The same thing happened to me last August (1975). When this man came to the door dressed in green, and said: 'I've come to read the gas meter.'

"I said, 'Fine,' opened the door and let him in.

"A week later another man came to read the gas meter, and I thought it was strange. A couple of weeks later a third man came to read my gas meter. When I got my gas bill it said 'estimated.' So I called the gas company and asked what was going on, and how could I get an estimated bill when they had sent three men here.

"'Oh no, Mrs. Hill, our gas meter man came around,' said the clerk, 'you weren't home, and he couldn't get in.'

"And when I said there were three meter checkers, the clerk asked if they were dressed in blue, and I said no; green. She said all their men wear blue. She said, 'I don't know who you had in your house, but don't

280

blame it on us. It wasn't anybody from our company.'

"So I had three men in my house, and I have no idea what, or who they were, or why they wanted to go downstairs!"

Possible creatures

Although Betty had neither seen nor heard Big Foot personally, she recalled an incident four or five years ago when her nephew and his wife, while camping out on a 4th of July weekend in some wooded area on her mother's property in New Hampshire, reported "That night it was particularly active. Like hearing a door slam. Metal hitting metal, and various lights appearing. So the next morning we started walking around to see what we could find, and on one side of the old cow hole, where years ago the cows used to drink, we found a huge footprint." Betty reported that it wasn't like the wax cast that Marianne Cascio* has of Big Foot, but that she thought there was another one Marianne had that was similar — something like a duck foot.

I (BES) had seen Marianne Cascio's paraffin cast of Big Foot obtained from the father's farm near Agawam, Massachusetts, and it was entirely similar to some of the plaster casts that Stan Gordon (5) and his group had made in western Pennsylvania. I later showed Betty a plaster cast of the abominable snowman presented to me by Bob Durant, President of the Society for the Investigation of the Unexplained, but she felt this was not similar to what her nephew had seen.

---

*See section entitled Paranormal Experiments (in a later part).

REFERENCES AND COMMENTS

1. Fuller, John G.: **The Interrupted Journey,** Berkley Publishing Corp., N.Y., 1973.
2. Fuller, John G.: **Incident at Exeter,** a Berkley Medallion Book (paperback), New York, 1967.
3. Simon, Benjamin: "Hypnosis in the Treatment of Military Neuroses," **Psychiatric Opinion,** Vol. 4, 24-29 (Oct. 2967).
4. Dickinson, Terrence: "The Zeta Reticuli Incident," in **Astronomy,** magazine, Zeta reprint, 757 N. Broadway, Suite 204, Milwaukee, WI 53202, 1975. Related material in this issue includes: Kretch, Jeffrey: "The Age of Nearby Stars;" "Center for UFO Studies Established," **Astro-News,** March, 1974; and Commentary, Discussions and Rebuttals from "In Focus," by Terrence Dickinson, Jeffrey Kretch, Carl Sagan, Steven Soter, Robert Schaeffer, Marjorie Fish, David Saunders, and Michael Peck. Among her other contributions to the Hill case, Marjorie Fish, with Betty's co-operation, made an anatomically sensible drawing and models of the UFO occupants' heads. She wrote me (BES) on

August 22, 1972, about the possibility that the occupants performed a pregnancy test on Betty by inserting a needle in the navel (**Interrupted Journey,** pp. 164-65). Betty wrote Miss Fish that she may have blacked out during this presumably traumatic incident. In response to Miss Fish's query to me, J.B. Skelton, M.D., a leading gynecologist, wrote that the laparoscope, a device that could provide a vision of the peritoneal cavity using fibro-optic light systems, was first introduced in the U.S. about 1964. Shortly afterwards the laparoscope was used by Dr. Steptoc in England for tubal sterilization procedures. The chronology of this information and technology was unknown to Betty in 1961, and it tended to support Miss Fish's contention that possibly the occupants were experimenting with human eggs.

5. In Schwarz, B.E.: ''Berserk: A UFO-creature Encounter.'' **FSR,** Vol. 20 No. 1: 3-11 (July 1974).

2 — The Things That Happen Around Here

On December 7, 1975, Marianne Cascio, a lady of Agawam, Massachusetts, who claimed that she was blinded by a UFO when eleven years of age, and that she had had possibly related psi experiences such as telekinesis, telephoned Betty Hill.

The Mystery Helicopter

Marianne wanted to speak about the Agawam mystery helicopters. Marianne said to Betty: "I'll try ESP to send the 'helicopter' to you so you can see what it looks like."

In her notes about Marianne's experience, which dovetailed with what Marianne and YD (pseudonym) had told me on the phone at the time, Betty wrote: "YD called from Marianne's home. He had gone to take her some doughnuts when they heard the helicopter. He went out with her Polaroid camera to get some pictures. He took three, but the helicopter did not appear on these. He was flabbergasted, for he had framed the pictures carefully, having a tree in one corner and a power line showing. The craft was between these two but did not appear on the film. The third picture he took was dark and overexposed."

[I (BES) later confirmed the conversation and notes by interviewing YD in person and also examining his memorandum and Polaroids. His notes stated: '. . .completely clear. Not a cloud in the sky. We called Betty Hill and reported it to her. Three pictures of a helicopter, yet when the Polaroid film was developed, no helicopter could be seen in the pictures."]

Betty received Marianne's "mystery helicopter" call when she was visiting her mother in Kingston, New Hampshire. Betty was preparing to leave for Portsmouth at 9:00 p.m., when she noticed a huge light that came up from the ground and stopped. Her mother and neighbors went out to watch it. When Betty got into the car and started the motor, the light ". . .started to toy with me. It went back to its former position. Two smaller lights were on each side of it, and they followed me for several miles in the direction of Exeter.

"Later, at 11:30 p.m., Marianne called again and said that she had made a mistake and that the 'copter' she tried to send did not arrive, but three UFOs did. True."

From 6:00 to 10:00 p.m., instead of 6:00 p.m., she had seen several small bright flashing lights in the sky. Betty recalled how Marianne also 'phoned Mrs. Stella Lansing who drove to Agawam and took motion pictures using three cameras.

Betty continued:

"Marianne said that she called Westover Air Force Base in Chicapee to report the UFOs. The base operator told her that everyone was calling in and that most of the lines were tied up. She was put through to Security Police, who told her that she was giving the twelfth report they received. We talked about my sighting this night, and it was agreed that we would try an experiment for me to obtain the book that was given to me on board my UFO. I would exchange my world atlas and my globe for this, or any possession they wished.

"The next night, on December 8, 1975, I [Betty] was returning home about dusk, when I saw two rows of puzzling lights in the sky. Four red lights on the right and four green lights on the left which formed a V. As I turned in my driveway, I discovered this was a helicopter, for it flew down low, over my car and the garage and barely missed the tree in my backyard. As it came down, the only light visible at that moment was one large white light in the front of the craft. No white light on the tail, and it disappeared swiftly from sight. I called OJ, a local UFO investigator, and he didn't believe it, but then the helicopter was over his house."

In her report Betty also included an additional mystery helicopter experience involving Marianne. "Marianne came on the phone to say that on Thursday night a helicopter had appeared and circled her house. She could hear the motor, which died and then returned later. Also, Its flight pattern was unusual in that it was not a true circle at times, but it seemed to be moving back and forth, making sharp angles. It appeared three times. . .While we were talking, the 'copter returned. Marianne's eleven-year-old daughter Chris stood at the door and described this one, different from the others, which were grey without markings. This one was blue and red with markings running in a vertical pattern. Chris described [and sketched the craft and the symbols]. The craft had a rectangular box in front from which a light was shining."

Betty's unpublished study *Mystery Helicopters* (6) (1976) presents this and much related data with documentation. She also wrote about another episode that she described to me during her Montclair visit: "A friend of mine in Wells, Maine, who is a commercial farmer had been seeing strange lights around her farm occasionally for about two years. Last summer she thought that one had landed in one of her fields but did not investigate this. On February 20, 1976, she said that increasing numbers of helicopters had been seen and heard around her farm and the cattle farm next door to her. That week she had seen two helicopters

284

side by side, over the highway, at night, during a severe snow-storm. They looked as though they were refueling in mid air as she could see a connection going from one to the other. Yet she knows that helicopters do not refuel this way and was puzzled by this, which was her purpose in reporting it to me. She did hear the sounds of the blades.

"About one year ago she found that all her pregnant rabbits had disappeared while her males and young females were left. She was never successful in finding out what happened to them, but apparently the rabbit building had been approached from the direction of the woods. If someone in the neighborhood had done this, it would probably have been known, as she had a large number of rare registered rabbits."

Microwave Tower

Betty recalled that once a UFO supposedly almost collided with a nearby microwave tower. This was a couple of years ago and was seen by several people.

"Batter Up"

NR (pseudonym), a well-known major-league baseball player, went to visit Betty and on the way up saw many strange lights in the sky. Immediately after he left Portsmouth, the street lights dimmed out over Betty's house and the neighboring area was completely out. According to newspaper accounts, no one knew why this happened.

"Pumpkin Head" and Odds and Ends

On February 18, 1976, Betty Hill wrote: "Personally I've seen numerous ones (UFOs) including the mystery helicopters and a large glowing 'pumpkin head' form which glides along beside my car while the UFO is above us. Now I have found an area on my mother's land (she owns 33 acres of meadows, swamp, brook and timberland) where I found two spots with three kidney-shaped marks in a triangle pattern. One of these marks sat down on the top of one of the flowering trees, breaking it off. The tree was too tall, and the stem too large to be broken in any ordinary way. We've suspected that UFOs have been landing in my mother's land for years, and have found traces in the past.

"Since I saw the pumpkin-head object, I seem to be filled with electricity for I have been getting electrical shocks from anything metal, or even if I touched wood. Immediately after seeing this object if I combed my hair or put on clothing, sparks are shooting all around. For example, as I was going through the security gates at the airport recently all the bells were ringing. When I was checked out with the hand gadget, it was buzzing everywhere, including my head and feet. The attendant said

285

this had never happened before and that the gadget was responding when no metal was involved. She shook her head and told me to go ahead. Today I can touch more things without getting a shock so it is lessening. But it is a real nuisance. In the midst of all this I went out on an errand, and when I returned, I found that my electric kitchen clock had set itself back ... three hours and fifteen minutes. I left it that way to check it out, but it operates accurately."

The tin box

"About 1970 or 1971, I had a little tin box with filing cards in it. I had kept this for eight years and had included all the [UFO-related] experiences that I had collected. I was going down to visit with Walter Webb, so I just grabbed the box, which was on top of my filing cabinet in the bedroom. However, when I opened it, all my cards and records were missing.

The purloined IRS papers

Shortly after Barney died, all the files containing bank statements, receipts for the apartments, forms pertaining to salaries, and everything else necessary for the accountant to fill out the income tax forms were put in a shopping bag. One day when Betty came home she noticed that the shopping bag with all records was gone. She immediately got in touch with the Internal Revenue Service to get an extension and she then had to write to all the companies and people involved to get duplicate copies for the income tax forms. She had to try to remember all the repairs and expenditures that had been made. Two days after she had done this and filed the income tax forms, she came home and found that the shopping bag was on top of the table and the contents had been strewn on the floor in the middle of the living room. Although the house had been locked, she said the man next door, an elderly gentleman, had noticed from his second floor window that two men entered Betty's house during the day. He saw them go up the steps and enter by apparently using keys. He could not recall any other distinguished features of this event.

Long, Long Ago

Betty received a letter from a lady in Kitchener, Ontario, who recalled how, as a child, she was abducted by a UFO. At the time, a neighbor boy was awakened in the middle of the night and he witnessed the event. He became hysterical, woke up his parents and told them. However, they passed if off as a nightmare. The UFO occupants supposedly gave the lady pictures, which she found had faded out over the

286

years. The lady wanted to have some support for her early experience, not knowing if it was a dream or reality, so she wrote many letters until she finally contacted the boy of long ago, who at that point no longer remembered the situation. However, this led to a correspondence, and she married a man who was helping her to investigate this.

Comic relief with a look-alike

Betty wrote: "I am also having another interesting thing happening. The last three times I have lectured the same man has attended. He was at Park Avenue, New York; Hartford, Connecticut, and Massachusetts. He looks very much like another person I know, so much so that I mistook him at first for this friend. He is almost a double for Ray Fowler, an investigator in Massachusetts. This reminds me of a time when my mother and I went to Montreal to do a TV program. The same man on the limousine out of Portsmouth; on the same plane, the same bus, the same hotel. At the hotel my mother spoke to him, and he lost his moustache in his soup when he nodded back! At times I have had some amusing things happen."

Possible Precognition

One of Betty's best high school friends was Louise. Betty once dreamed that she saw Louise killed. "I saw broken glass all over the road, and it amazed me to see teeth all over the road. I didn't tell Louise that I dreamt she was killed, but just said I had dreamt that she had been in an accident. I said, 'Be careful.' Shortly after I had dreamt this her mother called me and invited me to Louise's 16th birthday party, to be a surprise. Since it conflicted with something I had already agreed to do, I couldn't go. Her parents wanted an excuse to get her out of the house so that her friends could get in without her knowing it. They sent Louise to the store for a quart of milk. While she was walking to the store, she was hit by a truck and killed instantly. It was exactly as I had dreamed.

"I had many other dreams like that. I recall one when I was a senior in high school and was dating a fellow named Freddy, who went to another high school. I was going to go to his graduation exercises, and he was going to go to mine. Then I dreamed that he was killed in an automobile accident. It was so clear, I knew just where it happened — the whole bit. When I told him about it, I said, 'Keep away from that spot.' He just passed it off with a quip: 'OK, if I get killed, you go to my graduation with Rusty.' I did, for he was killed in the exact spot that I told him to stay away from. A driver ran through a stop sign, came out too far, and was going too fast. He side-swiped Freddy's car and that was it."

"Dreams, or seeing a scene flash in front of my eyes just before going to sleep at night, that's the way things come. For example, I was once ready to fall asleep when I saw a shadow come out in front of me and I hit it. All I could think of was, 'Oh, my God, a kid on a bicycle.' When I was driving I watched constantly for kids on bicycles. But one day, shortly afterwards, while I was watching for kids on bicycles, a deer jumped in front of my car and I hit it and killed it.

"My (maternal) grandmother had these things. Everyone used to say that she would be able to foretell the future. My (paternal) grandfather had a sister who was a psychic, or something. Also, when my parents first met — second date — my father took mother to a spiritualist meeting in Amesbury, Massachusetts, where they were told they were going to marry and have five children. This was very upsetting to my mother because she had just met Father, had only gone out with him once — and that only because she had nothing better to do at the moment. She really was not impressed by him. So 52 years later they were still married and had had five children. The motto is 'Keep away from Spiritualists!'

"My father was an atheist in regards to spiritualism and didn't believe in any of this stuff. My daughter, who is adopted, has psychic ability. She can tell how many people will drop in unexpectedly for Sunday dinner. And if we were planning a trip to the mountains or something, she would say, 'Forget it Mom, so-and-so is coming,' and she'd be right every time. There is nothing like this with my adopted son."

Psychic Healing

"I met Alex Tanous several years ago at a private home. Now he is travelling around doing lectures about his book (One Man's Experiences with Psychic Phenomena, Doubleday, NY, 1976) and he has been involved with psychic research — Karlis Osis, Ph.D., of the American Society of Psychical Research, and others. At this home, he squeezed my mother's hand and held it for a few moments, and her bursitis, of two years duration, left. This was four years ago and it has not returned. Last October or November, he and I were speaking to the same group in Boston, Mass. I told him about the health problems that I was having, after surgery last June, and how my doctor was unable to make a diagnosis. As a result I had to leave my job and was unable to work. During the day we were at this meeting, he put his arms around me three times, and I felt as though my circulation speeded up, a surge of energy. For the next two days, I had chest pains, followed by a bubbling sensation; this bubbling sensation increased to a point where I was beginning to become worried. Then I felt as though my chest had greatly expanded, the bubbling stopped, and I found myself taking deep gasps of air. It was suddenly a feeling of great relief, and I realized that I had been having a feeling of restricted breathing, which ended. My health has been fine since that time. I told my medical doctor about his, and he said that he heard about experiences like this."

Girl friend May

May is one of Betty's best friends, and her husband might be a distant relative of Betty's. The farm they lived on had been in May's husband's family for more than a hundred years. The people who owned the property before he bought it, had been wiped out by an epidemic. May and her husband were walking around one day when they got to a point of land which they thought might be a good place to build their house. So the husband took a picture of May, but when it was developed there was a man standing beside her dressed in Colonial clothes. "You could actually see the scenery and the river right through him."

The second 'spirit picture' was taken the first Christmas that May and her family were settled on their farm. "They had a huge Christmas tree which was decorated in an old-fashioned way. May took a picture of it to send to her mother, and when the picture was developed, there was a young woman standing in front of the Christmas tree, dressed in old-fashioned clothes." Although May and her husband have taken many pictures before and since, this is the only time they obtained such strange effects.

UFOs and Betty's family

"Before I saw a UFO, my sisters Janet and Norma saw one on Route 125 in Kingston, N.H. About 1954 they saw a large glowing green football-shaped object being circled by small lights, which merged with the large light. They stopped at the home of friends who came out and saw this. Later we learned that this specific area had many sightings like this one of which some were daylight sightings. Kingston has been a 'hot spot' of UFO activity for many years. OJ, an investigator, has investigated hundreds of reports.

"Actually, all my close family members have witnessed UFO sightings; my parents, my sisters and brother, my nieces and nephews."

Hapless Hannah

A good twenty years before Betty's UFO contact she recalls that her sister Janet repeatedly corrected her three children, then aged 2, 5, and 7, for mischief they denied doing. When they were older, they said that they had been punished for things they didn't do. But, at the time they could not figure out how these things were always happening. Silly things such as: who spilled the contents of the wastebasket all over the kitchen floor?

Finally Glenn, the middle child, whom Hannah the child ghost was particularly fond of, went away to service, and Hannah moved into his room. But, when Glenn came home, Hannah would have a fit. Night after night she would awaken him and throw his clothes across the room. If his clothes were hanging in the closet, they'd all fall off the hangers and be left in the middle of the closet with a bang, or they would tumble down just as if someone took them and swept them off the rod. Also, things would fall off the edge of the dresser. Betty saw some of these things happen herself.

"Sometimes you could hear Hannah sobbing. She would call, 'Mommy, Mommy.' One day, my sister Janet answered the door and it was the assistant scoutmaster dropping by to see her husband Donald. (Janet's brother-in-law was always active in the Boy Scouts.) Donald wasn't home, but while the scoutmaster was talking to Janet, Hannah started sobbing and crying, 'Mommy.' The man stopped and asked 'Is that your grandson?' Janet said 'No' and he said, 'You're taking care of some neighbor's child?' Janet still said, 'no.' Then he said, 'Well, where is the child crying?' And Janet said, 'Oh, I never told you, but that's our spirit Hannah.' And he took off!

"We realized something was going on, but we didn't know what. My sister went to a psychic, who said we had the ghost of a small child living in the house. He told us the story of Hannah — how she had lived with her parents somewhere in the vicinity about a hundred years ago and how there had been a fire in which both her parents burned to death. Hannah was rescued, and neighbors took her in and adopted her. The psychic said that Janet was living in Hannah's adoptive parents' home. Janet said, 'No, that couldn't be,' because she and her husband built the house themselves and there was no former house there. The psychic insisted that there had been a house there, but Janet disagreed because the land had been in their family since 1840. The psychic still insisted and said that the people adopted Hannah, and that one day while she was riding horseback, when she was about 5 or 6 years old, Hannah fell off, was injured and died.

"A few years later when Janet was digging a trench on the side of the house she found old cellar walls. That got her interested again and she checked through old records, deeds, and such, and found out that what the psychic said was true. She even discovered where Hannah was buried."

Betty continued: "One day Hannah got so obnoxious that Janet said, 'Look, Hannah, I've had it with you. You go over to Sheila's.' Sheila, who didn't know about this of course, was working at the kitchen sink at the time. All of a sudden the knobs on the front of the stove came off and fell on the floor, right in front of her eyes. Sheila got on the phone, dialed Janet, and said, 'Will you come over and get Hannah, or shall I bring her back?' Sheila is married to our nephew.

"In my mother's house Hannah is always knocking on the door. To the best of my knowledge, Hannah is never in two places at the same time. For example, when she was cutting up with me, there was no monkey business at my sister's. Once when Janet and I went to Ohio to visit my niece, we wondered what Hannah was going to do. About two days after we got to Ohio Janet was sitting on the bed, when all of a sudden, she felt Hannah grab her hand and she said, 'Hannah is here!' We'd say, 'Come on, Hannah,' and when we were leaving my niece said 'I hate to see you leave, but be sure to take Hannah with you.'

"My niece's [now ex-husband] was getting a Ph.D., in psychology at the University of Cincinnati. Of course, anyone getting a Ph.D. in psychology knows that there are no such things as ghosts. When they came to New Hampshire one summer for a couple of weeks, Tom (the husband) slept in Glenn's room, which Hannah objected to. At five in the morning Hannah would wake him up. We found Tom sitting in the front yard, and he wouldn't go back to the house. He said that Hannah kept him awake all night by rattling things in the closet and that he also heard a child crying. It suddenly dawned on him that it wasn't the grandson Danny, but, 'Oh, my God, it's Hannah. I'm not sleeping in any house with any ghosts.'

"Once, when Barney was alive, I gave Janet a rest by offering to take Hannah back to Portsmouth with me for two days. It was eerie. Hannah would walk in the room, cough, and you'd see the rocking chair rock but nobody was in it. This episode happened after the sighting.

"The rocking chair business also happened at Janet's, mother's and Sheila's house. Once, the first day of school, when the children left the house, and when Hannah was presumably with Janet, the mothers of the neighborhood got together at Janet's for coffee. They were sitting around the table when all of a sudden the storm door opened out, the house door opened in, the cat walked in, and the doors shut. Everyone just sat and looked without saying a word. Nobody mentioned it to Janet until two weeks later. They couldn't figure it out. Finally, somebody said, 'that was the strangest thing.' Janet said, 'Relax, it happens all the time.'"

"The latest happening was on the 28th wedding anniversary of Janet and her husband. Since they were separating, Janet had to go out and get a job. Janet had been on the new job two days when all of a sudden the file racks were moving by themselves. Everybody (in the office) was saying, 'What's going on? Look at those racks, they never moved before.' When Janet got home that night, she said to Hannah: 'Let me tell you, you stay home, or you can go to Grandmother's or to Sheila's, but you're not going to where I work.' But since some things have happened when Janet has been working, she has to keep reminding Hannah. In the meantime Janet's husband moved out. I guess Hannah was too much for him. He refused to admit Hannah's existence for a long time, and would say, 'Don't talk about your imaginations and all.' One night Hannah really did a job on Janet's husband Donald. His big feather pillow somehow got all torn apart, and when Donald went upstairs, he found the whole room strewn with feathers. Donald yelled, 'I'm going to get an exorcist! I'll get rid of you, you dirty (rascal).' Then the venetian blinds started shaking.

"Plants tip over, doors rattle, they open and shut." Recently (letter of March 28, 1976) Betty wrote, "My sister was with a psychic development teacher who taped the session . . . It is a most unusual tale, which includes a child's voice calling 'Mommy,' several times. This happened when they were talking about Hannah. Also, during the taping the batteries (new ones) failed to function and difficulties still developed when it was plugged into the electrical outlet. The tape might be defective although a new one, but this would not explain the batteries. My sister told me that she always has trouble with batteries if she was upset or tense."

NOTE

6. Keel, John A.: ''Mystery Aeroplanes of the 1930s, Part I,'' FSR **(Flying Saucer Review)** Vol. 16 (No. 3): 10-13, (May/June 1970); Part II, Vol. 16, (No. 4); 9-14 (July/Aug. 1970); Part III, Vol. 17 (No. 4) 17-19 (July/Aug. 1971). Part IV, Vol. 17 (No. 5): 20-22, 28 (Sept./Oct. 1971). See also, Druffel, Ann: "California Report: The Mystery Helicopters," **Skylook,** No. 99: 8-9 (Feb. 1976).

3 — Experiments and Conclusions

Documentation of the things that happen to and around Betty Hill were the subject matter of Parts 1 and 2. Herein I will close the chapter of those events, past and present [to July, 1976] and describe some interesting experiments.

Old Virginia Dungeon

As far as Betty knew, Barney had no past history for psychic phenomena, either for himself or other members of his family. However, Barney recalled an old house in Virginia which had belonged to a family who owned slaves. "When the slaves were freed, because they were all relatives, the owner wanted them to have his property, since he had never married or had children of his own except the black ones running around.

"Downstairs was a hangout — a carryover from the old slave days. It was like a dungeon. There were straps and chains where the runaway slaves had been taken for punishment. The dungeon was supposed to have been haunted and had clanking, moaning, groaning and other things like that. I heard Barney refer to it. He never heard the sound himself, but he said they always talked about it on the old farm in Virginia."

The wall came tumbling down

On April 25, 1976, Charles Bowen, editor of *Flying Saucer Review*, was a guest in my (BES) home. We phoned Betty Hill, who reported that she had just come back from California and had gone downstairs to her basement, and found '. . .the whole wall lying out on the floor. She said: 'I couldn't believe it. I was just astonished. There was no reason for it (no water leak, work in the street, extraneous vibrations or noises). The house had been all locked up. To get in, a person would have had to set off the burglar alarm. It didn't go off, as far as I know, but here's the wall. It's sturdy, and had been there for 20 years."

Current events: a letter of May 28, 1976

"I have had many unexplained things happen to me, but these happened when Barney and I were here, or when I was here alone; they have never happened when anyone else was here — until this past week. Just before Jim (pseudonym) arrived, I found under the hood of my car a paint stirrer, with an abstract kind of painting on it. Then, while Jim was here, a clock in my living room, which was not running, started operat-

293

ing — maybe it does have a loose wire somewhere, I do not know, however, it started and continues to run.

"Another thing, I have found something that looks like beige plastic. I put it in the trash several times and would find it again somewhere in the house. The last time this happened I had my upstairs tenant and friend Deb watch me put it in the trash then, while Jim was here, I slipped off my shoes and when I went to put them back on, I found the plastic thing in my shoe! We were both there all the time, within three feet of my shoes, when this happened.

"Then, a knife from my set of Towle silver disappeared. I have searched everywhere and it cannot be found. I am hoping it will be returned. Also, my car registration disappeared from my purse at one time, and about 10 days later I found it one morning lying on top of my purse. So I am hoping the knife will come back.

"On May 10 Marianne and I got together at my mother's home in Kingston. We went out to a well-known UFO area, and Marianne and I heard beeping sounds, loud and clear; however, the other two in the car could not hear these. We saw some strange lights in the sky and got out of the car, to get a better look. We were standing in the middle of a dirt road, no houses, sort of scary place, when we heard the most unforgettable snarling and growling of an animal. I was shaking, telling them to get in the car (only two doors and I wanted to get in the driver's seat). Marianne was standing there, calm, fascinated, and saying it was only a big foot. She hears them often in back of her home. I think I would move!

"As for mystery helicopters, Ron Wilson (pseudonym), whom I quoted in my report, saw a helicopter come down over a tree in his yard, so low that it was swirling the branches. He told me that helicopters are not easy to handle, but one thing that must be avoided is close contact with a tree. If a chopper comes too close, a down-draft is created and the chopper crashes. This one was not affected in any way, so he is now questioning the origin of it. He has a friend who has 4 or 5 flying around his home occasionally, at night. Another mystery he told me: a few days before he came to see me, a strange woman came into his business — he has a foreign cars franchise — she was small, wearing a long dress and carrying a pink briefcase. She asked directions to another town. She had the most unusual eyes he has ever seen, very large, dark pupils, but it seemed to him that they protruded to such an extent that he wondered if it was possible for her to close her eyes. As a car dealer, he noted the car she was driving — a dark green, 4 door, Dodge Dart, with a dent in the left front fender. He told me that the day he visited me he saw this same car parked in front of my house. Later this same car was seen about 40 miles from here, parked, again, in front of a home of an acquaintance of mine; however, Ron also knows this person, but was not aware of it until this past week. Now I have learned that Ron spent his summers at the lake which is close to my mother's home, and which is known as a 'hot spot' of UFO activity; also, the area where he lives. He refused to watch the movie of my book last October because he knew UFOs did not exist. Now he has 7 at a time flying around his home and he has become 'converted.'

"Incidentally, Jim took the paint stirrer and plastic home with him so I am hoping that this is the last time I will see them."

Paranormal tape experiments

Background: At 11:30 p.m., Friday, March 12, 1976, Betty Hill, Marianne Cascio, Georgia and Eddie Burns (pseudonyms), Hugh White, my wife Ardis and I were present with three tape recorders and fresh casettes. Eddie had a Contact, Betty had a solid state Sony, and I had a Sony Casette-Corder TC-55.

Prior to beginning our paranormal recording attempt, Georgia and Eddie told us about their prolonged period of allegedly UFO-related poltergeist experiences, including possible materialization, dematerial-ization, malodorous writing on a picture window, audible, purportedly paranormal taping sessions, bizarre phone harassment, and so on. Because of the terror, emotional complications, synchronistic factors, ouija board instructions, and bizarre spontaneous alleged cloning episodes involving some of the protagonists and UFO tie-ins, the group sought my professional assistance. Later, when the group and I were meeting together, the chief protagonist's telephone (7) was apparently violently disconnected and the police were called. I had been with Georgia, Eddie, and other members of their group of young adults, in-cluding the chief protagonist, when strange events took place, but I had been unable to get paranormal tapes. Because Georgia and Eddie were uncomfortably situated in the middle of the holocaust and seriously wondered about the UFO aspects, they were anxious to meet Betty Hill and get her opinion.

Marianne Cascio, who has already been described in this article, had been visited by Betty Hill over a period of several months. Whatever the realities of her claims and subsequent episodes involving, at times, other people and data, to Marianne the experiences were true. She was also apparently part of previously alleged paranormal recording effects. Although I was not present during these sessions, she played a tape that was recorded when she was in a hypnotic trance. The hypnotist's voice came through clear and loud, whereas Marianne's hypnotized voice sounded as though the recorder had gained speed giving her a high-

Marianne Cascio and Betty Hill

pitched tweety-bird-like sound.

Betty Hill said that she had tried paranormal tapings in the past and had obtained some nondescript but nevertheless recognizable effects. Hugh White had been experimenting with paranormal tapes for close to a year and had been obtaining many effects, including numerous voices for which he had no explanation.

Prior to Georgia's and Eddie's visit to my home, Marianne had been regaling Betty, Ardis and I at the dinner table with some of her experiences. Immediately after Hugh White's arrival from West Nyack, N.Y., the lights in the consulting room (adjacent to the dining room) suddenly flickered out. I discovered that a 20 amp cartridge fuse had blown. There was no ostensible reason for this, such as overloading a circuit, and it was a striking event because of the context of the table talk and Marianne's claims and spontaneous possible parapsychical (?) demonstrations of electrical and electronic effects. For example, on three occasions, earlier in the day, when Ardis had attempted to use the push-button phone to call Marianne's parents in Agawam, Massachusetts, she was immediately put in touch with the operator, who offered help, rather than having the call go through. This event also happened with Marianne at the National Institute of Rehabilitation Engineering at Pompton Lakes, N.J., when the call was dialed from there to Montclair,

N.J. Marianne said this was not an unusual experience for her. Months earlier I had a possibly related peculiar experience which involved a phone call from Mrs. Stella Lansing (8) of Massachusetts.

Results: With these background factors then, the group and I attempted a paranormal recording for approximately twenty minutes. During the middle of the recording Marianne waved her hand several inches above Betty's tape recorder and said that she'd change places. When the tapes were played back, nothing was heard on Eddie's tape; there might have been a distant mumble of hardly audible voices on my tape; but the introduction to the procedure that I had made, and which was clearly heard on Eddie's and my tape, was not heard at the beginning of Betty's tape. She seemed flustered about this and searched her tape looking for it. On playing her tape from beginning to end, she suddenly heard my announcement of who was present, the date, etc., in the *middle* of her tape. It seemed that Marianne had succeeded in transferring the announcement. Since this episode, Marianne has phoned me immediately after another similar episode and put her Uncle Dave on the wire who witnessed the second transposition from the beginning to the middle of the tape.

It is stressed that at no point in the experiment did Marianne, in her hand waving 'image passes' touch the tape recorder, and Betty Hill had a new cassette. Although this experiment is electronically indigestible, facts are facts, and it is not unlike many odd effects noted in ufology: for example, an automobile motor starting up spontaneously after it had been shut off, due to an alleged close UFO effect, and so on. It can be wondered why the taping transposition happened only between Marianne and Betty.

Discussion and Summary

This brief survey of some possibly previously omitted aspects of Betty Hill's life indicates that there are parallels between her and other people who have had reputed UFO experiences. Betty has had examples of bizarre harassment, many of which are probably in the realm of the here-and-now and explainable, and some of which might cross the border into UFO cat-and-mouse-like games and intriguing domains of psi.

In my sessions with Betty, I learned that she, members of her family, and close friends have been involved in nearly lifelong major psychic phenomena. Perhaps these events have increased since the abduction. It can be conjectured from her early reported early-life examples of precognition plus other episodes, which she could not readily remember, that she is an unwitting proscopist. This unique talent possibly ties in with her star-map experience while on board the UFO. For example, it is possible that, because of her likely prophetic ability, Betty received the star map information that was not known, or known incorrectly at the time, but which was later proved by Marjorie Fish to be true. We may ask, did Betty literally receive the information while on board the UFO, as she recalled during post-hypnotic suggestion, or was her experience in some way a projected thought from the occupants, or whatever force that is behind them? Could her experience have been a spectacular example of clairvoyance? It is obvious that her experience does not "prove" (nor does it disprove) an extraterrestrial origin for the information, because, for example, the prophetic elements from Jules Vern's science fiction come to mind; also the recent controversies stemming from Dr. Velikovsky's (9) successful projections; and paragnosts Harold Sherman's and Ingo Swan's (10) precognitive statements that apparently smashed time and space barriers. Since the prophetic theme is related to many UFO contacts, it can be wondered if this information was telepathically transmitted to Betty for reasons that are beyond our understanding at present. The riddle of precognition (11) might have much to offer ufology, just as ufology with its manifold psi manifestations might give clues to the mysteries of parapsychology.

In Betty's abduction case, as in some UFO contactee examples, there is the overall impression that the involved individual is a unique type of person whose talents (e.g., ability to rapidly enter a deep hypnotic trance, dissociative traits, and high quality psi potentialities), latent or otherwise, are necessary for the UFOs or the forces behind them, and that these factors might be vital to the generation of the apparent mind-matter interface experience.

On superficial scrutiny, many of Betty's isolated experiences would appear hard to accept, and perhaps to those who are inexperienced with such data they could conform solely to psychopathology. However, to one who is experienced in studying psychopathology, and who looks at the events in their totality, the problem is more complex. It can be seen how persons who have had UFO encounters like Betty and Barney Hill can as easily develop emotional disturbances as the other way around: viz., pre-existent psychodynamics can color and in some cases account for part or all of their alleged experience.

It is to Betty Hill's credit that she has a solid ego structure which has enabled her to maintain a healthy outlook and "inlook." Others with a less stable ego structure might have succumbed to the combination of psychopathology, psi, the UFO experience, associated harrassment, and in some cases the effects of a self-engendered superstitious "bad luck syndrome." It is a coincidence, if not synchronicity, that among all the psychiatrists in the United States, Betty and Barney Hill, after a few initial attempts elsewhere, chose a physician who was not only skilled in hypnotherapy, but who was familiar with the possibility of thought transference (12).

Whatever the force that induces such disparate effects above and beyond the close UFO encounter or the awesome abduction experience, these superficially trivial human details may really be the top of the iceberg. They should not be overlooked and could be the heart of the problem.

NOTES AND REFERENCES

7. As additional background information, in the course of the group's harassment I also became involved in a prolonged UFO sighting by the chief protagonist and her mother, and during the group's mystery phone calls I logged 87 mostly late-night calls with no one at the other end of the line, betweeen November 13, 1975, and December 3, 1975. Although I have an Answering Service, which reported no- or few-unexplainable calls when I was out of my office, on several occasions the phone would ring immediately when I entered the office from an outside engagement. This was at random intervals. Also, on two occasions my bedside office phone rang when it was supposedly impossible, since it was cut off by a switch in my secretary's office. My wife also witnessed this incident. Mrs. Crane of the Answering Service, who was unaware of what was going on but dutifully logged the calls, once reported: "The phone rang and there was no light on the board. It was funny because I was looking at the board at the time — there are two lights under each doctor's name — and this is the first time this happened in nine years at the exchange. Whoever the party is, he seems to know a lot about electrical equipment — the two lights didn't go on when they should have."

8. For comic relief, I had just finished hanging up on a "mystery call" when I received a call from Stella Lansing in Massachusetts. She was upset because she had just called me on reverse charges, and the operator repeated the correct number, but she got a man who accepted the call and initially sounded like me. When Stella became aware that it was the wrong number, she hung up and got the same operator again, who said she felt sure she had dialed the correct number and recalled the correct digits . . . coincidence, comic relief, or perhaps something else, when considerd within this broad context of specifically annotated events. For possibly related data see Creighton, Gordon: "Gobbledygook" FSR, Vol. 18 (No. 6): 25-27 (Nov./Dec. 1972); and Schwarz, B.E.: "Saucers, Psi and Psychiatry," MUFON, UFO Symposium Proceedings, Akron, Ohio (June 22, 1974), pp. 88-89.

9. Based on his studies of the world's ancient records, I. Velikovsky in his predictions of what would be found in space probes of Venus,

Mars and the moon was often correct when experts in astronomy and related sciences were wrong. See de Grazia, Alfred, Juergens, Ralph E.; Stecchini, Livio C. (editors): **The Velikovsky Affair: Scientism vs. Science!,** University Books, New Hyde Park, N.Y., 1966, Bowen, Charles (ed.): "The Leopard's Spots," FSR, Vol. 14 (No. 3): 1-2 (May/June 1968).

10. Harold Sherman and Ingo Swan, two gifted paragnosts, attempted psychic probes of the distant planet Jupiter on April 27, 1973. Their responses were monitored by Drs. H.E. Puthoff and Russell Targ of the Stanford Research Institute and later compared with feedback material from the Pioneer X space craft. Both paragnosts gave similar responses to each other and to data sent back from Jupiter (approximately December 3, 1973).

Later, Janet Mitchell, a parapsychologist with the American Society for Psychical Research, monitored Swan's out-of-body precognitive (?) observations of the planet Mercury, which were subsequently confirmed by the Mariner X's fly-by. Miss Mitchell wrote about this in the May/June 1975 issue of **Psychic.**

Therefore, it can be supposed that Betty Hill, whatever the nature of her star map experience, could have used her natural paragnostic abilities in analogous ways to Sherman and Swan, and the scholarship and intuition of Velikovsky, or that she possessed considerable latent psychic abilities which were precipitated by her life crisis: i.e., the abduction, and which were projected into the clairvoyant, precognitively perceived star map.

11. Guideposts for investigations into precognition can be found in chair tests by Professor Tenhaeff with the Dutch paragnost Gerard Croiset, and the contributions of Jule Eisenbud. See Tenhaeff, W.H.C.: "Seat Experiments with Gerard Croiset," **Proc.** of the **Parapsychology Institute of the State University of Utrecht,** No. 1: 53-65, 1960; and Eisenbud, Jule, in Dean, Stanley R. (ed.): **Psychiatry and Mysticism,** Nelson Hall, Chicago, 1975 (Chapter on "Research and Precognition," pp. 101-110).

12. Although Dr. Simon alluded to the possibility of telepathy as an important factor in explaining some of the events of the Betty and Barney Hill abduction, this theme was not developed. However, Betty Hill recalled, from her conversations with Dr. Simon, his mention of some hypnotic-telepathic experiments with other people. Therefore it would appear that this aspect of his opinion about the abduction was not just wild speculation.

About The Author...

Berthold Eric Schwarz graduated from Dartmouth College and Dartmouth Medical School and received his M.D. from New York University College of Medicine. After interning at Mary Hitchcock Memorial Hospital, Hanover, New Hampshire, Dr. Schwarz was a Fellow in Psychiatry at the Mayo Foundation, where he received an M.S.from the Mayo Graduate School of Medicine.

Dr. Schwarz is a Diplomate of the American Board of Psychiatry and Neurology, a Fellow of the American Psychiatric Association and also of the Academy of Medicine of New Jersey, as well as many other medical associations. He has contributed more than 96 professional articles to journals. His current interest, as UFO DYNAMICS/ Book I and Book II, reveal, is the investigation of various psychiatric and parapsychological phenomena related to UFO encounters.

If you would like to acquire additional copies of UFO-DYNAMICS, Book I & Book II, please direct your inquiries to:

Rainbow Books/Betty Wright
POB 1069
Moore Haven, Florida 33471